Managing Teaching and Learning in Further and Higher Education

To the past and present students on the 'Managing Teaching and Learning in Higher Education' and the 'Certificate in Adult Education and Training' courses at Westminster College, Oxford, without whose inspiration this book would never have been written.

Managing Teaching and Learning in Further and Higher Education

Kate Ashcroft and Lorraine Foreman-Peck

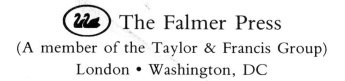 The Falmer Press

(A member of the Taylor & Francis Group)
London • Washington, DC

| UK | The Falmer Press, 4 John Street, London WC1N 2ET |
| USA | The Falmer Press, Taylor & Francis Inc., 1900 Frost Road, Suite 101, Bristol, PA 19007 |

First published in 1994

A catalogue record for this book is available from the British Library

Library of Congress Cataloging-in-Publication Data are available on request

ISBN 0 7507 0336 9 cased
ISBN 0 7507 0337 7 paper

Jacket design by Caroline Archer

Typeset in 9.5/11 pt Bembo by
Graphicraft Typesetters Ltd., Hong Kong.

Printed in Great Britain by Burgess Science Press, Basingstoke on paper which has a specified pH value on final paper manufacture of not less than 7.5 and is therefore 'acid free'.

Contents

Chapter 1

Teaching and Learning as a Management Process

This book is designed to appeal to open-minded and lively tutors who have a deep interest in developing their own teaching expertise within further or higher education, as well as in helping their students to become successful in their subject and able to make sense of the issues they will face in a diverse society.

Tutors new to teaching in colleges and universities are increasingly involved in new contracts requiring study and qualifications to develop basic and advanced teaching skills and an understanding of the learning process. More experienced tutors are facing a changing climate of quality control and academic standards. Some tutors recognize their need for professional updating. Many are interested in continuing professional development as part of their continuing quest for excellence in teaching. Yet others are leading professional development programmes for colleagues. You may fall into one of these categories; if so you will find this book useful.

We have tried to cover the management of teaching, and learning as it is related to any subject from the creative arts, through humanities to technical and vocational subjects. The book could be used in various ways. You might wish to explore new teaching, learning and assessment methods or consider models of the learning process itself and new ways of thinking about it. On the other hand you may decide to use the book for more specific purposes. You might work systematically through the book as a course or professional development text. Alternatively the book has been designed so you can dip into particular chapters to help you deal with a specific and immediate problem.

We have located the management of teaching and learning within the real, entrepreneurial climate of further and higher education in the 1990s. Thus the requirements many tutors face of having to meet the needs of new client groups and to build new kinds of educational programme are considered. The many interest groups who have some sort of relationship with or influence over the work of the tutor are recognized, including students, colleagues, institutional managers, employers, funding bodies and the community at large.

The book contains material about ways of managing the teaching, learning and assessment process to improve students' learning and benefit the learning process. This is seen as a process of management of self and others. It should help you to create an appropriate learning programme for your students and develop, through the process of enquiry and reflection, a range of teaching and learning strategies to meet your students' needs. We discuss the issues involved in the use of a wide range of assessment techniques to monitor student progress and enable self-assessment and a range of self, peer and student monitoring and evaluation techniques.

The book is written within a clear value framework, which includes the principles embedded within the reflective practitioner model (this is described later in this chapter) as they apply to further and higher education. We believe that part of the tutor's role is to help their students towards a reflexivity, also. This implies a valuing of student autonomy, collaboration and facilitation rather than an unqualified or simple didactic model of teaching or a transfer model of learning. Such a theory of teaching and learning emphasizes education as a holistic process, which recognizes feelings and relationships as well as ability as influences on learning. The real dilemmas that this model poses for a system of mass education are recognized, and some methods resolving some of the dilemmas discussed.

The Rationale for the Book

We wished to provide a handbook for teaching within the post-compulsory education and training sector with an emphasis on an entrepreneurial climate, but at the same time retaining a clear educational philosophy. We have aimed to provide an introduction to a model of informed action based on enquiry into teaching and learning as part of a management process. The main intention is to help you to reflect on your personal and professional practice and development in the light of evidence, assess your future development needs, and make plans for continuing professional development with the aim of improving practice through monitoring and evaluation.

Your practice and professional development is rooted in a personal and social context. The book should help you to understand what underlies your felt needs, satisfactions and dissatisfactions. At a time when external pressures seem to dictate educational decision making, this should help you to gain a sense of control over your own practice. The aim is to enable you to find out what sort of skills and values you need in order to do your job well. Although enquiry tasks are suggested, they should leave you scope to follow up your own concerns.

We wanted to develop material within the book which would address some of the difficult interpersonal and management issues often faced by tutors. These include the development of personal and professional coping strategies. In our view reflective practice involves developing key management skills and understandings, such as the management of people, resources and provision.

The Format of the Book

We do not intend to give a definitive guide to each issue. The chapters provide you with a starting point for development and enquiry or some starting points for dealing with immediate problems. In the second case you might refer to a synopsis of each chapter (and perhaps read the full chapter when you have more time). The style is practical, with concrete suggestions to try out and reflect upon. Research is quoted where appropriate, but it is not a research-based book.

We hope you will contextualize the material through the suggested enquiry tasks interspersed within each chapter. These have been designed to enable you to collect data from within your institution and reflect upon the operation of ideas contained within the section. You will need a trusted colleague to help you with some of the tasks. The ongoing reflective diary at the end of each chapter is designed to form one model of interaction with the material.

Because we can only touch upon many issues in a book of this length, there is a short annotated reading list at the end of each chapter, designed to help you to target further reading and take forward those issues you find particularly relevant.

If you are working through the book systematically as a personal development text, you may find it useful to find a more experienced colleague, or perhaps a colleague who is interested also in developing their teaching, who can act as a mentor and give you regular feedback on the enquiry tasks and your reflective diary.

The Reflective Teacher Model

Reflective teaching is an active process of learning from experience and evaluating your ideas, feelings and behaviour in the light of supporting evidence and discussion. It involves asking questions about your assumptions, your tacit definitions of knowledge and the basis for these ideas. It involves discovering and critically examining your beliefs and values. There are various models of this process (Dewey, 1916; Zeichner, 1982). The basic premise however is that you start with actual experience, and from that experience frame your own problems. Since our experience is different from yours and we bring our own experience to the situations we describe, we have found it hard to define problems which we could be sure would be relevant to you. The aspects we found salient in a particular situation, you might not. Therefore your learning from our descriptions of experience depends on you actively making sense of it in your own terms.

The starting point for your development as a reflective practitioner is the problems you face in relation to the way you construe your role and the dilemmas inherent in it for you. The usual motivation for examining beliefs and practices is a felt concern, worry or disharmony. The enquiry tasks in this book are meant to help you to investigate your own 'felt concerns'. For example, if you felt that something is amiss with the assessments you set, the enquiry tasks in Chapter 4 might help you to name your problems and suggest ways of investigating them. The reflective diary might help you to look at the emotional baggage that you bring with you to teaching, learning and assessment, which might be obstructing your acknowledgment of certain salient features in the situation. The tasks should ideally be discussed with a colleague, since they will be able to provide you with other viewpoints.

The critical point about reflective practice is that it requires a commitment to learning from experience and from evidence, rather than to learning certain 'recipes' for action. Even if you start with recipes, they need to be explored and analysed for their underlying assumptions and effects as you gain in confidence. This process of critical enquiry should be *reflexive*, that is responsive to your own needs and the context in which you work, but also critical of the existing educational provision and ideology (including your own). The analysis involves not just your practice, but also the social, moral and political context for that practice.

Reflective practice does not require a perfect setting. Indeed it is the means of finding solutions which transform the dilemmas inherent in teaching and the institutional context. The development of technical skills such as voice control and questioning are a necessary but not sufficient condition for reflective practice. It is essential to develop other skills including the ability to work as part of a team; to observe using a variety of methods; to communicate and exchange ideas; to analyse and evaluate data collected; and to criticize the status quo from a moral and a political point of view. Some issues will raise dilemmas for which transformational solutions must be found. For instance, certain solutions may require you to transform your definition of the problem, your existing view of yourself, other people or of education. We have found that it is possible to develop transformational solutions if you develop key qualities, in particular, open-mindedness, responsibility and wholeheartedness (see Zeichner and Teitlebaum, 1982; Isaac and Ashcroft, 1986; Ashcroft, 1987; Ashcroft and Tann 1988; Ashcroft and Griffiths, 1989).

Open-mindedness implies that you wish to seek out alternative viewpoints. You do not automatically accept or reject the prevailing educational orthodoxy of your institution or the educational system, but you do examine it in the light of your experience and compare your ideas with those of students, colleagues, educationalists and others outside of education. Reflective practice is therefore an active process of questioning and data collection. It may challenge existing systems. Many of the enquiry tasks within this book are designed to involve you in the systematic investigation of alternative perspectives and interpretations of your own practice and educational values and those prevailing within your institution. This is the reason that they sometimes require you to discuss your findings with a colleague.

Responsibility involves you in the consideration of the long-term as well as the short-term consequences of the actions of all those involved in the teaching situation, including your own practice. It requires you to move beyond utilitarian consequences of 'what seems to work' in order to take an essentially moral stance. It requires a consideration of the *worthwhileness* of action at all levels. The enquiry tasks and reflective diary entries in this book are designed to help you to build up and continuously examine your model of teaching, investigate your actions in the light of this model and to direct your attention to the social, political and economic context of educational decisions.

Wholeheartedness implies that responsibility and open-mindedness become constant attributes which are not confined to particular situations, but permeate the whole of your professional life. In particular, they are not assumed in order to gain personal advantage. Taking an open-minded and responsible stance will not automatically be good for your career prospects. Questioning the dominant hegemony and prevailing practices may result in better practice, but will not always make you popular. This can be particularly problematic if you are experiencing job insecurity or work in an institution with an ethos inimical to change. (It is not unknown for 'whistle blowers' to lose their jobs.) In these circumstances, your sphere of reflective action may be restricted to a developing expertise with students and developing an understanding of the dilemmas you face and ways of making them more manageable.

Reflective practice is an ideal to work towards throughout a professional lifetime. It may be only fleetingly achievable, but the journey towards it is the point. Its value is as a vehicle for a continuous renewal and development of your professional practice and understanding.

Enquiry Task 1.1

With a colleague you can trust undertake a SWOT (strengths, weaknesses, opportunities, threats) analysis of your professional practice. Identify together some of the strengths and weaknesses of your teaching and other practices and the opportunities for developing these further and the threats to their continuing quality.

	Teaching	*Other duties*
Strengths		
Weaknesses		
Opportunities		
Threats		

What use might you make of this analysis?

Teaching and Learning as a Management Process

We have suggested above that the most appropriate process for fostering many of the skills necessary for reflective practice is through that of critical enquiry. We have found that certain conditions facilitate this. These include group work and a consideration of the wider context for action (Ashcroft and Griffiths, 1989).

In order for you to take alternative viewpoints seriously and to research the perspectives of others it is necessary that you seek to work as part of a team. You may need to look for creative ways to build the reality of team work into the teaching and assessment system. Where institutional systems have been built on teacher autonomy or are resistant to change, any team work may have to be informal, for instance, through discussion and advice with trusted colleagues, as well as through collaborative work with your students.

New tutors are often overwhelmingly concerned with immediate survival. As a reflective practitioner, you may have to struggle to rise above this in order to root your practice in the real dilemmas facing society, including issues of equal opportunities, at a time of scarce resources, competing definitions of quality and cost effectiveness and so on. We believe that more frustration results from ignoring these dilemmas.

The sort of enquiry that underpins reflective practice is not for people who want simple answers to simple questions. Unfortunately, simple solutions tend to produce their own problems since reality is complex and educational reality is also relative. For instance, it is easy to be popular with students if you encourage them to rely on you. If you attempt more challenging and innovative teaching methods, you may need strategies for dealing with adverse criticism, at least in the early stages. Because it involves the values that underlie it, there may be few absolutes in education and none in reflective practice. Reflective practice is an ideal, albeit one that never seems to be achieved. We have found that working towards reflective practice is difficult, but never boring.

Reflective practice is about people and your experience of people. It requires that you develop a range of interpersonal skills and qualities. Although your enquiry will start with you, it must be essentially about people. Therefore, your access to data depends on your ability to communicate openly and honestly at some level. This can be very difficult in some contexts. The aim is to break down barriers created by your own and others' roles or by institutional systems or, if this is not possible, at least to understand the nature and effects of these barriers. If you work within a rigid institutional structure or in a climate of fear or insecurity, your ability to do this may be limited. You will be dealing with sensitive issues.

The implication of this is that the reflective practitioner will need to develop management skills and understandings. Perhaps the most important skill you can acquire is that of self-assessment. As a reflective practitioner, you will wish to investigate your strengths and weaknesses as a teacher and as a manager. You will need the perspectives of others on your personal style, and the ability to relate this openly and honestly to your stated theories of management. Other skills may relate to the management of students in classrooms, the management of the teaching and learning process and the development of good working relationships. These skills may include the ability to delegate to colleagues and students, to say 'No', to engage in meaningful consultation and to deal with stress and conflict. Key to the management process are listening skills and gauging when it is appropriate to listen without relating what people say to your own experiences. These skills are transferable to a variety of contexts. Skills you have developed for working with colleagues may be directly applicable to your work with students or senior managers. Understandings include an understanding of the management and committee systems and culture of your institution.

Enquiry Task 1.2

Do you know the following?

- What is the range of assessment methods used within your department?
- What staff development money is available for teaching and learning and how to access it?
- How to go about changing the teaching, learning or assessment methods on a course?
- What your department's policy is on course evaluation?
- What is recognized as good practice as far as written feedback on students' work?
- What counselling support is available to students for personal, financial, study skill or career problems, and how they can access it?

Find out the answers to any questions where you are not certain.

Skills and Reflective Practice

Your development as a reflective practitioner will inevitably lead to you rethink your role as an educator. You may begin to consider the implications of reflective practice for students. Should they also be developing as reflective practitioners? This consideration is likely to lead you to start to define the skills underpinning reflective practice, how these skills can be developed within yourself, and perhaps within your students, given your particular educational context.

The skills identified in one particular institution (Ashcroft and Griffiths, 1989) included skills of independent and collaborative learning; interpersonal skills; organizational skills; skills of self-awareness and self-assessment; communication skills; decision making skills; research skills; and skills of implementation and application. As a reflective practitioner, you will need to develop your own list of skills, (e.g. planning skills, negotiation skills) and consider how each of these can be operationalized within your own institution.

Each of these skills may be developed outside of a context of reflective practice. They are necessary but insufficient. In addition, you will need to develop a variety of attitudes such as a respect for the viewpoints of others, a commitment to particular human values, the willingness to consider, research and enquire into the long-term consequences of your actions.

This last attitude or quality suggests that reflective practice is not merely an intuitive process, but also one that requires that you develop areas of understanding. Some of this understanding may be acquired from a close study of your practice and its setting, but this can be enriched through a systematic exploration of understandings gleaned from other times and places, through a study of available research. It is through these two kinds of study that an in-depth understanding of issues such as cultural diversity and the interdependent nature of human society can be acquired.

The aim of reflective practice is to develop your understanding of the problematic nature of much of your 'knowledge' and an understanding of your own and your students' abilities, attitudes and needs. Through this you may become more aware of issues of responsibility and accountability and the difficulty of reconciling open-mindedness and value judgments.

More and more we have come to see truly 'objective' or value-free evaluation as impossible (Ashcroft and Griffiths, 1987). It can lead to self-deception and even intellectual dishonesty. It may be tempting to evaluate something easy to measure or something that will give you an answer which will support your prejudices. The only protection from this are the values and qualities you have developed and your willingness to risk an examination of both fundamental and surface features. Your values then become part of the enquiry itself. The enquiry should help you to define them more clearly as well as the conceptual frameworks you are using to analyse data. This implies that data collection and the initial analysis may be a private affair but evaluation is not. You will need to seek out critical examination of your data and conclusions.

Enquiry Task 1.3

Together with at least one colleague list the skills that are necessary for reflective practice and the sort of behaviour which would indicate that they had been acquired:

Skill   *Behavioural indicator*
e.g.
Planning skills;
Negotiation with colleagues;
Observation skills;
Organizational skills;
Listening skills etc.

Discuss your list with a colleague.

Are there aspects of the list that would apply irrespective of the educational context?
Are there others that are particularly applicable to your institutional context?

Reflective Practice and Student Learning

We apply the model of reflective practice within the book to student learning as well as to your teaching. We put forward the view that part of your role may be to facilitate your students' development as reflective practitioners of their subject. This applies within vocational courses, where students are learning to take responsibility for their actions and to look open-mindedly for ways to improve and develop their practice and understanding, but also within purely academic studies. The implication is that students learn to analyse alternative conceptions and models of their subject, its social implications and the views and perspectives on that subject of students, tutors and perhaps writers and researchers.

It also implies that they are willing to take responsibility for their own learning and to contribute to that of others. They will be expected to locate their actions and the subject within a moral framework and look at the values that underpin both.

Above all, there is an assumption that the ideal is for them to be whole-hearted about their studies: to seek after some definition of truth; to study for the intrinsic interest and pleasure and to abandon a purely instrumental model of study for the sake of advancement and grades. We have found that this kind of critical analysis and the development of the qualities for reflective action are possible at a variety of levels, with people of all ages and abilities, from children in the primary school to young school leavers and to students on masters degree and doctorate programmes.

It is our belief that part of your job as a tutor is to create the conditions to enable this development and ethos of study and analysis that is worthwhile for its own sake. It is also to help the students to develop the various skills (research, analysis, interpersonal skills, communication skills, and so on) which are prerequisite for reflective action. The ultimate intention is that your students will develop as *self-critical problem solvers*, who have the attitudes and skills for *lifelong learning and development*.

The Model and the Book

The format of the book implies that you wish to enquire into practice as an 'insider'. That is, that you wish to collect data, to research into your own practice, its effects on others and its relationship to your institutional context. Elliot (1993) suggests that this form of enquiry should involve a research model different from that of the scientific tradition. 'Insider research' implies that, within the constraints set by the nature of the courses you teach and the requirements of the discipline and validating bodies, you will be collecting evidence about your teaching and the students' learning. The production of generalizable knowledge about teaching and learning is not the motivation, but rather a realization of your own educational values. This implies that you may or may not be assessing data about your teaching and the data collection methods against the normal research 'production standards', but rather assessing them against your own goals. The aim is not to meet scientific standards of validity and reliability, but rather to come up with a clearer understanding of the context in which you work and to collect data that can be used to aid analysis, problem-solving and reflection. This is likely to be a process of enquiry into practice in which your goals and values may become changed by the process of enquiry, that is, it is a reflexive process.

We have assumed in this book that you are willing to enquire as to where your values lie, and where your actual practice stands in relation to them. Enquiry into such deep matters is likely to reveal more dilemmas than are resolved. It is probable that some mismatch between your stated values and those you operate in practice will be revealed. You may be frustrated by the fact that you are left with the question of how you can improve the relation between these two sets of values, but we believe that this is where real professional development lies.

Scientific enquiry works on the assumption that it is possible to detach yourself from your underlying values in assessing data and thus it is possible to eliminate bias. The kind of enquiry underpinning reflective practice presupposes that these values are articulated and examined in the light of the data. Your values are therefore part of the enquiry, and may (and perhaps should) be reconstructed as a result of the examination of practice, and an assessment of the 'bias' embedded within that practice. For example, you may find that you are not living up to your ideals as far as racial equality is concerned. Perhaps you give more (or a different form of) attention to white than to black students, or vice versa. You have to decide at this point whether this inequality is embedded in the situation, whether your definition of 'equality' is adequate, whether you change your theory, your practice or the situation and the costs and benefits of any change.

It is hard for the individual to examine the relationship between their practice and their values. This is why you are asked in many of the enquiry tasks to seek out alternative interpretations of your data and conclusions. Without the multi-perspectives of students, colleagues, parents, employers and senior managers you will be unlikely to reconstruct and modify the values that are embedded in your practice, and thus make deep changes to that practice.

The aim of reflective teaching is to facilitate your students' development as reflective practitioners of their subject, and so in Chapter 2 we focus on models of student learning. We seek to help you identify teaching methods to encourage deeper learning, consistent with the reflective practitioner model and examine the dilemmas raised by newer models of student learning implied by competency approaches to learning.

Because we believe that personal style is an issue in the management of teaching and learning as well as in building relationships, we use the third chapter to explore the thorny question of personal development and the development and monitoring of interpersonal skills, together with issues such as your time management, team working and management of change.

There seems to be a relationship between assessment methods and approaches, including group projects and self and peer assessment and the students' ability to develop as reflective practitioners of their subject. In Chapter 4 we look at models of monitoring student progress and the use of records of progress and achievement to support deeper levels of student learning.

Chapter 5 is very much focused on practical issues in 'reflective teaching' and its context, such as problems and opportunities presented by various methods of teaching, the role of instruction and facilitation and ways to address students' various needs.

Reflective practice is concerned with political and social issues. In Chapter 6 we deal with open learning and its relationship to assumptions about teaching and the politics of knowledge. We explore some of the ways you might use open learning to develop new opportunities and the management, teaching and student support problems it presents.

Chapter 7 focuses on aids to learning in the context of reflective practice, and in particular, how such aids may be used to encourage deeper learning. We look at ways that you might structure your students' learning through audio-visual aids and information technology, and also their use as an aid to your reflection and analysis of your own and your students' developing communication skills.

Because the reflective practitioner takes account of the emotional and practical issues students face in their learning, we have included counselling skills and student support as the main focus of Chapter 8. We introduce the use of appraisal, goal setting and ways of dealing with stress and conflict, such as analysing transactions to eliminate problems, assertiveness and stress management.

Reflective practice takes place within a values framework, which we believe should include issues of equal opportunities and therefore we have made this the focus of Chapter 9. Dilemmas raised in teaching, interviewing, assessment, content, publicity and language are explored, as well as ways you might foster equal opportunities amongst students and colleagues and the relationship between equal opportunities and institutional systems.

The reflective practitioner model is evaluation-led and therefore we decided that this should be the focus of Chapter 10. We explore evaluation methods in terms of your goals and values as well as issues of tutor and student control in the design of evaluation instruments.

As you become more familiar with the model of the reflective practitioner, we hope that you will wish to explore your values, teaching and the students' learning in a more systematic way. In our experience, action research provides a particularly useful framework for this exploration, and so in Chapter 11 we explore how you might go about setting up such an enquiry and examine how action research may empower you in institutional change.

The final chapter (Chapter 12) links the main issues within the book with the reflective practitioner model. We look at ways you might think about reflective practice in a cold political climate. We explore practical ways for developing the management of teaching and learning as part of a lifelong process, encompassing the aspects of the life of the educational institution, the community and the wider educational context.

Enquiry Task 1.4

Identify a priority area of development in each of the areas of your teaching; the students' learning and relationships with colleagues:

Area of development

Your teaching

The students' learning

Relationships
with colleagues

Reread the last section and refer to the table of contents. Identify which sections of this book may be of assistance in this development.

Summary

The book focuses on teaching, learning and assessment as management processes. There is a balance between the entrepreneurial context of education and the model of the reflective teacher. It does not give 'tips', but rather practical guidelines for action for you to relate and consider in the light of your particular values and context.

The reflective teacher model is based on three qualities: open-mindedness, responsibility, and wholeheartedness. Reflective practice is developed through a process of critical enquiry, which requires data collection and a public examination of practices. The aim is to bring your practice and your stated theories of teaching into closer relation. The process is likely to change both.

Reflective practice is an ideal towards which to work. It does not require a perfect setting, but is rather the means of finding transformational solutions to dilemmas inherent in teaching and the institutional context. It is rooted in a personal and social context and requires the development of a range of management skills and an understanding of the institutional and educational setting. It requires you to develop a range of skills, especially interpersonal, research and organizational ones. These must be related to a system of well articulated values that inform the evaluation process.

The content of the book includes discussion of student learning, personal development, interpersonal skills, assessment issues, teaching methods, open learning, aids to learning, counselling and support, equal opportunities, evaluation, and action research. Each chapter includes discussion of some of the main issues, a range of enquiry tasks, a summary of the contents of the chapter, an entry for an ongoing reflective diary, references and an annotated list of suggested reading.

Entry for the Reflective Diary

In discussion with a colleague list the various definitions and purposes of teaching learning and assessment at further or higher education level.

	Definition	*Purpose*
What is teaching?	1	
	2	
	3	
	. . .	
What is learning?	1	
	2	
	3	
	. . .	
What is assessment?	1	
	2	
	3	
	. . .	

How have definitions and purposes changed since you graduated or finished training?

In your reflective diary write about which of these concepts you value, why you value them and how you might need to change or develop in order to promote them.

References

ASHCROFT K. (1987) 'The history of an innovation', *Assessment and Evaluation in Higher Education*, **12**, 1, pp. 37–45.

ASHCROFT K. and GRIFFITHS M. (1987) 'The three faces of school experience: Teaching teaching skills in an enquiry-based initial teacher education course', British Educational Research Association Conference, Manchester, September.

ASHCROFT K. and GRIFFITHS M. (1989) 'Reflective teachers and reflective tutors: School experience in an initial teacher education course', *Journal of Education for Teachers*, **15**, 1, pp. 35–52.

ASHCROFT K. and TANN S. (1988) 'Beyond building better checklists: Staff development in a school experience programme', *Assessment and Evaluation in Higher Education*, **13**, 1, pp. 61–72.

DEWEY J. (1916) *Democracy and Education*, New York, The Free Press.

ELLIOT J. (1993) 'Towards a methodology of insider research', lecture, Oxford University.

ISAAC J. and ASHCROFT K. (1986) 'A leap into the practical', in NIAS, J. and

GROUNDWATER-SMITH, S. (Eds) *The Enquiring Teacher: Supporting and Sustaining Teacher Research*, London, Falmer Press.

ZEICHNER K.M. (1982) 'Reflective teaching and field-based experience in teacher education', *Interchange*, **12**, 4, pp. 1–22.

ZEICHNER K.M. and TEITLEBAUM K. (1982) 'Personalised and inquiry oriented teacher education: An analysis of two approaches to the development of curriculum for field-based experience', *Journal of Education for Teaching*, **8**, 2, pp. 95–117.

Suggested Reading

ARGYRIS C. and SCHÖN D. (1974) *Theory into Practice*, London: Croom Helm.
The definitive book on the relationship between espoused theories of teaching and theory in action.

ASHCROFT K. and GRIFFITHS M. (1989) 'Reflective teachers and reflective tutors: School experience in an initial teacher education course', *Journal of Education for Teachers*, **15**, 1, pp. 35–52.
A fairly short paper describing how one institution developed a model of reflective practice with both students and tutors and the implications for teaching, learning, assessment and evaluation.

Chapter 2

Learning and the Reflective Practitioner

Introduction

When the results or outcomes of learning are disappointing the responsibility for this is often assigned to the student. They are frequently labelled dull or idle or both. In reviewing study habits and achievement, Entwistle (1984) makes the point that successful students seem to be more intellectually able, more highly motivated, and better organized, but that these findings are supported by 'unconvincingly low levels of correlation' (p. 12). In general it is a mistake to place learning failure at the feet of students and ignore the shortcomings of teaching.

The question of how associated factors in the educational set-up (such as methods, group size, availability of resources) contribute to students' success or failure in learning is important for the reflective practitioner. Unfortunately there are no clear-cut prescriptions. For instance, there may be a mismatch between tutors' intentions and what students achieve. You may want to facilitate critical thinking but your teaching may encourage students to think in the same way as you do or to see learning purely as acquiring factual knowledge.

The existence of mismatch between intentions and actuality has long been realized. Snyder (1971) labelled it the difference between the formal and the 'hidden curriculum'. The hidden curriculum is embodied in the teaching methods, the assessment system and other arrangements such as the degree of independent learning expected on the course. Any aim, such as building student confidence, can be thwarted by inappropriate methods and course arrangements.

The aim of this chapter is to review briefly and critically ideas about learning derived from the research literature, which might help us answer the following key questions: 'How do students learn?' 'How can they be helped to learn?' and 'How are factors in the educational situation helping or hindering their learning?' Part of the way you teach is dependent upon an idea or set of ideas about what learning is. These ideas may be held implicitly or explicitly. This chapter should enable you to make these ideas explicit, know something of the research tradition from which they come, and to reconsider them in the light of the discussion. The ways in which researchers collect and organize information impose different definitions of learning and so it is useful to have an understanding of the origin of frameworks available for analysing and interpreting information.

We critically review various approaches to researching learning in this chapter. The complexity of the learning situation is discussed. We make some suggestions

Figure 2.1: A model of the complexity of the experience of learning

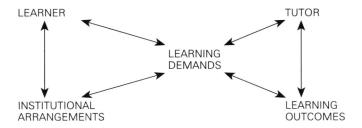

for collecting information on student learning that can be incorporated into every-day teaching. The last section offers advice on planning for learning.

The Complexity of the Learning Situation

Many factors influence the individual's experience of learning. The most obvious is the students' learning style and their goals and values. Equally important are institutional arrangements for learning, including size of groups, bureaucratic re-quirements, assessment systems and the opportunities for informal contact with tutors. Other factors to do with the institutional ethos are also important such as whether the institution is caring or distanced from the student.

The model in Figure 2.1 indicates the interdependence between elements of the experience of learning. For example the learner has to meet institutional requirements and in some way institutional requirements embody a view of the learner. It is a simple but useful model for thinking about elements of the learning situation or milieu.

Each element of the model interacts with the others to produce a complex learning situation. Student learning is embedded in a set of social expectations and bureaucratic arrangements. How the student fares depends not only on factors such as interest in the subject and personal goals in coming to college or univer-sity, but also how they perceive the totality of the situation.

However, the characterization of learning as a researchable subject has tended to reflect the requirement of the research model being used. Early research was experimental and directed to finding universal laws. Later research used natural-istic settings, which resembled normal learning situations while still having ele-ments of experimentation. Other studies have used natural settings where students are asked about their learning in situations that have not been controlled in some way. Over time there has been a shift away from the attempt to 'explain' learning to the attempt to provide authentic description grounded in real experience which is intended to give insight and illumination to the reflective practitioner.

Explaining Learning: Behaviourism

The following section reviews briefly some of the models of learning that have been used in an attempt to provide a theoretical understanding of the psychological processes of learning, divorced from social and institutional aspects of learning. For this reason they provide only partial accounts. They are important however since theories of instruction (e.g. programmed learning) and common sense (or implicit theories in use) can be traced back to them. They continue to underpin part of the craft of teaching, especially in dealing with discipline problems and structuring learning for students who find it hard to benefit from traditional education.

Conditioning theory is perhaps the most well known of these theories. Pavlov (1960) introduced the idea of classical conditioning. Here a stimulus is associated with a response or reflex. In Pavlov's experiment with a dog, an association was established between the stimulus of a sound and the reflex of salivation. The dog had previously responded to meat by salivating. The same response, a conditioned response, could be produced now by a sound associated with the original stimulus. This is an example of 'simple learning' that we may have all experienced. Hearing a dripping tap we might expect a flood in the bathroom like the last time our toddler turned one on. Fear of a certain teacher may be associated with the subject the teacher taught. This points to the crucial necessity of considering and protecting your students' feelings and avoiding teaching methods that set students up to fail.

Thorndike (1932) also took the view that behaviour could be conceptualized as an organism's response to a stimulus. Thorndike's experiments with cats led him to the conclusion that responses that are rewarded will be repeated. Responses which brought no satisfaction or reward are dropped.

It is now commonly accepted that reward is an effective way of motivating learning. This has crucial implications for the nature of the dialogue between tutors and students and for the quality of written feedback on assessments. A further development of conditioning theory became known as behaviourism. Watson (1925) showed that Pavlovian conditioning can be applied to people. Watson believed that emotions such as enjoyment of a teacher's presence could become associated with the subject. The subject becomes the object of pleasure. Watson developed the idea of second order conditioning whereby the conditioned stimulus is associated with another. His theories pointed to the inescapable emotional quality of learning that has been corroborated by later studies which do not employ the methods of experimental psychology.

Hull's (1952) work, which built on that of Pavlov's and Thorndike's, introduced the concept of reinforcement. The essential idea behind this concept is that we all have certain needs for satisfaction which are reduced if we are given attention and praise. He identified primary reinforcement, which occurs whenever a response follows quickly upon a stimulus, and secondary reinforcement, which occurs when this connection acquires the power to reinforce another connection. In an educational context the primary reinforcement could be the reduction of need that occurs when a task is successfully completed. The secondary reinforcement could be the grade achieved. Marks or grades reinforce the feeling of satisfaction. Hull claims that the majority of adults work for some form of social approval or financial reward, and the reduction of the need for these then takes on the characteristics of a secondary drive. In giving feedback on students' work we often employ phrases such as 'well done' to motivate students.

Early experimental work on the psychology of learning has highlighted the complexity of learning and the way in which many psychological concepts are involved, such as anxiety, interest, motivation and attitudes. The value of this work is the discovery that learning is essentially emotional. Teaching is not just the 'delivery' of the curriculum, without regard to the feelings, learning history, and aspirations of students.

Skinner (1954), building on the foundation of classical conditioning theory, produced a model of learning known as operant conditioning. The idea, very briefly stated, is that people learn when correct responses are immediately re-warded or reinforced. Complex behaviour can be evinced by reinforcing each step in a sequence of behaviours. Thus the object of learning has to be reduced to 'bits', each correct response being reinforced so that the desired outcome is 'shaped'. This is the fundamental idea behind programmed learning, which can take the form either of a programmed textbook where the student is assessed at intervals before being allowed to progress, or a 'teaching' machine which works on the same principle. Skinner's work might also be responsible for the very common idea in curriculum design that a complex skill is best taught by breaking it down into its component parts.

This review of conditioning theory points to the origins of some of our taken for granted ideas about learning, such as the importance of rewards, the centrality of emotions, and the importance of sequencing in learning. However, a behaviourist approach has important limitations. For example, emotions are thought of as needs that have to be reduced for an organism to feel in equilibrium. This completely ignores the fact that emotions are for the most part directed towards our understanding of an event or object. In other words they are dependent on how we perceive a situation. If I think I see a person coming at me with a knife, I will experience fear. If I realize that it is a toy, and that he is being playful my fear will go. The way we see 'rewards' and 'punishments' may vary between people. To characterize learning situations in terms of needs and rewards underplays the way in which learners perceive the learning situation and does not provide much help to the tutor who wishes to alleviate anxiety.

The behaviourist interpretation underestimates the central role of the learners' attempts to make meaning. In fact it rather implies that learners are not actively constructing meaning. In addition, some tutors would resent the idea of being manipulators of their students' learning. There is a moral dimension to learning that is not addressed by behaviourism. Tutors' behaviour is informed by a sense of care and the responsibility to provide worthwhile learning experiences. Conditioning is compatible with teaching immoral and educationally worthless knowledge, attitudes and skills. It has been used to ill effect in many totalitarian regimes. On the other hand, you do not have to be a dictator to have subconsciously picked up the routines of the teaching exchange learnt in the secondary school where questioning routines may involve students in guessing the teacher's meaning until the correct response is guessed at and rewarded.

The outcome of learning implied by a behaviourist model is problematic for some tutors who find it inadequate for explaining learning at anything but a simple level. The conception of knowledge it presupposes lacks some of the characteristics associated with higher or further education, such as analytical and critical ability. In many traditional psychological experiments, the content of learning has been low, or devoid of meaning. Thus outcomes of learning are characterized in 'quantitative' terms. Perry (1970) found that students early in their careers tended to expect higher education to help them distinguish between true and false, right and wrong. This dualist outlook was abandoned later in their careers, in favour of a relativistic conception in which it is recognized that there are often many competing explanations of phenomena and that they have to take responsibility for reaching their own conclusions.

In terms of the model presented in Figure 2.1, behaviourism does not value the learners' educational orientation to learning. In seeking to find law-like generalizations, the learner as an individual is neglected. The emphasis is on controlling learning rather than empowering learning.

Enquiry Task 2.1

The following ways of conceptualizing learning were identified in work by Saljo (Gibbs, 1992):

- Learning as being given knowledge. The (active) teacher has knowledge and transmits it to the (passive) student.
- Learning as memorizing. The student is active, and may take responsibility for their own learning, but the knowledge acquired is not transformed in any way, merely reproduced for assessment.
- Learning as acquiring skills, procedures that are applied.
- Learning as making sense. The student is trying to abstract meaning from the learning situation.
- Learning as understanding reality. The learning experience enables the student to see the world differently.

Which conceptions are compatible with a behaviourist model of learning?

Discuss with a student the way in which they see their learning.

Which definition most closely resembles what you are trying to achieve?

The Learner as an Individual: Conceptions of Learning

The literature that we have briefly reviewed goes some way to explain notions that you may have unconsciously picked up and used in your own teaching. We have pointed to the fact that the desire to get to underlying mechanisms involved in traditional conceptions of learning meant that the complexity of the learning situation was sometimes ignored. Naturalistic studies, those employing experimental methods but in situations very close to natural settings, have provided descriptions of learning which may have a more authentic feel for practitioners in higher and further education.

Saljo (1984), interviewed adults to find out what they thought about learning and found the five different conceptions which appear in Enquiry Task 2.1. He identified as a major division the conception of learning as increasing knowledge through the acquisition of facts by memorizing, (this represents a surface approach) and learning as understanding reality by abstracting meanings (a deep approach). He saw the idea of learning as acquiring skills as intermediate between the two major conceptions.

In an experiment by Marton and Saljo, reported in Entwistle (1984), involving reading a text, those students whose predominant approach to learning was to memorize failed to perform well. Those who concentrated on reading for meaning performed better. Those who failed to get the point of the text did so because they did not try to do so. In further experiments, it was shown that students have fundamental differences in approaches to learning. Even in situations where the assessment requirements demand a deep conception of learning the students employing surface approaches interpret the assessment demands in a surface way.

This should not be interpreted as implying that surface learning does not have a place but rather that it is not sufficient. Other approaches are also needed. You will probably have some students who will have great difficulty in seeing learning as anything other than characterized by a surface approach. For reasons which will be developed below, these students will tend not to be successful.

Enquiry Task 2.2

Brown and Atkins (1988) have identified two dominant orientations. Unlike the research from which the ideas of deep and surface approaches derives, their descriptions do not imply passivity as a characteristic of the surface learner, but do capture the essentially reproductive nature of the learning.

Look at some of the learning demands required by one of the courses you teach.

Tick off from the following list the processes that are required by the learning demands of your course.

Knowledge seekers
Storing facts
Collecting skills, procedures
Breaking down problems and tasks into separate subunits
Making links within units of knowledge
Working methodically through logical order of task or problem
Analysing
Using systematic trial and error
Evaluating data

Understanding seekers
Relating information to own experience
Linking to other knowledge
Restructuring for personal meaning
Working from whole picture
Searching for underlying structure, pupose, and meaning
Intuitive use of evidence
Using analogies and metaphors

Does the course require students to be seekers after information or seekers after understanding?

The Learners' Educational Orientation

There are other sorts of studies that attempt to capture more of the meaning students are making of their learning and their learning processes in natural situations. Case study research has provided a valuable way to interpret student behaviour. The central intention of these studies is not to explain by discovering general laws or cognitive processes, but to provide descriptions that will illuminate and inform the practitioners' judgments in practical situations.

However, in thinking about the learner as an individual you may wish to reflect on more general considerations than students' conceptions of learning. The illumination of these factors go some way to helping us understand differences in attitude and motivation between students, for instance, case studies of students' perceptions, focused on aspects such as their personal goals, values and purposes in studying. Gibbs, Morgan and Taylor, reported in Entwistle (1984) found that students typically have a complex mix of personal views, ideas about learning and ways of going about learning, which can change over time.

You have probably found that students get different things from the same course. Some students not only gain an understanding of the course content but also gain in confidence, change in attitude, increase their critical awareness and so on.

From the point of educational orientation, the student's success or failure is judged in personal terms according to the student's own agenda. The analysis of educational orientation does not presuppose types of student but types of orientation which might inform our understanding as tutors. An understanding of these helps us to understand the approach to learning a student might adopt. Taylor (1978) identified four distinct types of orientation. These are academic orientation, where students' goals are to do with the academic aspect of higher education; the vocational orientation, where students' concerns are with getting a job; personal orientation, where the goal is personal development; and social orientation, where goals are to do with the student's lifestyle. The categories were further refined. The academic orientation could be divided into two subtypes, intrinsic orientation where the student is interested in the content of the course; and extrinsic orientation where the student is primarily interested in educational progression through the system. Enquiry Task 2.3 sets out all the categories.

Enquiry Task 2.3

Choose a small group of students you teach and through discussion try to locate the orientation of each of them below.

Students' Educational Orientations

Orientation	Interest	Aim	Concerns
Vocational	Intrinsic	Training	Relevance of course to future career
Vocational	Extrinsic	Qualification	Recognition of worth of qualification
Academic	Intrinsic	Follow intellectual interest	Room to choose stimulating lectures

---

Academic	Extrinsic	Educational progression	
Personal	Intrinsic	Self-improvement	Challenging, interesting material
Personal	Extrinsic	Compensation or feedback	Passing course, proof of capability
Social	Intrinsic	Having a good time	Facilities for sport and social activities

How well did you know them?

Write about the implications of knowing your students' educational orientation for your practice.

Approaches to Learning: Deep Learners and Surface Learners

In an influential series of studies carried out by Marton and Saljo reported in Entwistle (1984) categories were derived from observing the way in which a group of students went about learning an article for a test. Those whose main strategy was to look for facts that might appear in the test (a surface approach to learning) were less successful than those whose strategy was to try to understand the meaning of the article (a deep approach to learning).

The student who takes a deep approach will be able to relate previous knowledge to new knowledge and become involved in an active process of comparing, contrasting, testing and relating knowledge from different courses. Theoretical ideas will be related to the student's everyday experience. The student will try to relate and distinguish evidence and argument, and organize and structure content into a coherent whole. The emphasis will be internal and the impulse to learn comes from within the student.

In contrast to this, in the surface approach to learning, the student focus is on the 'signs', for example, the words and sentences of the text, or the formulae needed to solve the problem. The focus is on unrelated parts of the task. Information for assessment is simply memorized and acts and concepts are associated unreflectively. Principles are not distinguished from examples. The task is treated as an external imposition, and the emphasis is external and the impulse to learn comes from the demands of assessment.

The idea that surface learning is a less effective approach is an oversimplification of a complex field of study. Each attribution needs to be thought about in context. Not all learning tasks require a deep approach, for instance learning keyboard skills. Not all learning tasks are problem-solving ones. We learn for example, data, laws, principles and propositions, which might require us to adopt both deep and surface approaches. A successful learner is likely to have a repertoire of learning approaches which match to the requirements of the learning task. An important role of the tutor is to help students become aware of different approaches to learning tasks and to provide key elements of a curriculum that foster a deep approach.

Although Marton and Saljo found a close connection between approach to learning and the quality of the learning outcome. However, it seems to be difficult to 'change' students who continue to adopt a surface approach even if they are required to answer questions designed to encourage an attention to meaning. In Marton and Saljo's study (1984), surface learners answered 'deep' questions in a superficial way and missed the opportunity for reflection. Questions that were intended to help the student to a deep approach became the object towards which the learning was directed in an expedient way, as an end rather than as a means. They concluded that it is easy to induce a surface, reproductive approach by structuring the learning demand, but very difficult to induce a deep approach. In the experiment only half the students interpreted the demands in the way intended. Others were solely concerned with the requirements of the test.

It may be possible to promote a deep approach by altering the learning demands for some but not all students. This implies that the reflective practitioner may need to find ways to make the nature of the learning approach required for learning tasks quite explicit. Some surface learners' inability to switch to a deep approach may result from inexperience or from their perception of the assessment system.

Learners begin their studies with their own educational orientations. Taylor (1978) found that intrinsic motivation, or interest, leads to a deep approach over time, but it may be that intrinsic interest is 'found' in students rather than 'created'.

Fransson's (1977) finding, that a deep approach is associated with absence of threat and absence of anxiety has important implications for tutors. It seems that in order to promote a deep approach, the climate of learning is a crucial factor and one over which you have some degree of influence. You may decide to keep in mind the students' interests and try to eliminate factors, such as anxiety, that lead to an overreliance on a surface approach.

Enquiry Task 2.4

Examine a course handbook that is given to students.

- What views of learning are transmitted by your department's handbook?
- What hidden messages are transmitted by the assessment scheme?
- What explicit messages are there about models of learning?
- Write down any phrases you find that might give the student a clue about the department's view on learning.
- Are there phrases that are ambiguous?

Remember the absence of information can be significant.

What was left out which you would wish to add?

Helping Students to Learn More Effectively

You may find the idea of matching teaching to the present level of understanding of your students daunting, especially where large classes inhibit the kind of interaction possible in small groups. However it may be possible to investigate whether there is a mismatch between your aims for your courses and your students' orientations. Finding out what your students expect and what their purposes for study are can explain why they can evaluate the same event in different ways.

You may also find the idea of providing for different learning needs in the same class highly problematic. You may be unfamiliar with differentiation in learning at further or higher education level. Nevertheless, with increasing numbers of mature students and students from diverse backgrounds it is an idea that should be considered.

It is possible to differentiate either by setting a common task with extension tasks for those who are more able, or by setting different tasks for those at different stages in their learning. Both approaches have drawbacks. The common task may be beyond some, and fail to challenge others. If some are required to tackle more challenging, additional work, it may encourage unhelpful stratification among students and can lead to resentment all round. Setting work appropriate to a student's level of development presupposes you know them well enough. It is very unlikely that you would have the information to sustain such an approach.

It has been suggested that a better way of dealing with the problem is to set a common group task, where students work collaboratively and the more experienced student is enabled to contribute more for the benefit of the whole group. Differential student input can be reflected in the assessment rubric (see Chapter 4) whereby students are invited to allot marks equally or differentially according to how they perceived the relative contributions of the group. Differentiation can also be achieved by asking students to choose their own assessment criteria from a menu.

Many problem-solving tasks can be achieved at a variety of levels, if they are designed to be open-ended. For instance, in a first year degree course in environmental science, at the start of the physical science strand, students are presented with various substances and told to work in small groups to 'find out all you can about each substance'. Those with a biological background can find out some quite basic things about the substances and about experimentation in chemistry, whereas those with chemistry qualifications can perform more sophisticated experiments. At the end of the session, each group shares their practice and results, and each is likely to have discovered something valuable and particular to itself. At the end of the session the tutor can draw out some general principles about processes in physical science and the main items of knowledge acquired.

Gibbs (1992) suggests that it is possible to build into course design, methods that foster deeper approaches through the encouragement of independent learning, (negotiated between student and tutor), personal development and problem-based learning. You might think about whether to require explicit reflection by students on their learning or to include opportunities for independent group work. In any case, it seems that students are more likely to adopt deeper approaches to learning where they learn by doing or through project work and where tutors have deliberate strategies for developing learning skills.

Enquiry Task 2.5

With a colleague, discuss a course you are currently both teaching and try to identify those elements of it that require a deep approach and those which require a surface approach.

List them below.

Elements encouraging a deep approach

1
2
3
4
5
6

Elements encouraging a surface approach

1
2
3
4
5
6

Is it possible to make a tentative statement about the quality of learning on the course?

What criteria do you think indicate quality in learning?

An element of independent learning, negotiated between the tutor and the students can be achieved in a variety of ways. For example, some items in the syllabus can be categorized as core and compulsory and others as open to negotiation. You might also leave vacant slots in the course outline to be filled by content requested by students as they become more certain of their needs.

Personal development is often achieved through the development of interpersonal and group working skills (see Chapter 3). Reflection can be encouraged by asking students to keep reflective diaries, portfolios of work, and to engage in self and peer assessment exercises (see Chapter 4). Independent group work, when it works well, can be very productive. It does, however, require careful management if you are to manage those students who are unable to contribute in a fair and responsible way and those alarmed at being given a measure of responsibility for their own learning. Some students and some teaching staff tend to see such methods as 'pooled ignorance', but if carefully structured, they can provide more opportunities for real attitude change as well as for intellectual and interpersonal development.

You may find that you need to help students by talking about the processes involved in learning and the attendant emotions of disorientation and anxiety. You may find it is very useful to create a five minute slot at the start of sessions, to invite students to bring up any problems, worries or anxieties that they may be experiencing. Furthermore you might invite students to reflect on theirs ideas of what learning, knowledge and being good at a subject actually means. You could invite students to become aware of their learning strategies and ask them to consider how effective they are.

Techniques for Active Learning and the Student as Reflective Practitioner

There are useful techniques for helping students to read in an active way, for helping them to participate in class discussion, and for tracking and evaluating their own learning progress. Some are discussed very briefly below.

Concept Mapping

The basic idea of concept mapping is to ask students to draw a circle with a key concept in it that you want to explore and then to produce or brainstorm related ideas, which are then arranged spoke-like around the circle. This is a very quick way of assessing your students' current understanding. It is useful to ask students to modify their concept maps as the course and their understanding develops. It can also be used by students as a form of note taking. Each key idea on the map can be cross-referenced to source material or more detailed notes. This technique encourages deep learning, (but does not of course guarantee it) by mapping connections, charting development of thinking, providing an easily accessible *aide-mémoire*. It could provide you with evidence of a student's approach to learning and give you a basis for intervention.

Jigsaw Reading

Jigsaw reading provides the opportunity to talk about reading and the difference between passive approaches and interrogative approaches. In this method a complex piece of reading is divided into parts and groups are invited to summarize each part without having read the other parts. From the summary a composite reading is formed and recorded on a flip chart. Students, having gone through this process, are better able to tackle the reading of difficult articles. You might use this method to assess the present level of understanding of the class or to help the students to deepen their understanding through discussion of the composite record of the reading. Above all it encourages an active, interrogative approach to reading.

Student summaries

It is usual for the tutor to summarize what has been achieved in a class. It is very instructive to allot this task to the students. You could invite them to write a short paragraph and then ask for some volunteers to read their summaries out. This should give some instant feedback on what has been understood and what needs to be covered again. Allowing for opportunities for students to speak out loud may also help build confidence in speaking in front of the group. The requirement to represent for themselves in their own words what they have learnt, encourages deep learning, since it presupposes or requires understanding.

Enquiry Task 2.6

Using the ideas of concept mapping, jigsaw reading and student summaries *either* think of a way you might apply one of the ideas above *or* design and try out a new technique.

Your technique should embody the following features:

- Student activity
- Minimizes anxiety
- Encourages deep learning
- Addresses student interests
- Allows for student diversity

What kind of feedback did the technique you tried give you about your students?

Biggs (cited in Entwistle, 1992) argues that the activity of the student is the most important factor in the learning situation. He suggests that to create the right conditions for effective student activity, there should be a 'felt need to know' by the student, which can be created by making the curriculum task-focused. In addition there should be a warm interpersonal climate; students should feel some degree of ownership or control over their studies; students should be enabled to interact with others; and they should be encouraged to think about their own thinking and learning processes. One to one contact with a tutor should be available, and the knowledge base should be well structured. This implies that the context, or institutional factors and how they are perceived by individuals on learning is centrally important to learning.

Institutional Factors in Learning

In a study of the effects of assessment in the USA, Becker *et al.* (1968) showed that the 'grade-point average' permeated the entire college experience for students and provided the backdrop to their studies. This perspective defined the learning situation for students, who saw grades as defining success. They found that there was a real conflict between getting the grade and really learning. Whatever tutors believed themselves to be doing, the assessment system was overriding their intentions and driving students into coping strategies.

It could be argued that tests which elicit a surface approach block the development of any interest in the material to be learned and therefore tend to preclude a deep approach. Saljo (1984) showed that two groups in his study read differently because of the way they expected to be assessed. However there was a great variation both in the processes of learning and outcome of learning within the group that was given questions intended to induce a deep approach, perhaps due to the participants' different perceptions of what was required of them. Some of the differences may reflect something that the students brought with them, such as their past experiences of similar situations and ideas of what it takes to learn. It seems important therefore that students are given messages that help them to formulate more adequate and appropriate views of learning. Where this does not happen, for instance where contradictory messages are conveyed by the hidden curriculum, learning pathologies may occur.

Entwistle *et al.* (1979) developed carefully designed surveys of study methods and student perceptions of academic environments. They also conducted in-depth interviews of students on study methods. Their findings showed that deep and surface learning are distinctive processes, although both may be necessary to achieve understanding. They also identified three stable orientations or styles of learning, 'personal meaning', 'reproducing' and 'achieving'. Personal meaning is associated with intrinsic motivation, a preference for autonomy, and a deep or versatile approach to learning. Reproducing is associated with extrinsic motivation, fear of failure, anxiety, syllabus-boundedness, and surface approaches. Achieving is associated with hope for success, a calculative approach to study, a willingness to adopt any method that leads to high grades. Low scores on achieving are associated with dilatoriness, personal disorganization, and random study methods.

Ramsden and Entwistle (1981) related these orientations to student perceptions of their academic departments. Using a sample of 2200 students from arts, social science and engineering courses within higher education, they found that departments considered to give good teaching were strongly orientated towards personal meaning. In departments thought to be poor on teaching the teaching was directed to reproducing. These findings held for all departments and took account of differences in the pre-university qualifications of the sample.

Competency, National Vocational Qualifications and Learning in Workplace Settings

It is interesting in the light of the above discussions of the optimum conditions for learning to consider the move to competency-based models of the curriculum for courses concerned with professional development. The key issues for the reflective practitioner that we posed at the beginning of the chapter were 'How do students learn?', 'How can they be helped to learn?' and 'How are factors in the educational situation helping or hindering learning?'

Competencies are those behaviours that are deemed necessary to the effective discharge of an activity or work role. The thinking behind this model is located in the behaviourist tradition, in the sense that it casts learning outcomes as behaviours.

Many areas of industry and the professions in Britain now have lead bodies which are responsible for defining 'standards' within a system for National Vocational Qualifications (NVQs). The standards are sets of competences that define the job at various levels of seniority and responsibility. Thus a student or a worker can obtain NVQs that define their level of competence, from level one, the novice's stage, to level five, which is equivalent to the post-graduate stage.

One feature of the NVQ system is that there is no associated prescribed scheme of study that complements the standards. This is a strength and a weakness, in that it allows people without formal qualifications to be accredited for what they already know, but it does not provide them with the guidance and the tuition to progress.

So far we have discussed the problems arising for learning partly in an institutional setting. However, that institutional setting usually includes people whose primary responsibility is the learning and the welfare of their learners. In the work setting, responsibility is primarily elsewhere, since the main business of the workplace is not usually education or training. Work mentors are therefore in a difficult position. Assessors under the NVQ scheme simply assess. They do not have the responsibility for sorting out next steps. The outcomes are defined (and doing this is also problematic) but other factors such as the characteristics of the student, the nature of the workplace, relationships with higher and further education, the nature of the learning tasks, and so on, are all missing.

It could be said that it does not matter how students arrive at the competences, but this ignores the way understanding governs intelligent action and the moral dimension to action. For example, in learning to teach it isn't enough to be competent, you also need to be compassionate. Compassion is built on deep understanding of for example, student development, the problems of family life, the reasons for learning failure, as well as how to manage students' learning and structure the substantive content in such a way as to make it accessible.

Understanding may not develop unless students are given the time to reflect, read and discuss. The tutor's role within further and higher education is to facilitate learning as well as to instruct. It may be unreasonable to expect untrained workplace trainers to fulfil this role. We have implied that the good tutor is someone who can use learners' concepts; challenge students' thinking; set goals; encourage independence and responsibility in learning; maintain dialogue; give meaningful feedback; and monitor progress. This level of involvement is not captured by the NVQ model as it tends to be presented in the literature. There are, however, more sophisticated models of workplace learning, using learning contracts (Knowles, 1986) and based on the theoretical ideas of Kolb (1984). In these, the idea of competences is supplemented with strategies to encourage reflection and self-knowledge.

Andragogy and Tutors' Views of Their Place in the Learning Milieu

An alternative way of thinking about learning has been derived from work by Carl Rogers (1983). His views seem to overcome the negative aspects of other models we have been considering so far and give weight to students' orientations, the context of learning and the tutor perspective. His work has been influential in thinking about the needs of learners for a climate of trust in the classroom, a say in what is learnt, the development of confidence and self-esteem, the discovery of the excitement of learning, and the need to become independent learners.

Unlike behaviourist theories, which imply manipulation of the environment to produce certain behaviours, the emphasis is on self-determination and free choice in learning. Rogers reached these conclusions from reflecting upon his own experiences of working with people as a psychotherapist and university teacher. He believes that, in order for learning to be meaningful and rewarding, the student must be allowed freedom of expression and the tutor's unqualified positive regard. Rogers argues that these needs are best met by tutors adopting a facilitative stance towards their practice. He is critical of traditional didactic or expository methods, unless they are part of a different approach to education.

These ideas can best be illustrated by drawing a comparison between traditional, (although in many respects outmoded), definition of pedagogy and what Knowles (1984) termed andragogy, or the study of teaching adults. Knowles uses the term 'pedagogy' in a sense that is different from most other researchers. In his definition of a 'pedagogical' scheme, the tutor accepts that the learner will be dependent. The presumption of the way Knowles defines 'andragogy' is that learners should be encouraged to become increasingly self directive. Pedagogically oriented tutors will tend to be more authoritative, formal and develop a competitive environment. The andragogically inclined tutor will wish for a climate that is collaborative, informal, respectful and involves the tutor in learning as well as the students. Pedagogical approaches assume that the learner's previous experience is of little worth. The andragogical tutor sees learners' experiences as a rich resource for learning. Furthermore, they, unlike the pedagogical tutor, will involve the students in planning, diagnosis of needs and the negotiation of sequence.

This approach to teaching has sometimes been called 'open'. Rogers (1983) has reported research that supports the argument that a facilitative approach is effective. He argues that students should be taught how to learn, since information rapidly becomes obsolete. Above all Rogers wants students and tutors to recognize that emotions are an essential part of 'significant' learning: that is learning which develops the whole person as well as the intellect.

Being a facilitator is often misinterpreted as not transmitting any information at all. Rogers pointed out that some learning is threatening, especially learning that implies a re-evaluation of one's idea of oneself. The students may experience an external threat if they are not able to take a deep approach to learning because the subject matter is so new, complex and extensive. The desire for students to become autonomous learners has to be balanced by taking on board the idea of students evaluating their own learning needs. Therefore, it may be important not to be overtaken by evangelical zeal in pursuit of the ideals in Rogers's thinking. Students' access to the knowledge-base of their subject has to be carefully structured and presented.

Ausubel (1968) drew attention to the fact that the learner's pre-existing knowledge was crucial in determining what new information could be assimilated and how. New information has to be constructed by the individual, and concepts contain a mixture of shared knowledge and knowledge that is unique to the individual. This gives credence to the view that the best starting point for learning is with the knowledge, skills and understandings that a student brings. It implies that you are able to diagnose the place the student is starting from and has implications for assessment and evaluation methods. Diagnostic methods are only a starting point. Material needs to be appropriately structured and sequenced. This clearly has implications for the role of the tutor.

Rogers' view of the aim of education as one of unleashing a sense of inquiry, opening everything to questioning and exploration and recognizing that everything is in a process of change is a commonly held ideal. On the other hand, his claim that facilitation of significant learning rests upon attitudinal qualities of tutors, and the accepting, empathetic relationship tutors establish with their students, ignores the tutors' crucial role in the management of learning for whole cohorts in a climate of reduced resources for higher and further education.

There is an important dimension to learning, especially in the context of teaching adults, that has not been addressed so far in this chapter and that is its potential for emancipation. Mezirow (1981) interviewed women returning to education about the processes they underwent. Their responses led Mezirow to his view of 'perspective transformation'. This is the process of becoming critically aware of how and why assumptions arising from the psychological and cultural environment restrict the way we see ourselves and our relationships. Emancipation involves reconstituting this structure to enable us to develop a more inclusive and discriminating integration of experience and to act upon these new understandings. Part of the learning for the group he studied involved a re-evaluation of their previously taken for granted assumptions about their gender roles.

This process may involve students in a painful and disorienting dilemma. There may be a period of self-examination, followed by a critical assessment of role assumptions and a sense of alienation from traditional expectations. Students may wish to explore new ways of acting to build competence and self-confidence in new roles. Emancipation can enable them to plan courses of action, acquire relevant knowledge and skills, and finally reintegrate themselves into society on the basis of conditions dictated by their new perspectives.

In our experience the emancipatory dimension of learning is particularly visible on professional development courses where people who have proved competence in their field face again the risk of highly visible failure. For example a headteacher on an MEd course will have to re-evaluate his or her view of themselves if it seems that they are failing to cope. Where a person's self-concept is tied to a highly visible role, anxiety may be very marked. It may help to talk to the group about the probability of experiencing a 'disorienting dilemma' and to allow time on the course for students to express their anxieties, so that reassurances can be given.

Planning for Learning

Effective planning for learning involves taking the factors relating to student learning into account and considering these in the light of the material or syllabus to be taught. There are many approaches to the planning of schemes of work and lessons, and you will need to develop your own. Some of these approaches are dealt with in the context of designing open learning programmes in Chapter 6, but all seem to include common elements.

In the design of a scheme of work for a group of students it is important to consider the aims of the programme. These aims can be conceptualized in terms of the model of the student you wish to develop; the qualities, skills and knowledge you want the student to acquire; or the 'job' which the programme is designed to achieve. For instance, if we took the first model, the aim of this book could be said to be 'to develop readers as reflective practitioners'. In the second model, the aim might be 'to enable the reader to function as an effective teacher in a variety of contexts and with a variety of students'. In the third model, the aim might be stated as 'to provide the reader with the tools for them to enquire into and develop their own teaching and values and student learning'.

It is also important to develop objectives for a scheme of work or a lesson. An objective describes the criteria by which you would recognize that desired learning has taken place. Objectives should be related to, but are not the same as, your overall aims. For instance, one objective for this chapter might be 'to encourage the reader to take action to match the delivery of parts of curriculum to differing levels of student ability'. Another objective might be 'to develop an awareness of the relationships of teaching methods to deep and surface approaches to learning'. The first of these objectives is expressed in behavioural terms, and therefore might be broken down into demonstrable competences. The second objective is not, and therefore success can only be inferred through discussion and reflection.

Planning for learning involves long-term, medium term and short-term planning. The long-term planning is important if you are not to deliver a 'Blue Peter' curriculum, one that contains lots of interesting 'things to do' but does not include notions of progression and integration of experiences. Medium term planning is important so that you and your students can see the next stage in their learning in a manageable form, so that they and you can plan for the use of time and to develop the particular skills and understandings needed to reach the next stage in learning. Short term planning is important because you and your students will work better if you know what you are going to do today, why you are going to do it and how you will know whether you have been successful.

It is our experience that in the early stages tutors tend to plan too much content and focus too little on management and organization. If you try to cover too much material, most of it will not get through to your students. You can probably achieve only one or two objectives (or items of learning) in one lesson. One of us gave one of her best lectures when she had to step into the breach at a moment's notice due to the illness of the normal teacher. Since she only had three ideas on the subject to be taught, she had to find several ways of using these ideas with the students. At the end of the session they said that they had learned more from that lecture than from the rest of the programmes altogether!

It is important to explore resources for learning in your planning. We outline opportunities for resource-based learning in some detail in Chapter 6, but it is important to remember that in many programmes, the time you are teaching the students is only a fraction of the time which is available for learning. It is our experience that tutors who help the students to structure their students' non-contact time help them to achieve better results.

In Chapter 7 we go into the use of audio-visual aids in some detail. These and other resources need planning but, effectively used, they can facilitate students' learning, perhaps through the involvement of more than one of their senses, or perhaps through the use of material to illustrate or manipulate an idea.

Most tutors build up their own bank of resources for learning. These may include overhead projector transparencies, useful papers, handouts and activity sheets, posters, videos and so on. We have learned from long and bitter experience that it is a good idea to set up an effective cataloguing and retrieval system from the start. One of us has her transparencies in plastic wallets in lever arch files, one file for each programme and each file organized into sections with labelled file dividers. Where a transparency might be included in more than one section, she makes a photocopy of it with a note as to where the original has been stored. She keeps other paper-based teaching materials in box files related to various broad topics. Within each box file, the paper is organized into plastic wallets, each carefully labelled. Her partner has a card index system for video-taped items, cross-referenced where an item might be used to illustrate more than one idea. The position of each item on each tape is also noted.

However you organize your materials, it is important to be systematic (overflowing cardboard boxes waste an enormous amount of tutor time) and for your systems to take account of the fact that many resources have application within several topics. The difficulties of management and organization can easily be underestimated. Audio-visual aids which have not been checked seem always to malfunction. If it is possible to misunderstand an instruction students will do so. Really good open and challenging questions seldom occur to inexperienced tutors off the top of their heads. Resources will be locked away in a cupboard without the key if they can be.

Enquiry Task 2.7

Undertake a resource audit of your department. List:

- the resources that are available for your subject;
- general resources available (such as computers).

Think about how you might use each resource in your teaching.

Find out:

- how you access each resource;
- what resources you are allowed to order;
- how you go about ordering resources yourself;
- how you put in a bid for more expensive equipment.

You need to think through each phase of the lesson or activity. How will you introduce the lesson? How will you link it to what came before? What will you need to get ready? What ground rules do you need to establish? What stimulus might you use to catch and keep the students' interest? What questions might you ask to make them really think? How will you vary the pace and teaching method so that the students are not doing the same type of thing for an hour? How can you make sure that all the students are working hard and fast (students seem to hate tutors who waste their time)? How will you deal with those students who work faster or slower than others? How long should each part of the lesson take? What will you do if one part takes longer than you expect? This last problem is very important. We have found that tutors often leave out the consideration of phases of a lesson. This is often where you order, 'name' and reinforce the students' learning. Without this, much of the learning will tend to be lost.

Enquiry Task 2.8

Plan a session using the following headings:

- Name of activity
- Nature of student group
- Objectives
- Resources required
- Ground rules/health and safety issues to be emphasized
- Introductory phase: Description, provision of cognitive challenge and timing
- Activity phase: Description, provision of cognitive challenge and timing
- Consolidation phase: Description and timing
- Evidence of success to be collected

How useful were the headings in structuring your thinking?
How would you adapt them?

Summary

Learning problems often reside in the teaching rather than the learners' ability. Factors in learning may include the match between teaching intentions and methods.

Behaviourism is one model of learning. Its features include:

- stimulus/response conditioning;
- reward and punishments as motivators;
- emotions as secondary reinforcers of learning; and
- a linear model of learning.

Criticisms of the model include a lack of emphasis on:

- the social and institutional setting for learning;
- complexity and individuality of individual's responses to stimuli;
- the learner's role in the active construction of meaning;
- the moral framework for learning;
- individual orientation to learning; and
- the laboratory setting of much of the basic research.

More recent research has focused on naturalistic settings and the exploration of students' goals (intrinsic and extrinsic) and orientation (vocational, academic, social and personal) to learning. Surface and deep approaches to learning have been identified. Surface approaches are characterized by:

- a focus on memorization, signs and formulae, and on parts rather than the whole task;
- particularization rather than abstraction;
- extrinsic motivation.

A deep approach is characterized by:

- the ability to relate new and previous knowledge and theory to experience;
- learning as an active process of comparing, testing and integrating knowledge;
- the ability to distinguish evidence and argument and to generalize;
- a holistic approach to understanding;
- intrinsic motivation.

Approaches to learning are influenced by:

- assessment forms;
- nature of the learning task;
- presence or absence of threat.

Deeper approaches are encouraged by:

- independent negotiated learning or groupwork;
- a focus on personal development;
- problem or project-based learning;
- encouraging students' explicit reflection;
- experimental learning methods.

Tutors have to cater for students with different abilities. Differentiation in learning may be achieved by:

- setting a variety of tasks;
- setting cooperative groupwork;
- differential assessment criteria;
- problem-solving achievable at different levels.

Institutional factors in learning include:

- assessment systems;
- the hidden curriculum;
- approaches to learning (meaning, reproducing and achieving).

The National Vocational Qualification scheme has the following features:

- a competency outcome-based approach;
- location in the behaviourist tradition;
- independence from particular educational settings.

The emotional factors in learning include:

- the meaning of the learning for the student;
- the pedagogic or andragogic approach of the tutor;
- the opportunities for self-evaluation;
- the respect accorded for the students' prior knowledge or experience;
- the student/tutor relationship.

Where the conditions are right, learning can be emancipatory and make the learner look at 'self' and the culture in new ways. Where the student's sense of self is very tied to success, learning can be particularly stressful. Planning for learning should include:

- the assessment of the students' needs and level;
- the identification of aims and objectives;
- progression;
- the specification of content;
- the specification of phasing and timing;
- resources;
- organization and management.

Entry for the Reflective Diary

Write about your conceptions of learning and orientation when you were an undergraduate or training for your career.

Did you experience any learning failure?

What did it feel like, and why did it occur?

References

AUSUBEL, D.P. (1968) *Educational Psychology: A Cognitive View*, New York, Holt, Rinehart and Winston.

BECKER, H.S., GREER, B. and HUGHES, E.C. (1968) *Making the Grade: The Academic Side of College Life*, New York, Wiley

BROWN, G. and ATKINS, M. (1988) *Effective Teaching in Higher Education*, London, Methuen.

CURZON, L.B. (1985) *Teaching in Further Education: An Outline of Principles and Practice*, London, Cassell, 3rd Edition.

ENTWISTLE, N.J. (1984) 'Contrasting perspectives on learning', in MARTON, F. HOUNSELL, D.J. and ENTWISTLE, N.J. (Eds) *The Experience of Learning*, Edinburgh, Scottish Academic Press.

ENTWISTLE, N.J. (1992) *The Impact of Teaching on Learning Outcomes in Higher Education: A Literature Review*, Sheffield, CVCP.

ENTWISTLE, N.J., HANLEY, M. and HOUNSELL, D.J. (1979) 'Identifying distinctive approaches to studying', *Higher Education*, **8**, pp. 365–80.

FRANSSON, A. (1977) 'On qualitative differences in learning. Effects of motivation and test anxiety on process and outcome'. *British Journal of Educational Psychology*, **47**, pp. 244–57.

GIBBS, G. (1992) *Improving the Quality of Student Learning*, Bristol, Technical and Educational Services, Bristol.

HULL, C.L. (1952) *A Behaviour System*, Yale University Press.

KNOWLES, M.S. (1984) *The Adult Learner: A Neglected Species*, Houston, TX, Gulf.

KNOWLES, M.S. (1986) *Using Learning Contracts: Practical Approaches to Individualizing and Structuring Learning*, San Francisco, CA, Jossey-Bass.

KOLB, D. (1984) *Experiential Learning*, Hemel Hempstead, Prentice-Hall.

MARTON, F. and SALJO, R. (1984) 'Approaches to learning', in MARTON, F., HOUNSELL, D.J. and ENTWISTLE, N.J. (Eds) *The Experience of Learning*, Edinburgh, Scottish Academic Press.

MEZIROW, J. (1981) 'A critical theory of adult learning and education', *Education*, **32**, 1, pp. 3–24.

PAVLOV, I. (1960) 'Conditioned Reflexes: An Investigation of the Physiological Activity of the Cerebral Cortex' translated from the Russian and edited by G.V. Antrep, New York, Dover Publications.

PERRY, W.G. (1970) *Forms of Intellectual and Ethical Development in the College Years*, New York, Holt, Rinehart and Winston.

RAMSDEN, P. and ENTWISTLE, N.J. (1981) 'Effects of academic departments and students' approaches to studying', *British Journal of Educational Psychology*, **51**, 1, pp. 368–83.

ROGERS, C. (1983) *Freedom to Learn for the '80s*, Columbus, OH, Charles E. Merrill.

SALJO, R. (1984) 'Learning from reading', in MARTON, F., HOUNSELL, D.J. and ENTWISTLE, N.J. (Eds) *The Experience of Learning*, Edinburgh, Scottish Academic Press.

SKINNER, B.F. (1954) 'The science of learning and the art of teaching', *Harvard Educational Review*, **24**, pp. 88–97.

SNYDER, B.R. (1971) *The Hidden Curriculum*, New York, Knopf.

TAYLOR, E. (1978) 'Orientations to study: A longitudinal interview investigation of students in two human studies degree courses at Surrey University', unpublished PhD thesis, Guildford, University of Surrey.

THORNDIKE, E.L. (1932) *The Fundamentals of Learning*, New York, Teachers' College.

WATSON, J.B. (1925) *Behaviourism*, London, Norton.

WALKER, S.W. (1984) *Learning Theory and Behaviour Modification*, London and New York, Methuen.

Suggested Reading

O'CONNELL, B. (1973) *Aspects of Learning*, London, George Allen and Unwin Ltd. Good introductions to the work of Pavlov, Thorndike, Watson, Hull and Skinner.

Chapter 3

Personal Development and Interpersonal Skills

Introduction

The personal development of students and their development of interpersonal skills are perhaps areas which most engage and most infuriate teachers in all sectors. Until recently they were considered by some to be beyond the remit of tutors in further and higher education. Many tutors have now become interested in the way they can affect learning. Definitions of learning which include qualities prerequisite for the reflective practice of a subject, open-mindedness, responsibility and wholeheartedness, depend on the students' personal development. Similarly, the skills underpinning the development of such qualities, especially communication skills and cooperative skills depend upon the development of interpersonal skills.

Personal development and the facilitation of interpersonal skills centrally concerns your sense of self and your definition of yourself as a teacher. It may lead you into vitally important, often rewarding but occasionally frightening involvement with your students and their problems (for instance, if you have to deal with verbal, racist aggression). If you engage with your students as people and believe that you and they should develop qualities of open-mindedness and responsibility, or believe that teaching and learning is sometimes focused on relationships and groupwork, this is an area that you cannot avoid.

In this chapter we argue that your role in the personal development of students and the development of their interpersonal skills is to enable students to become more aware of the assumptions, values and perspectives that influence them as learners. We look at the personal development and the development of interpersonal skills of the tutor and the facilitation of students' development as a unitary and reflexive process. In order to act effectively in interpersonal contexts, you and your students may need to develop an understanding of the various forces that affect the ways in which groups of people work together, in order that you and they can develop an awareness of the options open to them in choosing how to behave towards others. This may develop the inability to deal with the issues facing them. The intention is to enable students to develop a greater sensitivity to their own learning and to the situations in which they find themselves. For this to happen you may find you need a range of cognitive frameworks to help you analyse interpersonal situations. You may wish to introduce your students to these frameworks so that they refer to them while they develop the understandings and skills necessary to form and put options into action, and to reflect on the processes involved in interaction and the feelings which accompany it.

Issues within personal development and the development of interpersonal skills can seem deceptively simple or highly theoretical and general, depending upon how they are defined. It is an area that is concerned with the way learning is acquired and used in interaction rather than with knowledge itself. In particular, it is an area that focuses on how people behave and feel, rather than a more narrowly academic focus on what they know and understand. If personal development and the development of interpersonal skills are to be tackled in any depth, you may find that they represent problems that are embedded in the tutor and student roles. You may find yourself facing real dilemmas about the boundaries of your roles and responsibilities. These can and should be tackled, but you may need to study and experiment in order to develop the skill and understanding to handle them.

A concern for personal development and the development of interpersonal abilities implies a belief in encouraging individuals to become more involved in their own learning. It emphasizes the importance of the change process and involves you and your students in choices about the pace and direction of learning. This chapter is based on ideas outlined by Kolb (1984) and the humanist tradition, rather than (say) a behaviourist approach (see Chapter 2). In particular we focus on the identification of learner needs and goals; on the analysis of learning and management styles and the learning opportunities these present; and on group processes in achieving goals. There is an assumption that effective learning involves you and your students in reviewing your own experiences, collecting data and observations about that experience, analysing that data and finally modifying your behaviour. It implies that part of your role is to show your students how to evaluate their own learning, feelings and interactions as a student of a subject. In this respect it is similar to the evaluation-led approach to reflective practice that underpins much of the thinking about teaching within this book. You are, in effect, facilitating your students' development as reflective practitioners at the same time as they help you to do the same. Thus you may become less of a detached facilitator of learning and more involved in the learning itself. You may find yourself confronted by difficult personal and professional issues in this process.

The chapter rests on the assumption that the development of interpersonal skills involves looking inwards. This presupposes that until you and your students can understand yourselves, you will have difficulties in improving your relations with others. The onus for personal development and the development of inter-personal skills is thus placed on the individual. You are responsible for your own learning and the direction of your development and ultimately, your students are responsible for theirs. This does not mean that you are irrelevant to the students' learning in this area. You can provide structure and support for students, but you cannot be in control of the individual learning in this area in the same way as you might be in subject learning. Similarly, you may need the help of an experienced colleague whom you can trust in your own personal development.

Interpersonal skills and personal development are concerned with feelings as much as with ideas. You may decide that workshops focusing on this area should be protected places, where students are free to experiment and try out new ways of working. This kind of development will be facilitated where group members are supportive of each other, extend trust towards one another and avoid competitive and defensive behaviour. It is part of your skill to facilitate such an atmosphere.

Personal Development

Amongst the most interesting dimensions for tutors and students to explore are the approaches to learning described by Entwistle (1981). Some students have a strong 'achievement orientation'. These students tend to be competitive and to have well organized study habits. They are motivated by a desire to do well and will do whatever this involves. Some students have a 'meaning orientation' to learning. This implies that they have a deep approach to learning and an intention to make sense of the subject, an interest in the subject matter and a desire to learn. They follow up interests whether or not they are part of the assessment of the course. They are motivated by a strong desire to understand what they are studying and find what they are learning interesting. Students who combine an achievement with a meaning orientation tend to do very well indeed. Some students have a 'reproducing orientation'. This indicates a surface approach to learning (see Chapter 2). Students with this approach tend to be extrinsically motivated. Because they are studying to achieve a pass or a qualification, rather than because of an interest in the subject, they focus on instrumental learning. They do not explore beyond the syllabus boundaries. They tend to memorize, rather than understand subject matter. Despite focusing on the assessed course they tend to do badly.

Personal development is a broad topic that may be taken to include all the non-subject learning that we hope that our students will achieve, having non-work interests and a good social life. We define it more narrowly. The aspects which, for the purposes of this chapter, are included within the category 'personal development', are those non-subject specific aspects of student learning you might intentionally teach through the classroom and other processes that you employ. Non-subject specific skills and understanding that are directly related to the education process and affect student performance in learning are included. Thus student learning about how to attract the opposite sex would not be included, but the ability to work as part of a team would.

The chapter is premised upon the view that if you wish to foster your students' personal development, you will need to develop an understanding both of yourself as a manager of student learning and of the students' strengths and weaknesses. Furthermore, there is an assumption that it is part of your role to encourage students to reflect on their present skills and their styles of learning and interaction in order to analyse and remedy weaknesses for themselves and identify and build upon strengths.

This may be problematic, or even impossible in systems that rely on mass lecturing as the main teaching method, or where teaching is restricted to short modules that give little time to develop relationships. In these circumstances, the best you may be able to do is to provide your students with starting points for their own self-assessment.

Personal development depends on a mixture of feedback and reflection. To a great extent the students are responsible for their own reflection (although you can aid the process by the way you structure material and questioning), but you are likely to be mainly responsible for giving or organizing feedback (although you may be interested to find ways that students can also provide each other with supportive and structured feedback). The business of providing feedback on personal (rather than academic) issues is a delicate one. You might decide to indicate that feedback is available, but only give it when requested to do so. For instance, you may have set up some group work which is not successful because some of the students are not listening to others. You might wait until your advice was sought or risk their hostility and point to the problem and suggest solutions. On the other hand you may decide that it is better to ask the group to assess the way they are functioning (perhaps using a checklist) as a starting point, since they may be aware of weaknesses. It is usually less painful to admit to faults than to have them pointed out. In these circumstances, you may be able to help the student to focus on action points rather than judgment.

In providing feedback you might decide to focus on a very limited range of specific behaviour that is in the student's control. Sweeping, judgmental statements about a person's character or personality are likely to be damaging and may well be wrong. For instance, in the case above, an insensitive tutor might tell a student that they are domineering, intolerant and a poor listener, when part or all of the real problem might lie with a lack of time management or poor preparation on the part of the other students.

Feedback is likely to lose part of its value unless it is immediate. It may be more useful if it is given as soon as possible after an event or behaviour and focuses on the positive as well as the negative. Personal development stems from building on strengths as much as remedying weaknesses. Personal development is difficult and time consuming. It may be unreasonable to expect people to work on more than one tightly defined aspect at a time. We believe that it is essential that the receiver of the feedback should be invited to react to and evaluate the feedback, immediately and after they have had time to think about it with others.

Personal Style and Teaching and Learning

Part of personal development is the expansion of the learning repertoire available to each student. An understanding of your own personal style and the variety of styles that students may manifest may be necessary if you are to foster this kind of personal development in learning. In addition, you may wish to encourage your students to start to think about their personal learning styles and to consider strategies for developing them.

Messick (1976) describes a wide variety of dimensions which might be explored. You may wish to encourage students to analyse whether they are habitually reflective or impulsive. That is, whether they tend to evaluate a response before making it, rather than responding immediately. Students may also have sensory modes that they prefer and through which they learn best. Many tutors rely on speaking, or the auditory mode, to help students' understanding, when the students may learn better through the use of kinesthetic or visual material. Students who do not understand an explanation may need to 'see' or 'experience' a solution. For instance, some of our students recently assembled themselves into a car to illustrate the idea of an extended metaphor or conceit during an English session.

Some students learn better in a serialist way. They need to grasp new material through a step by step approach. Others prefer a holistic approach and prefer to grasp the whole picture before analysing the parts. Students vary in their ability to process complex situations. Some prefer simple or well patterned situations. This may be related to convergent and divergent thinking, that is, a tendency to look for a single outcome against the tendency to entertain multiple possibilities. There is a general (though not exclusive) tendency for the approach at higher education levels to be more appropriate to holistic learners who can process complex situations. It may be part of your role as a tutor to present material in a way that encourages a flexible approach.

A further dimension that may be related to this is the extent to which students tend towards taking chances as opposed to seeking certainty. This is described as 'risk-taking continuousness'. It may be related to students' tolerance for unrealistic experiences. Some students seem to be more willing than others to accept information that is improbable or unconventional. Others faced with such information will reject it or define out such information.

Methods for Developing Interpersonal Skills

It is not easy to define interpersonal competence. It is a skill area, as can be seen by thinking about such matters as communication, although this may also involve knowledge (as in the case of intercultural communication) or 'collateral' knowledge (understanding about behaviour, such as a doctor's interview, which is governed by conventions). It also seems to include qualities such as personal warmth and an ability to project a genuine interest in others. Much educational management theory implies that the ability to promote the owning and sharing of personal ideas and feelings with appropriate others, and being receptive to the need of others to do the same are all important. This implies a 'good' interpersonal climate that is relatively free of power differentials, competition and unfavourable comparison of one individual with another. This is not the case in many educational settings. It is part of your skill to encourage students away from an instrumental grades and competition focus towards cooperative learning motivated by the intrinsic interest and value of the material. This can be particularly difficult in some assessment and institutional climates.

Tutors in colleges and universities tend to be interested in helping their students to develop a range of interpersonal skills for a variety of reasons. These include the deepening of the understanding of subject matter which often takes place when groups of students discuss, explore and apply it. Tutors usually feel that they are preparing students for a personal and professional life outside of the college or university, but, whether they feel it or not transferable skills are valuable and wanted by employers. These skills are behind the entrepreneurial thrust of much recent development in further and higher education. The range of competences that may be defined as 'interpersonal skills' may be centrally important to success and satisfaction in many careers and personal life.

The application of the subject to real life situations is an important issue in reflection. Dilemmas can be explored within the context of group work and learning. Subject understanding may be enhanced and interpersonal skills developed through group work. Priestly *et al.* (1978) suggest interpersonal skill learning will be facilitated if students perceive the learning to be voluntary and the learning situation is sufficiently open for the students to feel free to ask for and challenge information about the aims, content, methods and assessment involved in their learning. This implies that the tutor models interpersonal competence and accepts that his or her authority is always open to challenge. Such challenge is important for the tutor's development as well. As a reflective practitioner you will be seeking out alternative viewpoints on the value system that underpins your practice and on the practice itself.

When students are learning to solve problems, you may find that they are also teaching you how to present the course more effectively. You may wish to encourage them to suggest ways of making their learning more effective. This is essential data for reflective action. The conditions above imply an assumption of optimism on your part and that you assume that your students are capable of changing, growing and learning and that they will influence the learning environment in positive ways. Personal competence and the development of interpersonal skills seem to be best achieved in an atmosphere of optimism. The institutional climate may affect the way in which you achieve this. It is difficult, but remains important, to maintain an optimism about students and colleagues in systems which seem relatively impervious to change or where autonomy is limited.

Work within management contexts implies that failures in interpersonal situations are often not the fault of the participants. An understanding of some of the likely causes may enable you to set up situations where students can work more effectively towards success. Malone (1988) stated that there may be a failure to identify the criteria for successful performance. For instance, we sometimes talk about cooperative skills without defining the subskills (e.g. listening skills, assertiveness, organization, time management) or being sure ourselves how we would recognize them. In addition, you may not have assessed the learning needs of the student accurately or you may not have obtained the student's commitment to those needs. This may be particularly likely to happen in interpersonal skill learning, and since we largely define ourselves through our interaction with others, recognizing and facing the need to change patterns of interaction can be a painful process. It may seem obvious to you that a student lacks a particular skill, but not to him or her. You may need to set up situations where the student can explore the issues at a distance (for instance in hypothetical settings), before he or she is ready to look closely at themselves.

A failure by you or the course structure to support the students' learning process may be damaging. This is especially true where there is a lack of congruence between the learning process the student is exposed to and their particular needs. Students are particularly vulnerable to being set up to fail in the area of interpersonal development, especially if the learning process is set up on an assessment by the tutor of what they think would be useful for 'most' students.

The final difficulty identified by Malone is the problem of timing an experience in the development process. Students may not be emotionally or intellectually 'ready' for the experience, or the learning may not be immediately applied and therefore lost.

Malone's work implies that successful interpersonal skill learning depends on a programme managed by a tutor who has collected careful observational and other evidence about the students' interpersonal skill development and ensured that the students have the information necessary for success and, as far as possible, an immediate opportunity to apply their learning.

Enquiry Task 3.1

Identify one each of the following:

- The silent student
- The student who talks too much
- A student presenting another interpersonal problem (e.g. aggression)

Discuss the problems with an experienced colleague and together list strategies which may:

- Influence the aspects of behaviour of each student that you consider to be problematic;
- Enable each to develop a greater awareness of the effect of their behaviour on their own learning; and
- Enable each to develop a greater awareness of the effect of their behaviour on the learning of others.

Design an observation schedule to collect evidence of the effectiveness of each strategy.

Use the observation schedule and analyse the results.

What strategies did you find to be useful in helping yourself and your students to use seminar time more effectively?

What might be the long-term effects of these strategies?
How might you justify your interventions on educational grounds?

Monitoring Interpersonal Skill Development

In monitoring interpersonal skill development it is important to identify the skills that are required by you and your students in particular situations. You may find it useful to reflect on the aspects of group work which you and your students find cause difficulties. You might, for example, find it difficult to avoid dominating the talk in seminars. You might consider the reasons for this. For instance, are you worried about the difficulty of getting a discussion going? Discussion and group work require more skill, flexibility and mental alertness on the part of the tutor than more formal types of taught session. Part of the skill lies in the way you enable students to see each other as repositories of knowledge and understanding and to see you as more nearly equal in the process. Some students may be afraid of saying the wrong thing. Others may be afraid of the resentment that dominant students often incur. You may need to develop the skill of bringing in the quiet and meek and preventing domination by a small group of students. You may also act in some way as chairperson, and so have a responsibility to ensure that discussion is kept on track and necessary points covered.

Some students dislike being exposed in group situations. They find vague questions difficult to respond to and do not like being asked to contribute unless they feel ready to do so. On the other hand, they may be impatient of being held up by the queries or problems of others. They usually require an atmosphere of trust in order to fully explore issues. They may feel threatened if they believe that you are using questioning to assess their attitudes and knowledge.

Enquiry Task 3.2

Identify an aspect of your teaching and a group of students where group work plays a prominent part.
Consider what key interpersonal skills you wish the students to develop in interaction with each other and what behaviours would indicate that the skill is being achieved at an appropriate level.

Design a research instrument to monitor the extent to which certain students are developing each identified skill.

Record your findings as follows:
Student 1
                    Evidence of skill development
Skill 1
(e.g. Supporting   Yes – encouraged a quiet student to give an opinion)
Skill 2

Student 2
                    Evidence of skill development
Skill 1
Skill 2

How might you justify the use of tutorless groups to a colleague who thinks that such groups are non-productive?

Management of Yourself and Others

It seems approaches to teaching that take into account the students' need for dignity and self-esteem are more likely to facilitate learning. The same is true of working with colleagues. Both situations depend on the management skills of the participants. The tutor who is able to see the potential for growth in students and colleagues and who can respond positively to the excitement provided by the challenges and constraints of the workplace, will facilitate positive development. You may find it useful to develop your understanding of the needs of your colleagues and students for task and social satisfaction and the role of self-concept and self-actualization in the way that learning and work processes operate.

You may find that students and colleagues tend to respond more positively to challenges if they feel that they are involved in the decisions affecting their work. This depends on developing a 'faith' that people, students and colleagues, are both able and wish to achieve well. Such faith is often founded on competence in interpersonal management, which enables openness about ideas, feelings and difficulties so that trust from all parties can be fostered and the manager is secure that if difficulties do emerge, she or he will know about them before they become real problems.

People's lifestyle preference seems to affect both their management and learning style. There are various ways of describing and measuring dimensions of this style. Friedlander (1975) defined three lifestyle preferences which have direct applications to management issues. These are the formalistic style, the sociocentric style and the personalistic style. These styles are not 'fixed'. People can choose to understand the strengths and weaknesses implied by particular preferences and broaden the repertoire of responses available to them.

People who have a strong preference for a formalistic style tend to look for outside structures and rules by which to regulate their working and social lives. Their strength is the ability to work systematically and to organize a lot of information. Their weaknesses include an impatience with the ambiguities that working with people involves. They may see the solution to problems solely in terms of systems and may ignore the importance of interpersonal skills and people's perceptions in finding appropriate solutions.

Strongly sociocentric people tend to look to the group for motivation for their working and personal lives. Their strength lies in the ability to make the groups with which they work cohesive and supportive. Their weaknesses may include the valuing of social harmony at the expense of the task in hand. They are too willing to give up their own opinion to that of the group, even if the result is to make the group's goal more difficult to obtain.

People strong on the personalistic style look to their own feelings as the guide to how to respond to the outside world. Their strength lies in their willingness to express strong views, even where these are unpopular. They may be the institution's most difficult members, but also its main source of creativity, innovation and challenge. They do not mind taking risks and will consider what is right rather than what is good for their career. Their weaknesses may include a willingness to ignore rules and systems. Perhaps more importantly, if their inner-directedness becomes self-centredness, they may not listen to or value the opinions of others. If they do not agree with institutional goals, they may not be willing to cooperate in working towards them.

It is important to realize that each style has equal value, each is essential to effective group working. Each of us has the capacity to operate in all three styles in the appropriate situation. On the other hand most of us do not habitually use the full repertoire available. If you and your students develop an awareness of your own preferred styles, take action to work on the implied weaknesses while preserving the strengths of that style, and take account of the styles of others, you may find you are part of the way forward in the development of interpersonal skills. Unfortunately, too often we tend to value people who have a style similar to our own. Because people with a preference for the formalistic style tend to have clear career goals and to value achievement and prestige, many senior managers in education seem to have this style. This may explain why there always seem to be so many colleges and universities that are in the process of changing their management structure.

An analysis of your preferred style may enable you to seek ways of developing a broader repertoire and also analyse sources of stress. For instance, if you have a strong sociocentric preference, you may experience stress if working alone. On the other hand, if you have a strong preference for both personalistic and formalistic styles you may prefer to work alone and may experience stress and frustration if participative management is expected. In general, people with a strong formalistic preference will tend to experience lower levels of stress than those with a strong sociocentric preference. If you are the formalistic type you may need to make a special effort to understand the stresses your colleagues and students experience.

Enquiry Task 3.3

Consider your lifestyle preference. Do you prefer to:

- make professional decisions by yourself?
- seek the help of your friends or colleagues in making decisions about your career?
- like clear pathways for career progression?
- strive for freedom and independence?
- strive for friendship and colleagueship?
- strive for promotion?
- look to your own conscience for moral direction?
- take the advice of others about what is the moral course of action?
- look to the rules of society or religion for moral direction?

Do you believe that management is most often improved through:

- getting systems right;
- getting interpersonal relations right; or
- individual creativity and innovation?

What have you learnt about your preferred style(s)?
List action you could take to broaden the repertoire of your styles of interaction.

Give small groups of students the task of representing a complex idea or process in diagrammatic form within a very limited amount of time. Observe the groups working and analyse their products.

What have you learnt about your students' preferred styles?
List strategies for encouraging them to develop a broad repertoire of styles of interaction.

Time Management

Time management is essential for effective teaching and learning. There is some evidence that those students who organize their study time and stick to their plans achieve the higher grades (Entwistle, 1981). You may need to develop an understanding of some of the principles of time management if you are to help your students develop appropriate study skills. It may also help you to manage the ever increasing level and complexity of work demanded within further and higher education.

Time management involves managing yourself and managing others. The person anxious to improve their time management, whether they are a tutor or a student, might usefully explore how they see themselves in relation to their work. For instance, do they feel that they are always delegated to, or are they the sort of person who delegates? This question is more complex than it appears at first sight. It involves fundamental approaches to management that often relate very closely to aspects of your self-concept.

Each of us achieves satisfaction from our work differently. Some of us focus on satisfaction from the completion of tasks, and some social satisfaction. The nature of this satisfaction has an impact on time management. For instance, if your task satisfaction comes from doing the work better than others would, you may find it hard to delegate. If your satisfaction comes from working as near to perfectly as possible, deadlines may be hard to meet. You may find social satisfaction from being the sort of person who always says 'yes'. This is likely to interfere with the planning and organization of tasks and you may find you cannot complete tasks on time. On the other hand, if your social satisfaction comes from solicitous care of students and colleagues, you may be encouraging dependency and other essential tasks may be neglected during the normal working day.

Poor time management may result in others being inconvenienced, the institution losing efficiency and in you working long hours to the detriment of your personal life. In the longer term it will therefore interfere with your social and task satisfaction. One of the great problems with poor time management, which will affect students and tutors, is that it leads to important tasks being neglected in favour of urgent ones.

Effective time management requires organization, planning, communication, trust and discipline. Organization and planning go hand in hand and need to be tackled at a fundamental level as well as day to day. You may find it necessary to assess what is the real purpose of your life and the extent that the way you are conducting your career is furthering that purpose. Long and shorter term goals may need to be defined and steps taken to reach them. Rational planning is not the whole answer. Plans must be reviewed and adapted in the light of opportunities or difficulties, for instance, in response to the needs and wants of a family or to possibilities that open up as a result of new developments.

The only certain thing in life is that the unexpected happens. It is important that you and your students build some slack into your schedules to take account of unplanned events and problems. Within the time available, it is often useful to assess the tasks and deal with those that are important and urgent first. You may find that it is helpful to set your own deadlines for starting and for completion of each task. We have found that on the whole, tasks done well in advance of the deadline and as close to their arrival as possible take less time than if they are left until later. This is because the instructions and background materials are less likely to have become lost or buried. We have also found that a quick 'good enough' response is usually more useful and appreciated than a highly detailed one that arrives rather late. Speed of response depends upon two main factors: your willingness to tackle unpleasant tasks as soon as they come in and your willingness to complete tasks only as well as is necessary.

Unpleasant tasks seem to be the enemy of time management. Unless they are dealt with quickly, they seem to dissipate energy in guilt feelings, encourage trivial displacement activity and tend to be done at a late stage, when much of the information may not be at hand and it is embarrassing to ask for it.

Perfectionism may be incompatible with effective time management. There is a cost as well as a benefit to achieving perfection. It usually means that the task is achieved late, or another is neglected. For instance, tutors in higher and further education may resist time saving assessment techniques such as peer assessment, on the grounds that it will not be as accurate as their own carefully documented gradings and comments. At certain stages of the course, this may not be as important as the understanding that students get of the critical process from assessing each others' work. In addition, a small time saving is achieved which may be used to benefit student learning in other ways, for instance through the tutor engaging in personal research or preparing taught sessions a little more thoroughly.

There are some tasks that we know will never be done. There are reports which will never be read and commented upon, there will be working parties which will never get off the ground. It may be better for all concerned if you are honest about this, to yourself so that you do not feel guilty, and to others if they are involved, so that they are not held up.

Other tasks are so simple that they can be done within seconds of receipt. We have found that it is useful to have a diary and pen when visiting the institutional pigeon holes. Many memos can be replied to by scribbling on the memo itself a short message, such as 'Fine by me' and a signature before returning it to the sender's pigeon hole. This is much quicker and more efficient than taking the memo back to your office and writing the sort of memo which begins 'With reference to your memo today about . . .'.

Organization and planning on a day to day basis can help time management. A common system is the 'to do' list, which is kept constantly in sight. As tasks are completed, they can be ticked off. It may be useful to have daily and longer term 'to do' lists. The act of writing such lists and reviewing them regularly forces some kind of organization and prioritization. It may be useful to arrange the 'to dos' into four categories of priority, and perhaps to abandon the lowest priority ones. Large tasks can sometimes be subdivided to make them less daunting. We have found that the ones in the 'class two' category tend to slip through the net. These are likely to be important rather than urgent and should be monitored carefully. They might not get done unless you are fairly ruthless about binning paper that you know you will never read or deal with.

It is important to leave sufficient time to undertake the tasks without interruption. For this reason 'open door' policies may be incompatible with time management. You may decide that it is better for all concerned to set time aside to see students or colleagues at specific times. Accurate estimation of the time that should be set aside for each task is important. Poor time managers may tend to underestimate this. Setting and keeping deadlines for each task and building in some slack for complications is a useful planning activity. Once a plan is drawn up, you need to stick to it. You may need a 'setting up' or orientation period when starting a task. If this is the case, it may be a better use of time to complete one task or subtask at a time.

Your efficiency in filing and organizing notes and materials will affect your use of time. If you keep things needed constantly in a way that makes them accessible and know where other material is, you may waste less time looking for things. A notebook to take down information from the telephone or conversations and self-duplicating memo pads for keeping copies of messages to others can save time and anxiety at a later date. You may be the sort of person who works better if you organize your desk and update the 'to do' at the end of each day.

Paperwork affects you and your students. The ability to organize and respond to written material is important. The aim should be to handle each bit of paper once. Ideally it should be dealt with as soon as you pick it up. Otherwise, it could be filed, referred elsewhere, thrown away or analysed and put into a date handling system. The date handling system can be as simple as putting a 'to do' date on it, filing it in a date ordered pile, which you review daily. This type of system should bring things up automatically on specified dates.

Memos tend to cause you and others work. For this reason you may choose to use them only for announcing, confirming or reminding. If a more complex interaction is required, such as a negotiation or complaint, you may find a telephone call or face to face discussion is more time efficient. Memos used in these circumstances seem to lead to more memos that have to be composed, written, sent and filed. We have found that much filing is unnecessary. Most paper could be dealt with and binned without serious consequences. Perhaps papers should be filed only if they are likely to be referred to later or if you are the only person who possesses the information. One of us empties her filing system each year into a series of box files. Each box is taped with masking tape. If at the end of the year the tape has not been removed, the contents of the box can usually be binned.

Discipline is probably the most important factor on time management. Above all, avoiding procrastination and sticking to task seem to be the essence of time management. Thinking regularly about your aims and objectives may help you to keep on track. You may find that doing unpleasant tasks as soon as possible leads to more satisfaction and increased energy.

You may need to be firm with others and sometimes say 'No'. In return, perhaps you owe it to others to tackle tasks as far in advance of the final deadline as possible and to be on time. This implies that you do not set off for a meeting or a taught session at the last minute and that you allow a small cushion of time for unexpected delays.

Other people can also be undisciplined. Some students and colleagues can be unnecessarily garrulous. You may need to develop strategies to deal with this. It may be helpful to meet them in a place where it is easy to make your escape. It is difficult to tell someone that you want them to leave your office, but easier to tell them that it is time you left their's. Sometimes it may be necessary to explain that you can spare a specified amount of time to deal with their problem.

Where an office is shared, it may be helpful if you lay down ground rules about working time and social time. If your work relies on the cooperation of others, it is essential to allow for some slippage of deadlines. When coordinating projects, a system of automatic reminders of deadlines may minimize this problem. You may be able to help colleagues and students manage their time better by producing clear and structured material and information with tasks and time precisely defined.

Enquiry Task 3.4

For one week make a note of the tasks that you do and how long each one takes.
Decide the following:

- Which tasks were important?
- Which tasks were urgent?
- Which tasks were not important or urgent?
- How much time did you spend on each type of task?

Think about the work that you asked the students to do during the same period:

- Which tasks were important?
- Which tasks were urgent?
- Which tasks were not important or urgent?
- How much time would you like them to spend on each type of task?

Ask the students to log the work they do over one week related to your teaching outside of the taught sessions and to categorize it as important, urgent or neither.

Write down your reflections on this exercise and what you learned about the ways you and your students manage time.

What might you do to help yourself and your students to increase the proportion of time spent on important tasks?

Summary

Personal development and interpersonal skills focus on behaviour and feelings rather than knowledge. They emphasize the responsibility and control of the individual over their own learning and development. They involve:

- change and choices;
- sensitive personal and professional issues;
- group support; and
- empowerment.

Personal development focuses on a range of transferable skills and understandings. It requires that the tutor develops an understanding of himself or herself as a person and as a manager; and skills in reflection, giving feedback, and the facilitation of students' diagnoses of their own strengths, weaknesses and needs.
Personal development should broaden the learning repertoire available to students. This may involve various dimensions such as:

- impulsive/reflective approaches to learning;
- serialist/holistic approaches to learning;
- preference for auditory/kinesthetic/visual modes;
- achievement/meaning/reproducing approaches to learning.

The conditions for fostering interpersonal competence include:

- warmth and optimism on the part of the tutor;
- a climate relatively free of power differentials; and
- student control of content and methods.

Failure may result from:

- a lack of criteria for success;
- a lack of congruence between learning processes and student needs; or
- a lack of 'readiness' on the part of the students.

Team work requires that others' need for dignity and self-esteem is recognized. This implies an involvement in decision making and an openness to others' ideas and feelings.

Personal style affects our ability to work as part of a team. One's personal style may be categorized as personalistic, sociocentric or formalistic. Each style has its strengths and weaknesses.

Time management involves:

- the management of others and the ability to delegate;
- organization and planning;
- discipline;
- the ability to manage paper;
- the ability to say 'No'; and
- a willingness to be a 'good enough' tutor.

Entry for the Reflective Diary

Write about what kind of a 'manager' of learning you are and what kind you
   would like to be.
What personal qualities do you believe you have?
Which qualities do you lack which you value?
Which interpersonal skills do you believe you have?
Which interpersonal skills do you lack which you value?
What positive action do you take to:

a)   ensure you demonstrate the skills and qualities you value; and
b)   develop those you know you lack?

What personal qualities and interpersonal skills do you expect from your
   students?
How explicit are you about these expectations?

What action do you expect them to take to acquire personal and interpersonal skills they lack?
How explicit are you about this action?

How do your expectations of your students compare with those for youself?

References

ENTWISTLE, N. (1981) *Styles of Learning and Teaching*, London, Wiley.
FRIEDLANDER, F. (1975) 'Emergent and contemporary life styles: An inter-generational issue' *Human Relations*, **28**, 4, pp. 329–47.
KOLB, D.A. (1975) 'Towards an applied theory of experiential learning' in COOPER, C.L. (Ed) *Theories of Group Processes*, London, Wiley.
KOLB, D.A. (1984) *Experiential Learning: Experience as the Source of Learning and Development*, Englewood Cliffs, Prentice Hall.
MALONE, S.A. (1988) *Learning to Learn*, London, Institute of Management Accountants.
MESSICK, S. (1976) *Individuality in Learning*, London, Jossey-Bass.
PRIESTLY, P. *et al.* (1978) *Social Skills and Personal Problem Solving*, London, Tavistock Publications.

Suggested Reading

JOHNSON, D.W. and JOHNSON, F.P (1982) *Joining Together: Group Theory and Group Skills*, Englewood Cliffs, NJ, Prentice Hall.
PRIESTLY, P. *et al.* (1978) *Social Skills and Personal Problem Solving*, London, Tavistock Publications.
Both of these books analyse the relationship between personal development and interpersonal skills. They each outline a theoretical framework for work within these areas and contain a variety of practical exercises for students, which the creative tutor may be able to adapt to a range of educational contexts and subject areas.

Chapter 4

Assessment

Introduction

Many of us have had the experience of receiving work which is graded but without an explanation of the reasoning behind the grade. In the past it was possible for some students to take courses and qualifications without being told of the examination regulations or the criteria for success in course work. Strengths in other areas of such courses could not compensate for this omission, which seriously disadvantaged students.

Assessment is a key element in the effective management of learning. We have already seen in Chapter 2 that assessment design can encourage deep or surface approaches to learning. Successful courses are those which have integrated teaching aims, methods, content, outcomes and assessment. If course aims and content for example do not relate directly and obviously to what is assessed, students will become confused and demotivated. In other words, assessments should be seen to be valid.

Tutors may give mixed messages about what is required for assessment purposes, unless the criteria are clearly stated and shared. This lack of reliability is a common source of student discontent (Clift and Imrie, 1981). All tutors involved in assessment should be using the same criteria. Ideally, there should be arrangements for double marking samples of work between tutors in order to 'check' judgments.

Assessment can be used for diagnostic or formative purposes, providing information needed for appropriate teaching interventions. Such formative assessments enable you to be responsive to the learning needs of your students. This form of assessment may be particularly important from the learner's point of view since it signals what has been and what is to be learnt. This is an advantage of staged course work assessments that can be used to help the student practice and prepare for final judgments on achievement (summative assessments). An assessment scheme should be designed so that the learning process is improved during the course as well as being used for final assessments of achievement (Crooks 1988).

In this chapter, we will define terms that can cause confusion, suggest enquiry tasks that will help you to evaluate assessment schemes on your present courses and describe some assessment methods. Some typical difficulties will be described and we will outline some general principles that should be kept in mind when designing assessment schemes. The social purposes of assessment, such as selection, control of curricula, imposition of standards and public accountability of institutions will not be addressed.

Definitions: What Does Assessment Mean?

Assessment is often confused with evaluation. Assessment is generally taken to mean a judgment about the progress (formative assessment) or achievement (summative assessment) of a particular student's learning. Evaluation is a term usually referring to judgments about the merits of a particular course of study or a particular teaching intervention. Evaluative judgments may therefore include comments about the assessment component of a course. Course evaluations are usually part of an institution's course review process. Both assessment methods and evaluation methods can be used to monitor the general state of 'health' of a course and its participants.

Another common cause of initial confusion is the difference between criterion referenced and normative assessment. Criteria are an attempt to make explicit (ideally to students as well as staff) what exactly is being looked at for assessment purposes. Criterion referenced testing is designed to check that a student has mastered an area of knowledge or skill. Normative assessment makes qualitative judgments about the level of achievement relative to other students. For example a criterion might be 'accuracy' at a basic level and 'accuracy and originality' at a higher level of achievement. The conditions for a satisfactory through to an excellent outcome should ideally be understood in the same way by students and tutors. Criterion referenced testing is particularly important in the area of professional education where a minimum level of competence is essential. They can, however, be difficult to specify and interpret. An element of subjective judgment is inevitable even in apparently simple cases. For example, the criterion 'driving at a speed appropriate to traffic conditions' has to be interpreted by the assessor and the student (Gibbs *et al.*, 1986, p. 159). Students can get a better idea of the meaning of essay criteria by being shown examples of past essays that exemplify them and the different levels of achievement. Their assessments can be compared with the tutor's.

Normative assessments can work with suppressed criteria ('impression marks') or with an itemized marking scheme. The underlying question for the assessor is not what has the student achieved but that person's achievement relative to others undertaking the same assessment. The assessor may compare the work assessed with the work of others to get a rank order. This ranking usually goes with a system of allocating marks or grades.

Criterion referenced assessment usually goes with giving qualitative feedback to students about their achievement. Numerical marks can be given in criterion referenced assessment in addition to the qualitative feedback. It could be argued that this gives the student a better sense of progress. However, an unintentional aspect of this is that you are in fact ranking students.

Final ranking may be justified by the social necessity of selection where goods (jobs, post-graduate awards) are scarce. Where there is no such social purpose, but simply an educational one a pass/fail judgment with qualitative feedback may go some way to ameliorate 'grade dependency' (see Chapter 2), anxiety and unnecessary competition in the learning group (Gibbs *et al.*, 1986).

There is almost inevitably an element of norm referencing in all but the simplest assessment. If you include words such as 'well' or 'good' within your criteria, you are implying a standard that is relative to the expectations you would have of an average student at this stage of this kind of course. In other words, you are assessing the individual student relative to a 'norm'.

Where groups are large enough, a normal distribution of ability and achievement may be assumed. Norm referencing may be used to maintain standards and to prevent 'grade inflation', which can be the result of internal marking and moderation. One of us used to be a course leader and found a tendency for tutors to see each year's students as 'above average'. Where a particular group had been awarded an average mark by the internal assessors which was way above the predetermined course mean (55 per cent), or where less than 3 per cent of students had been awarded a mark above 70 per cent, she used to require that the tutor re-examine the assessment, in order to ascertain whether the student group was in fact unusual in some way, whether the marking had been at fault or whether the assessment was inappropriate in some way. When performance indicators were related to the proportion of first class honours degrees awarded, this vigilance was relaxed and the average mark crept up year by year.

A major problem with designing assessment schemes is deciding what is to be assessed, how and when. This is not just a matter of having insufficiently well specified aims and objectives, or learning outcomes. Decisions have to be made about what is worth assessing. This is particularly important since assessment defines the 'real' curriculum for students.

On some courses a student's potential and attitudes are being assessed in a way that is not made explicit by the assessment scheme. This is true of some teacher education courses. For example, where students are supervised in schools, it may not be apparent that a student's rapport with children or their ability to evaluate what is going on in the classroom is being assessed. It may be that a course team values independence in thought, commitment and interest. If this is so, these attitudes ought to be part of the explicit assessment scheme.

Enquiry Task 4.1

Look at the assessment requirements on a course that you teach.

- Are assessment criteria clearly stated and made explicit to students?
- If grades are used, is it clear to students what they mean and how different parts of the course are weighted?
- Are there formative assessments on the course and do these prepare students for summative assessments?
- Are any skills or attitudes important to your course left out of the official assessment scheme?

Choosing Assessment Methods

There are many assessment methods apart from the essay or traditional examination paper. The methods used on your courses should be a fair reflection of the course aims and content and appropriate to what it is that you wish to assess. Methods may also be used which enable you to find out about student progress.

In Britain, teacher discontent over key stage 3 assessments for English was the result of a lack of congruence with the English course prescribed by the

National Curriculum. In other words the test did not have content validity. On the whole, teachers were not claiming the right to 'teach to the test', but the right of students to be fairly prepared for a test. Sometimes assessments can be inappropriate because they test at the wrong level, for example at the level of factual recall rather than at the level of analysis. Some can be inappropriate because they are unnecessarily expensive in terms of tutor time. If we wish simply to assess someone's recall of information (e.g. the names of the bones in the forearm), a prose essay may be unnecessarily time consuming. If however we wish to test analytical and critical ability, a discursive form of writing might be appropriate. On the other hand, analytical and critical abilities could be assessed in more creative ways (see Chapters 2 and 7).

Different methods of assessment also have various advantages. For example, 'blind' examinations may appear to guarantee equal opportunities, although the definitions of knowledge implied in the questions or the competition created by the examination process may favour one group of students (see Chapter 9). Projects may allow for deep reflection, planning, research and the chance to work on a personal interest. A further advantage of introducing variety into assessment schemes is that it can help reduce student anxiety (Heywood, 1989).

Enquiry Task 4.2

Think about the variety of assessment methods used on a course that you teach:

What are the advantages and disadvantages of each method?
(You could think in terms of their efficiency, their appropriateness, and the quality of learning they encourage.)

Method	Advantages	Disadvantages
1		
2		
3		

Assessment methods may be critically evaluated in terms of the statement of aims or outcomes or objectives for the course. You might find that the assessment scheme gives conflicting messages about the overall direction and purpose of the course. The social and political environment may change quite radically over a period of time. For example, it might be that a degree in librarianship is structured around the idea of what makes a good librarian. Given the rapid developments in information technology, there maybe some uncertainty about the qualities and skills librarians will need. The Enterprise in Higher Education Initiative has encouraged institutions to meet the perceived needs of the employers by producing 'enterprising' graduates and diploma students (Foreman-Peck, 1993). This has led to a positive emphasis on the so-called transferable skills such as communication skills, team working, leadership and increased autonomy in learning. Changes in assessment in further education, with the introduction of National Vocational Qualifications (NVQs), inevitably raise questions about the overall purpose, direction and underlying values of the course.

This explicit attempt to focus on vocational values has led to relatively new methods of managing teaching and learning and associated assessment challenges (Foreman-Peck *et al.*, 1992). For example, a common strategy to foster collaboration and to reduce tutor dependency is to use group work methods.

The next section provides an introduction to a selection of assessment methods indicating advantages, disadvantages and possible problems.

Assessment Methods

The Essay

Essays take a variety of forms, from the open-ended type ('Write an essay on an author of your choice') to the narrowly directed type ('Analyse the contribution of . . .'). The latter type usually requires reasoned argument. Open-ended essay titles allow the good student the freedom to develop their own line of interests but the weaker student may flounder. This weakness can be overcome to some extent by identifying for the student what should appear in the essay. The structure of the essay can also be indicated. An example in Gibbs *et al.* (1986, p. 18) illustrates this clearly:

> Is the *Heart of Darkness* a Victorian novel? Discuss the characteristic features of Victorian novels. Identify the key differences of post-Victorian novels. Highlight the main characteristics of *Heart of Darkness*. On the basis of the preceding three sections, draw conclusions about the extent to which *Heart of Darkness* is a Victorian novel.

This kind of highly structured essay assesses content rather than the ability to strucure. It is a good way of building confidence in students who may lack confidence. A variant of the traditional essay is the role play essay where students are asked to write in a non-student role, for example as a journalist, lawyer, parent. This can encourage a sense of the relevance of issues to concerns outside the course.

Objective Tests

Objective tests produce answers which do not require an element of subjective interpretation, that is the 'correct' answer is not open to doubt. For example the question 'What is the name of the present Prime Minister?' should produce an answer that is either correct or incorrect. This form of assessment may be appropriate for certain aspects of the learning on a course. However, it tends to trivialize the content since low level abilities tend to be tested. Furthermore, if a student gives the wrong answer they will not necessarily be told the reason. Some multiple choice tests allow for guessing and therefore are not a true reflection of the student's knowledge.

Objective tests can be set up on the computer. The computer can be programmed to give a test score and to provide commentary for those items that have been failed. The Keller plan (see Chapter 5) makes use of the computer to test objectives of each unit of work. The pass mark is high and students are not allowed to go on to the next unit until they have passed. Tutor time is used for 'remedial support' and for devising tests. Students only sit the tests when they feel ready (Gibbs *et al.*, 1986).

Examinations

Examinations often take the form of the unseen, essay answer type. These have the disadvantage of assessing memory rather than some other higher order skills. Many students find this form of assessment daunting and may perform below their capability.

These problems can be alleviated to some extent through a variety of alternative approaches, such as the seen examination paper. Here students are allowed to see the exam paper in advance (usually one week) of the examination. During this time they can prepare for the questions. The point is to reduce student anxiety and to prevent pointless memorizing. The disadvantages are an increased risk of cheating. Where there is cause for concern, this may be offset by using the viva, or oral examination.

Alternatively, students may be allowed to take reference sources that will help them to answer the questions into the examination. This discourages memorization and enables students to demonstrate their analytical skills and ability to apply concepts to the material.

Assessing Group Work

There are a number of forms of group work which may be assessed. These include project work and student-led presentations. With group assessment, it is particularly important that the assessment requirements are thoroughly thought through and discussed with students before they start.

In group projects students work in small groups. Each group collaborates on a project and produces a report. The same mark is usually awarded to each member of the group. There may be problems, however, within and between the groups.

One way of encouraging autonomy and collaboration is through the use of a syndicate approach. A syndicate-based course groups students into teams of up to four students and much of the work of the course is carried out cooperatively through assignments, often in the absence of the tutor. A group of students have to allocate tasks, organize themselves, research and put together a report or a product (Collier, 1983). Some common problems include dysfunctional group dynamics (for example the group contains a 'shirker'), difficulties associated with cultural factors or gender, or some members of the course may be unconvinced of the value of working in groups. If the report receives a mark, other aspects of the experience may be seen as unimportant by the students, whatever the views of the tutor.

A solution to the problem of giving marks where there has been unequal effort or contribution is to assign a shared group mark. For example, if a group of four were to be given 40 per cent for a group report they would be given 4 ×

40 = 160 to distribute amongst themselves. In order for this to work smoothly students may need to work out the criteria for the allocation of individual marks. Students can be assessed on the way they fulfilled their roles in the group (e.g. note taker and monitor) or they can be assessed in terms of their contribution to all aspects of the project. A list of criteria is given by Gibbs *et al*. (1986, p. 108) together with a method of calculating how differential contributions should be rewarded, including leadership and direction, organization and management, ideas and suggestions, data collection, data analysis and report writing.

The student-led seminar can be taken by an individual or a group. It can be a particularly appropriate form of assessment if you are interested in promoting communication skills or the ability to synthesize and order material. It also tends to be quick and interesting for you to mark and (provided clear and high expect- ations are communicated about presentation standards), interesting for the student audience. We have found that where two or more students share the presentation further advantages are presented, such as the development of students' ability to work as part of a team and to organize people and material. Again, it is important that the ground rules for the assessment, as well as the criteria, should be abso- lutely clear. Whenever we have used this form of assessment, we have included criteria related to presentational skills (such as the variety and appropriateness of presentation methods), as well as those related to content and analysis. We have also been quite clear about how the marks are determined and moderated and what happens where students make a differential contribution to the assessment.

Diaries

A student diary is a record of their experience during the course (or a part of it). It can be set as an alternative to more traditional forms of assessed writing. It is an appropriate form of assessment where the learning is focusing on the processes of doing something rather than the outcome. For example, it might be used during a literature course as a record of the way in which a student comes to a reading of a text. It could be used on professional development courses as a record of thinking in practical situations. The diary might contain sections where the student tries to summarize learning so far. A few minutes at the end of taught sessions might be set aside for diary entries.

You may need to make it clear at the outset if the diaries are to be read by others. One of the authors asked students to keep a diary of their experiences and to hand in an extract that they did not mind being made public, and which in their view reflected some interesting learning. Students might also be told that personal writing is likely to be relatively unstructured compared to more formal writing. Diary writing can be a way of building up students' confidence in their own thoughts and feelings, rather than taking on other people's in an uncritical fashion. It could be said therefore to encourage independent thinking.

Criteria for assessing diaries can be the same as for other written work. Criteria such as originality, depth of analysis and self-knowledge could apply. As with other assessments it helps students if they know the criteria in advance. In this particular form of assessment it might be useful for students to contribute to decisions about the criteria. If you wish students to record their feelings as well as their ideas, it is important to reduce any feeling of vulnerability.

Self-Assessment

If it is well structured and supported, self-assessment can be very productive. In a formative context it can be a positive way of encouraging reflection on experience and achievement and the setting of new targets. Self-assessment is particularly useful in contexts of professional development where competencies and work habits are concerned. Students should first of all be involved in generating criteria for assessing work or the way in which they work. For example, you might look at the quality of team working by asking: 'Am I building on other people's comments?', 'Do I involve everybody in discussion?' or 'Am I positive rather than negative in my contributions?' Similarly, students can use checklists to assess whether the group as a whole is working effectively (see Falchikov in Brown and Dove, 1991).

Students can generate criteria for the assessment of written work with the tutor. This in itself is a useful exercise since students are required to think explicitly in terms of success criteria. They are then in a better position to evaluate their own work. Andresen *et al.* (1993, p. 51) suggest the use of self-assessment attachment sheets which students can put in with work to be marked. This might consist of prompts such as 'the strengths of this work are . . .' and 'the weaknesses of this work are . . .'. The blank spaces would be finished using the criteria previously discussed. The tutor can note points of agreement, disagreement and give more meaningful feedback.

Peer Assessment

Peer assessment can be used in a number of situations, for example, in giving feedback on student presentations; giving qualitative feedback on written work; and in assessing contributions to project work. In every case it is essential that criteria are discussed and agreed beforehand.

Feedback from peers is a useful way of looking at a range of viewpoints. However, there can be problems. Giving feedback sensitively and in a way that helps rather than destroys confidence is difficult. Givers have to be trained or briefed to do it well. Equally, it can be difficult to receive critical messages, the authority of the peer might not be accepted and an automatic reaction to criticism is defence. We can alert givers of feedback to their responsibility to help with constructive criticism by suggesting that they identify three areas of strength and one suggestion for improvement, without making value judgments. This should encourage reflection rather than dismay. Another way of trying to pre-empt a defensive reaction is to explain to students that comments do not have to be accepted *or* rejected. The most useful stance to take is one of open-minded consideration: that is, to acknowledge that there may be some truth in what is being said but that it is information that does not chime with your own feelings/needs at the moment or that it seems to confirm what you half suspected. If all members of the groups receive three comments on strengths and one suggestion for improvement, they will not be likely to make invidious comparisons between themselves and others and so they may be able to consider the viewpoint or information without accepting a damaging negative value judgment such as, 'I always mess things up'.

Peers can assess not only presentations but also written work or other products.

However, as has been said, it is very important that peer assessments should be given according to *criteria* that are made explicit and agreed with students before-hand. This eliminates irrelevant and damaging feedback such as 'You have no dress sense'.

Bond (1985) reports a study of a third year undergraduate class on electronic circuits. Students assessed their own performance and one of each of their peers in a mid-session examination. Students were given detailed model answers and commentaries with which to compare their own solutions and those of their peers and could thus allocate marks. Their peers' exam scripts were anonymized. They had to indicate on the marking sheet where the answer deviated from the model and to award a mark for each section on a scale provided. The papers and marking sheets were returned a week later, when they received their own script. They then applied the same procedure to their own script without knowing what mark had been allocated. The self and peer generated marks were then compared. If the marks were within 10 per cent of each other the self-awarded mark was given. If there was a greater discrepancy the paper was marked by staff. As a precaution against cheating, a random selection was also marked.

Enquiry Task 4.3

Select an assessment procedure that is in use on your course.

Can you think of modest innovations to try out?
How do you think the change will improve the assessment scheme?

- What will the students gain?
- What will you gain?

Describe present practice.
(Before you take any action it is probably wise to consult your course leader.)

- Describe the change you wish to try.
- What will students gain?
- What will you gain?

Student Records: Purposes, Formats and Access

Tutors need to keep good records since they may be needed for a variety of predictable and unpredictable purposes, such as material for references or reports to examination boards or appeal committees. You need to monitor the progress of students to inform teaching and learning and to pick up any serious difficulties students may be facing. It is as important to know which assessments have not been attempted as it is to know which have been fulfilled. Recording is therefore an extremely important aspect of the intelligent management of student learning. In short, one needs to keep records for accountability (for example, you may need to provide evidence that a student never turned up to tutorials), to be part of the evaluation of the course in progress (for example, if the students are all getting very low marks), for teaching intervention and as a record of summative assessments (you might be called upon to write a reference or report). All these forms of record keeping can provide a deeper understanding of your students and enhance your professional capabilities.

Enquiry Task 4.4

Ask your colleagues how they monitor and record student progress.
Design a pro forma which fulfills some of the following purposes:

- dates of assignments set and due;
- marks or grades assigned;
- notes on qualities or attitudes;
- attendance;
- contributions to seminars;
- participation in group work;
- contribution to group projects.

Does your record keeping system cover all three purposes, accountability, course and student monitoring, information for reporting on student progress?

Learning Contracts

Well designed pro forma can be useful in making explicit what learning should be going on and how it is to be assessed and by whom. For example, a learning contract may be an agreement between a student and a tutor about what and how a student will learn. The pro forma used usually has headings that require both parties to set out objectives, activities, deadlines, outcomes, evidence for learning, and assessment criteria in writing (see for example Cork, 1993, p. 11–13).

Learning contracts are especially suitable for structuring the learning on work placements, where students are likely to experience a wide variety of work environments and demands. The learning contract may form part of an explicit three way agreement between the tutor, the student and the employer. This has the advantage of helping the employer determine what sort of experience, information and people are likely to be of most use to the student. The contract also allows the tutor to monitor the situation more effectively, since there are clear and realistic expectations. They can also be used to help structure and monitor syndicate work on projects. This form of monitoring could be helpful in deciding on the distribution of marks. More formally, learning contracts can be used to define an individually negotiated programme of study in preparation for advanced entry to a course. Failure to comply with the contract would lead to disqualification.

Learning contracts can also be used in situations where the objectives, methods and assessment methods are all to some extent flexible. The advantage of learning contracts (which can be renegotiated at intervals) as with records of progress is that they record progress over time and can therefore enhance a sense of achievement.

Records of Achievement

Records of achievement (sometimes called profiles) are systematic attempts to involve students in recording, reviewing, and evaluating their academic and personal progress and development throughout their college careers. Central to this process is conversation with a tutor who encourages the student to reflect on experience, diagnose strengths and weaknesses and formulate action plans. In Chapters 3 and 8 we discuss the form of this kind of conversation and its relationship to learning in more detail. The record itself can be used by employers and others as another source of information about the student. Records of achievement have the potential to provide a much fuller picture of the student than a set of examination marks. On professional development courses they can be used to direct reflection, encourage self-assessment and target areas for development.

Since 1993, all school leavers must be provided with a record of achievement. It seems likely that students will enter higher and further education with a new level of awareness about assessment, learning and personal development.

The Council for National Academic Awards (CNAA) undertook a study of systems already in use between 1990 and 1992. From a possible 250 courses they investigated twenty-four. They found three types of profiling system, which can be interlinked. These were the prescribed learning outcomes profile, the negotiated learning outcomes profile and the personal development profile (Assiter and Shaw, 1993). The first set out the learning outcomes and defined the teaching, learning and assessment processes. This is particularly useful on professional courses where there are objectives that practitioners must achieve in order to enter a profession. The second involves not only negotiated outcomes, but also evidence to be collected, criteria for success and resources to be used. This may be most appropriate where course members have different experiences and levels of achievement. As in learning contracts, students could be involved in negotiating not only learning outcomes, but the form of assessment and the nature of the evidence required. The third variety is much more like a diary where students reflect on and assess their experience according to a framework of course objectives. The CNAA study found that this kind of system was taken more seriously if it was integrated into the course in some way. They recommend that all systems be fully integrated into teaching and learning processes.

In order to work effectively records of achievement or profiling systems require training in their use, including training for the students, the tutors, workplace assessors, mentors and external examiners.

Portfolios and the National Vocational Qualifications (NVQs)

Candidates for NVQs collect evidence from the workplace to show that they have met the competencies for that level laid down in the standards (see Chapter 2). The portfolio can consist of work done in the past to demonstrate that a certain competence has already been acquired. This is generally called the accreditation of prior learning (APL). The evidence can consist of a variety of documents, such as memos, letters, flip charts, minutes of meetings. It may be helpful if the evidence is linked by a narrative which makes clear how it meets the standards required for a particular competence. In the NVQ scheme, the standards set targets for the collection of evidence where competencies have yet to be achieved. New evidence recording new learning has to be collected to advance to the next element or level. Foster (in Assiter and Shaw 1993, p. 53) claims that 'candidates develop themselves'. Where the workplace does not allow the right experiences for progression, simulated workplace experience could be set up.

Summary

Assessment schemes should:

- closely mirror the aim, objectives or intentions of the course;
- include formative assessment points so that progress in learning can be gauged;
- have no hidden assessments on courses;
- have criteria that are shared between staff themselves and shown to students;
- be fit for their purpose;
- be practically feasible and cost and time efficient.

You need to develop records which will help you monitor student's progress and give you sufficient information for various purposes. You should be aware of:

- the underlying values of assessment schemes you have to work with;
- qualities that are not currently assessed by your scheme;
- any centrally held records and who has the right of access to them;
- the hand-in dates of assignments set on your students' other courses.

Assessment may be summative or formative, criterion referenced or norm referenced. Assessment methods include:

- various forms of examination;
- essays;
- objective tests;
- group projects;
- group or individual student-led seminars;
- diaries;
- self-assessment;
- peer assessment.

Forms of formative assessment which support student learning include:

- records of achievement;
- learning contracts;
- portfolio record of competence.

Entry for the Reflective Diary

Write about your own experience of being assessed.

- Which aspects of your experience were positive?
- Which were negative or even destructive?

What can you learn from your experience that could affect your practice?

References

ANDRESEN, L., NIGHTINGALE, P., BOND, D. and MAGIN, D. (1993) (Eds) *Strategies for Addressing Students*, SCED Paper 78, Birmingham, SEDA Publications.

ASSITER, A. and SHAW, E. (Eds) (1993) *Using Records of Achievement in Higher Education*, London, Kogan Page.

BOUD, D. (1985) *Studies in Self Assessment: Implications of Teachers in Higher Education*, Occasional Publication No. 26, Tertiary Education Research Centre, Kensington, NSW, The University of New South Wales.

BROWN, S. and DOVE, P. (Eds) (1991) *Self and Peer Assessment: Standing Conference for Educational Development Paper No. 63*, Birmingham, SCED.

CLIFT, J.C. and IMRIE, B.W. (1981) *Assessing Students, Appraising Teaching*, London, Croom Helm Ltd.

COLLIER, G. (1983) *The Management of Peer-Group Learning, Syndicate Methods in Higher Education*, Guildford, SHRE.

CORK, A. (1993) *Learning Contracts*, Self Study pack series, Student Learning Resources Development, Leicester, De Montfort University.

CROOKS, T. (1988) *Addressing Student Performance*, HERDSA Green Guide No. 8, Kensington, Higher Education Research and Development Society of Australia.

FOREMAN-PECK, L., TALLANTYRE, F. and BOYNE, N. (1992) *Six Case Studies of Enterprising Courses at the University of Northumbria in Newcastle*, Newcastle, University of Northumbria at Newcastle.

FOREMAN-PECK, L. (1993) 'Enterprise education: A new social ethic for higher education', *The Vocational Aspects of Education*, **45**, 2, pp. 99–111.

GIBBS, G., HABESHAW, S. and HABESHAW, T. (1986) *53 Interesting Ways to Assess Your Students*, Bristol, Technical and Educational Services.

HEYWOOD, J. (1989) *Assessment in Higher Education*, Chichester, John Wiley and Sons Ltd.

Suggested Reading

ASSITER, A. and SHAW, E. (Eds) (1993) *Using Records of Achievement in Higher Education*, London: Kogan Page.

A very useful collection of short articles and case studies on all aspects of using records of achievement: access, admissions, accreditation of prior learning, the development of skills, and workplace learning.

BOUD, D. (1985) *Studies in Self Assessment: Implications for Teachers in Higher Education*, Occasional Publication No. 26, Tertiary Education Research Centre, The University of New South Wales.

A very useful discussion of the rationale and implications of self assessment. A good discussion of the practical problems, and suggestions for implementation.

CLIFT, J.C. and IMRIE, B.W. (1981) *Assessing Students, Appraising Teaching*, London, Croom Helm Ltd.

Good introduction to assessment, with chapters on assessment time tabling, non-traditional exam formats, writing examination questions, technical aspects of marking and grading. Written as a practical guide but also contains interesting discussion on the limitations of assessment practices.

COLLIER, G. (1983) *The Management of Peer-Group Learning, Syndicate Methods in Higher Education*, Guildford, SRHE.

Introductory chapter defines distinctive features of 'syndicate methods' in the context of other 'group-teaching' methods. A clear exposition located in a discussion about the aims of higher education.

CORK. A. (1993) *Learning Contracts*, Self Study pack series, Student Learning Resources Development, Leicester, De Montfort University.

A very clear introduction with good examples.

FENNELL, E. (Ed) (1992) *Competence and Assessment Compendium, No. 2*, Employment Department, Sheffield, S1 4PQ.

This is a current digest of the latest thinking on the assessment of competencies as embodied in occupational standards. The compendium contains articles addressing the following: how to determine and develop standards; assessment models and principles; delivery issues and practice. A copy can be obtained by writing to Rik Martin, room W644, Employment Dept, Sheffield, S1 4PQ.

FOREMAN-PECK L., TALLANTYRE, F. and BOYNE, N. (1992) *Six Case Studies of Enterprising Courses at the University of Northumberland in Newcastle*, available from MARCET, EDS, University of Northumberland at Newcastle.

This provides six case studies of non traditional approaches to assessment.

GIBBS, G. (1992) *Developing Teaching: Teaching More Students, No. 3 Discussion with More Students*, London, Polytechnics and Colleges Funding Council.

On p. 37 there is a description of peer assessment of a student-led seminar which counts for 20 per cent of the marks for the course. Each seminar group produced its own criteria.

GIBBS, G., HABESHAW, S. and HABESHAW, T. (1986) *53 Interesting Ways to Assess Your Students*, Bristol, Technical & Educational Services.

This is a quick and painless way of reading about assessment *methods*. The methods are categorized under the following heading: essays, objectives, tests, alternative exams, computer-based assessment, assessing practical and project work, criteria, feedback to students.

Chapter 5

Teaching

Introduction

Anyone who wants to make teaching his/her profession is faced with two fundamental questions. The first is 'What does a person need to know in order to become a tutor?' The second is 'How is this knowledge achieved?' In the first part of this chapter these two questions are explored and practical suggestions are made for going about learning to teach; in the second part, some teaching methods are described.

One way of answering the first question is to consider a description of what it is that tutors do and compile a list of competences that constitute the job. Winters and Maisch (1991, p. 3) define a competency as 'the ability to carry out to an acceptable standard a specified activity which is required in the occupational role'. The Staff and Educational Development Association (Baume, 1992) have put forward a list of competences that one would expect to find in a professional development course for tutors in higher education which is also applicable to tutors in further education.

We address each of these competences within the present book. In this chapter the competency of most relevance is the ability to use a wide and appropriate range of teaching and learning methods effectively and efficiently, to work with large groups, small groups and one to one. This 'competency' is more complex than it appears at first sight. It includes the ability to make presentations (e.g. lectures, demonstrations); facilitate group learning (e.g. through seminars, discussion groups, projects); work with individual learners; facilitate practical or laboratory classes; contribute to team teaching; and use the appropriate technology for the teaching and learning method (e.g. overhead projectors, handouts or information technology).

A similar approach has been adopted for the professional education of trainers in industry. Here the Training and Development Lead Body has set the standards that constitute the work of a trainer.

Effective Teaching

While competencies are a useful tool for defining what we would expect to see in a professional development programme, they are of necessity an incomplete account of the knowledge needed by the tutor since they only describe behaviour. In order to be a minimally competent teacher your teaching has to be effective. This implies that learning has to take place, not just learning of anything but learning of a content or process predetermined by the tutor. Hence a prerequisite of effective teaching is having a very clear notion of what the aims of the activity are. Stating aims that are appropriate is something that has to be learned since it requires a very good grasp of the nature of your discipline, a good grasp of the level of understanding of your students and an understanding of the most appropriate teaching methods taking into account both factors. This is important because you can only judge how effective you have been in the light of your teaching and learning intentions, that is, in terms of your aims. Formulating aims is therefore a key prerequisite of being effective and it is potentially misleading to think of it as a simple matter of learning teaching techniques and picking up tips.

Finding out about your learners requires some investigative work and an actively enquiring engagement with them. Knowing your subject or discipline, in the sense of understanding its key concepts, modes of reasoning and its uncertainties, is necessary in order to know what learning it includes. This requires conceptual investigation.

Enquiry Task 5.1

Discuss the following questions with a colleague:

- What do you expect your best students to achieve?
- What intellectual skills do you expect your students to develop?
- What counts as learning your subject?
- What counts as progress and development in your subject?
- What sort of commitment to knowledge and what sort of values do you want your students to acquire?

These questions are prior to and constitute a major part of our judgment of the effectiveness of any 'technical' or management solution.

What is the link between reflection and effectiveness?

Effective teaching requires a knowledge about ends. Without this knowledge you will find it hard to provide reasons for employing one teaching method rather than another. Methods of teaching are like 'horses for courses', in that the method, like the horse, has to be suitable for the job you want it to do. This knowledge is gained through actual practice and reflection. Regarding teaching methods as tools for various purposes and being aware of the 'political' implications in the notion of choosing methods are marks of the more proficient tutor. The culture of your department may be conservative. The pressure to follow custom and practice is not to be underestimated. However, you may need to question this practice in order to come to conclusions about the appropriateness of teaching methods to the material and your aims if you are to be fully effective. In achieving this, you should not underestimate the complexity of learning and life in educational institutions. In some circumstances the idea that you are free to choose your method of teaching may be seen as 'romantic'. Even where this is the case, you may feel that it is part of your professionalism to know what the likely effects of various methods on your students' learning will be.

Enquiry Task 5.2

What are the principal methods of teaching in your department or on the courses you contribute to?
What kind of learning outcome do they seem to encourage?
What do they require the student to do?

Methods   *Outcome*   *Students' Role*

Which methods seem to be most appropriate for the learning outcomes you believe to be desirable?

Developing into a Reflective Practitioner

Ramsden's (1992) notion of three distinctive ways of understanding teaching seem applicable to both higher and further education. He illustrates these ways of understanding through three vignettes based on recent research. In the first vignette the tutor holds a simple 'transmission' theory of teaching. She or he sees the job of teaching as the unproblematic transmission of information. The traditional didactic lecture may be favoured as the best way of imparting a body of knowledge. In this model the students are passive recipients of teaching, recording what is said. If you believe that the principal teaching virtues are being an expert and communicating well, you may hold a transmission theory of teaching. Failure to learn may be attributed to the students. The teachers' interest in methods is more likely to be focused on polishing performances than helping students to learn.

In the second vignette the teacher is seen as the organizer of student activity. The focus has shifted from what the tutor does, to what the student does and the tutor sees her or his job as supervisory. Interest in teaching methods is now focused on ensuring that students learn. The tutor's main concern may be with motivating students to be actively engaged. The teaching method may include indirect reward and sanctions within assessment, techniques requiring students to make connections between theoretical knowledge and experience and techniques for promoting discussion in class.

In the third vignette the tutor is concerned with 'making learning possible'. Teaching is understood to be a cooperative process. The tutor finds out about student misunderstandings and intervenes to put them right, in a context where students are actively engaged in their learning. She or he is very much concerned with obstacles to understanding in the context of what has to be learnt. The content to be taught and the way in which students interact with it determine the methods she or he uses.

The tutor operating with this last model has a different relationship towards methods than the tutors in the other vignettes. Methods will not be seen as instrumental, but as problematic in themselves. There will be a constant effort to match teaching methods to the learning needs of all students. Methods are judged by the learning they promote and may be modified as feedback on student learning becomes available. The tutor will explore factors which have been shown to be conducive to student learning in various settings and actively modify them to fit specific circumstances, particular students and the subject matter.

In other words the view of teaching taken here is that effective teaching entails reflective teaching. However, this does not mean that the reflective practitioner does not need to be an expert or a good communicator or skilled in techniques for promoting student activity. We believe that as a reflective practitioner you need to be able to learn from experience. This implies the ability to reflect for different purposes: for conceptual understanding about ends; to interpret information about learning processes and outcomes; to improve your management and communication skills; and to develop and explore your own theories of teaching and learning in order to guide future action.

Ramsden claims that there is a rational line of development in tutors' careers implied from the first to the third vignette. At first glance this is not wholly convincing. The superiority of the third is not self-evident in all circumstances and with all material. For instance, it might not be the best model for teaching beginners to ski. The third vignette may simply embody a preference. However, in many circumstances, the third model seems to be the most appropriate model, provided the others are available where the material makes them appropriate. The third model may be particularly useful as an ideal of professionalism if we consider other factors in learning to teach within further and higher education.

The Development of Situational Understanding: Learning from Experience

Moral judgments and judgments about what is salient in your experience are among the key factors in learning to teach. Settings involving communicative interaction have limited predictability. Thus, these judgments have to be achieved in an environment that is inherently unstable.

Elliott, drawing on the work of Pearson (1984), (cited in Elliott, 1991) makes a useful distinction between 'habitual skill knowledge' and 'intelligent skill knowledge' that makes this point. Pearson claims that only habitual skill knowledge can be derived from an analysis of the tasks involved in doing a specific job. These are the necessary but unreflective routines, which are a necessary but not a sufficient condition of competence. In order to be judged competent one has to display a 'situational' understanding, which underpins the notion of 'intelligent skill knowledge'. This involves the ability to discern, discriminate and act. In situations that are complex and dynamic, the appropriate response is dependent on the discretion of the tutor and so it may not be possible to predict what a good practitioner will do in certain circumstances. This model reveals a fundamental problem with behaviourist accounts of competences, since it is likely that individual practitioners, each of whom are fully competent, will find different solutions to the same problem.

Dreyfus (1981, (cited in Winters and Manish, 1991) quoted in Elliott, 1991) argues that there are four capacities involved in judging and understanding complex situations. These are component recognition; salience recognition; whole situation recognition; and decision making. He claims that the career progression of the caring professional involves a movement through the stages of novice, advanced beginner, competent practitioner, proficient practitioner and expert. Each stage is characterized by a growing ability to see factors of a situation as interdependent and to discriminate those factors in the situation that are important and have to be attended to and acted upon. If we accept this as an accurate portrayal of the way in which the expert develops, then the logical progression implied by Ramsden (1992) in his three vignettes becomes more plausible.

The components of a situation can be seen as either objective context-free attributes or subjectively experienced context-dependent aspects. The novice can be taught to recognize objective attributes without the benefit of experience. This kind of component recognition is 'non-situational'. Here the novice tries to operate with facts and rules. It is at this stage that learning about methods of teaching are necessary and useful. However, it would be a mistake to suggest that professional training ought to stop there. Factors that are salient to the situation are not 'seen' by the novice simply because their conceptualizing of the situation is insufficiently comprehensive.

The ability to recognize context-dependent aspects depends on a prior experience of real situations where recurrent meaningful components are noted by the novice or pointed out by a mentor. An example referred to elsewhere in this book would be the incidence of high anxiety among students whose status could be compromised by failure. Salience recognition involves discriminating those aspects of a situation that should be considered in order to decide on an appropriate response. For example, you might recognize that your students are anxious but not realize that it is something on which you should act. The way in which you have conceptualized your role as a tutor may exclude responsibility for negative feelings in the group.

'Whole situation recognition' encompasses all the salient attributes and aspects of a situation. Dreyfus (cited in Winters and Maisch 1991) argues that at the expert stage the practitioner's skill is often intuitive and inaccessible except through the skilful practices where it is embodied. Winters and Maisch (1991) argues that while Dreyfus's model rightly points to the experienced practitioner's work as a valuable learning resource, difficulties in articulating it may prevent it from being utilized for the benefit of others, or indeed for the practitioners themselves. If you are unable to verbalize what you do and why you do it you are likely to remain trapped in a 'self-reproducing ideology'.

Enquiry Task 5.3

The following lists situational factors in teaching:

- the predominant teaching methods students have experienced in the courses before yours;
- other stake holders in the course, such as employers;
- if your course is taken by more than one tutor, differences there are in course organization;
- assumptions about the students' prior experiences, for example their entry qualifications.

Can you list how each of these factors affects each student?
If not, find out.

Figure 5.1: A model of experiential learning

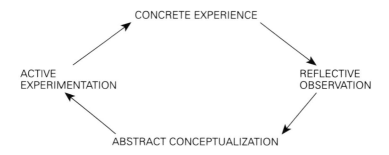

Learning from Experience

Professional knowledge is acquired through the interaction of thought-about ends, reflection on experience and a gradual development of the ability to reflect in action. A model of the general process of experiential learning has been described by Kolb (1984). (Later we will consider other models which address the more specific needs of the novice.) A simplified version is presented in Figure 5.1. We can use this model to describe how professionals develop their expertise. The most problematic aspect of the model is 'reflective observation'. It is a skill that is difficult to achieve. Although it can be said to characterize the expert's way of learning, it is not necessarily something that is immediately possible for the novice.

It may be more helpful to break down reflection into stages, before action, during action and after action, as discussed in the following subsections.

Reflecting Before Action

The novice typically is concerned with survival or 'getting through the day'. The most useful professional development step here is to consider practical aspects of teaching such as preparation, planning the teaching event, timing, resources, and recording. Key organizational tools are the lesson plan and the longer term scheme of work, which should also provide information about the aims and objectives of the course, the assessment requirements, reading lists, and any other information about course expectations. These organizational aspects can be evaluated for their appropriateness and their effective communication.

Enquiry Task 5.4

One way of organizing the preparation stage of a lecture is given by Brown and Atkins (1988) and reproduced below.

When you next prepare a lecture, try to follow these steps and talk them over with your mentor or a colleague working in the same area.

Step 1 What is the topic?

Step 2 Free associate. Make a note of any ideas, facts, questions. Group and organize them.

Step 3 State a working title. Are there any hidden variables in the title?

Step 4 Prepare a rough outline of the lecture.

Step 5 Directed reading. Read only that which is relevant to your plan. Make notes about ideas, important areas, facts that you left out in the first plan.

Step 6 Structure the lecture. Set the lecture out under clear headings. Add structuring moves and examples. Prepare handouts, audio-visual aids and activities that you are going to introduce. Summarize the main points of the lecture. Make a list of resources that you might need such as an overhead projector.*

Step 7 Check opening and ending. You will probably find it easier to construct the opening when the lecture has been largely devised. A good question to ask yourself is what do you expect the students to take away from the lecture? The ending should draw the themes together.

Step 8 Check equipment and the room if you have time. If worried about timing you could rehearse what you have to say. Give the lecture.

Step 9 Reflect on any changes you think you ought to make.

* It is best not to write out a script to read out loud as this is difficult to follow, often sounds stilted and stops you from maintaining contact with the audience, but rather to have your lecture set out in short notes with the points you want to make listed and notes to yourself about illustrative material. Some lecturers talk to key points on overhead transparencies which has the advantage of being available to students as well.

An alternative way of structuring a lecture is given by Gibbs and Jenkins (1992, p. 65).

There are numerous ways of preparing for and structuring small group methods. A list of useful references is given in the annotated bibliography. Many of the steps outlined above are likely to be the same, except that the role of the tutor may be less dominant. An advantage of small group size is that students can take a more active part (see Brown and Atkins, 1988, p. 63, for a description of small group teaching methods in terms of their structure and tutor dominance).

Another aspect of preparation that should come before action is a consideration of how the course you are working on relates to what is to be assessed. (This has been dealt with more fully in Chapter 4). Equally important is the requirement for continuity and progression, especially where course components are taught by different tutors, sometimes from different departments.

Reflection During Action

The key interactional skill at this stage will be managing the interaction in an orderly and coherent way. This implies some facility with questioning techniques

— explaining, listening and responding appropriately — in other words, communicative competence. Schön (1987) suggests that the expert practitioner may be thought of as someone who has developed the ability to reflect in action.

Reflecting After Action

Boud *et al.* (1985) suggests that a useful way to conceptualize reflective activity is to 'return to the experience', 'attend to the feelings' and 're-evaluate the experience' after the event. Returning to experience is not unproblematic however. There is a danger that we may not be able to transcend our descriptions of the event to find anything new or interesting, especially if the learning event was uneventful. Attending to feelings may also be unfruitful in the sense that for the novice they can be extreme and puzzling; at one time anxiety is experienced, at another boredom. The effort of managing the content and the interaction seems to militate against the relatively detached stance you need to develop in order to notice salient events or to really listen and respond appropriately to what a student is saying. Above all you need a good reason to get beyond managing well enough to get by.

Once the organizational aspects of teaching have been more or less sorted out, you may find that it is necessary to formulate a focus for reflection. This focus may be found by considering your experience of the teaching event. It may be that you felt that the interaction could have been better. This could be a useful starting point for reflective activity.

Reflection after action is usually more productive if you have collected some evidence of what went on. Methods of doing this are described in some detail in Chapter 10 but include video or audio tapes of your teaching, fly on the wall or structured observation by a colleague you can trust, student feedback or an examination of the work produced by your students.

Enquiry Task 5.5

The following items are taken from Luker's (1987) list of tutor's difficulties (cited in Brown and Atkins, 1988, p. 55).

Thinking over your recent experiences with classes can you add to this list?

- getting a discussion going;
- quietening the vociferous;
- bringing in the meek;
- dealing with a poor or irrelevant answer.

It often requires considerable skill to direct discussion in fruitful directions. List reasons why you should be concerned with the quality of interaction.

What criteria would you use to evaluate whether the interaction in a class was good?

You might characterize a teaching interaction as good if it reflected certain values such as care, accuracy, encouraging learning, active attention and participation by all members. The exercise of values often utilizes technical knowledge, but the key skill is the ability to judge and evaluate the significance of situations encountered and to respond appropriately. Your ability to realize your values in teaching establishes the conditions for it to be a worthwhile process. Part of the expertise in reflection in action is realizing when the conditions for worthwhile

---

Enquiry Task 5.6

Audiotape or videotape a taught session.
Select one or two of the aspects of a taught session listed below and judge your performance.

What criteria are you basing your judgments on in each case?

What is the source of these criteria?

	Good	Room for improvement
Opening remarks		
Structure		
Interest		
Pace of delivery		
Pitch of voice		
Clarity of explanation		
Use of illustrative examples		
Use of techniques to help students follow		
Use of techniques to allow students to be active 'meaning makers'		
Use of visual aids, handouts		
Questioning techniques		
Responding to questions		
Level of analytical thinking encouraged		

Discuss your thinking with your mentor or a colleague.

Discuss why you thought an aspect of the teaching needed to be improved and ways in which you might effect the improvement.

Describe an aspect that you thought was good. Give reasons.
Check your perceptions with your mentor or colleague.

interaction are missing and taking steps to remedy this. In terms of Kolb's (1984) learning cycle, reflective observation would lead to a conceptualization of the experience and experimentation in order to improve. If you aim for improvement, you will need to have a clear idea of what good practice might look like.

The process of reflecting in action can be developed through acting in a deliberate way as a result of the kind of reflective practice suggested above. The enquiry tasks above are directing attention to the likely quality of the learning event. A more systematic approach that incorporates the idea of the interpretation and evaluation of data about processes and outcomes is found in the literature on action research. This is explored in Chapter 11.

Teaching Methods

This part of the chapter provides a brief introduction to the basic methods of organizing teaching. The size of the group is likely to be a major consideration in your decision as to the most appropriate teaching method. Group size to a large extent determines the kind of interaction that is appropriate or possible.

Each of the methods described below has advantages and disadvantages. Part of the expertise of the reflective practitioner is in maximizing the potential of each method and minimizing its disadvantages.

Teaching Large Groups: Lecturing

Bligh (1972) suggests that the lecture is the most ubiquitous method of teaching in higher education. Traditionally this method involved reading aloud from a prepared text, particularly in the humanities. In science, engineering and medicine demonstrations and audio-visual aids were more common. Fortunately today more interesting ways of presenting lectures are becoming more normal (Gibbs *et al.*, 1992).

The large lecture is less costly in terms of tutor–student contact time than other methods. However, if used inappropriately and without a degree of proficiency in the skills of lecturing, the real costs in terms of student learning may be high. In situations of increased student numbers and a reduction of resources it seems likely that lecturing will be increasingly used for some time to come. It is therefore important that you consider its advantages, disadvantages, its degree of fit with the structure of your discipline, what it implies for student learning and what it implies for your ability to care for your students.

Gibbs (1992) enumerates eight student difficulties that can accompany an emphasis on large group teaching and a decrease in small group teaching. Among the most important may be students' lack information about their progress and learning. Even if they are coping, they still need to know how to improve. Advice given by the tutor may be necessarily of a general nature, addressed to the whole group.

Library resources may be unable to cope with surges in demand stimulated by mass lectures. One librarian we know described seeing students throwing themselves like lemmings at book shelves in a desperate attempt to get books out before their peers.

Exclusive reliance on lectures may deny students the opportunity for discussion. This may be particularly damaging, since knowledge is not the same as information. Information is often unproblematic, but theories, concepts and principles of disciplines are open to a variety of interpretations which may need to be clarified through discussion. Lectures tend to be an unsuitable forum for the discussion of complex or contested issues.

These problems are exacerbated by the fact that students' backgrounds tend to be less homogeneous than used to be the case. Mass lecturing tends to assume that all students have reached the same level of understanding. The problems this causes have been recognized and have led to a recent interest in the possibilities of the lecture, and methods for minimizing its disadvantages have been suggested.

The most effective use of the lecture, when properly planned and presented, is in the transmission of information and ideas which provide a conceptual overview of the subject. This seems to be an educationally defensible use of tutors' time since the expertise of the specialist can be utilized to give a synthesis that may not be available from any other source. However, detailed or complex information may be more usefully presented in the form of handouts, books or other materials. The use of lectures to present original work may be inappropriate, except where the audience has the necessary conceptual understanding.

Entwistle and Hounsell (1975) propose a model of lecturing that reduces it to key components. This simple model (Figure 5.2) is useful in that it allows us to examine aspects of lecturing in turn.

Figure 5.2: Model for exploring lectures

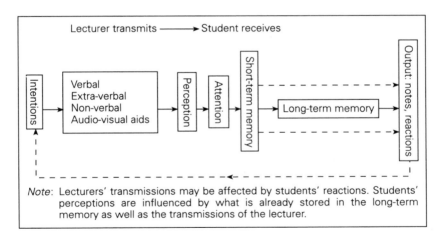

Note: Lecturers' transmissions may be affected by students' reactions. Students' perceptions are influenced by what is already stored in the long-term memory as well as the transmissions of the lecturer.

Intentions

Brown and Atkins (1988) suggest that there are three points to lecturing: to provide coverage of a topic, to generate understanding and to stimulate interest. These three uses are interdependent, but may vary in emphasis. The less experienced lecturer is likely to find difficulty in using the lecture to achieve higher cognitive objectives.

Work by Janssen (cited in Entwistle, 1992) suggests that successful lecturing has close links with effective learning and studying. He found that students need a deliberate focus on the assessment requirements. Assessment and task demands have to be clarified. Students need to feel confident that they can master the course content. Lecturers here have to be supportive and to anticipate likely difficulties. Confidence also depends on knowledge acquisition. Here the assessment requirements will encourage either a deep or a surface approach to learning (see Chapter 2).

Lecturers can challenge students to think critically and analytically. One way is for the lecturer to model the thinking processes characteristic of the discipline (Sheffield, 1974). Critical thinking can also be encouraged by the use of challenging questions within the lecture (Cryer and Elton, 1992).

Part of the answer to the use of the lecture to promote cognitive challenge is to find ways of encouraging students to interact with each other and with the material. Techniques for involving students in higher levels of thinking include setting small group problems and exercises (Gibbs and Jenkins, 1992, p. 65). For instance, in a lecture about gender in education, one of us asked students to work in twos or threes to brainstorm some of the reasons for the differential achievements of boys and girls in the physical sciences. Some of these ideas were collected onto an overhead transparency and matched with the biological, social learning and sociological theories of gender differentiation later in the lecture.

The use of interactive handouts to encourage the students to structure their learning, to interact with the material being presented or to do additional work are described in Chapter 7. These include gapped handouts which require the student to fill in carefully selected missing sections. Lecture outlines, which give the structure of the lecture, an explanation of key concepts, and follow up references may enable students to follow the lecture and alleviate the anxiety of those who find it difficult.

There are also techniques for collecting and answering students' questions. Students can be asked to write down and hand in at the end of the lecture any points that they would like answered in the next lecture. Students can be asked to write down questions and invited to spend a few minutes discussing the answer with their neighbours (Gibbs, 1992).

Each of these techniques may help your students to internalize the material and work with it to relate it to their context. They have the additional advantage of helping to redirect the students' attention and to change the pace of the presentation. Macmanaway (1970) reports that the majority of students can only attend to a lecture for twenty to thirty minutes. If you are giving an hour-long lecture, you may need to think about ways of breaking it up, so that students listen for periods of about twenty minutes interspersed with short active periods when they discuss the material in small groups, 'buzz' lists of ideas, read handouts, fill in questionnaires and so on. Without these techniques, perhaps the most common intention of the lecture, that of getting material covered, will not be achieved. The material will be 'sent', in the sense that the lecturer will have stated it, but most of it will not be received.

Transmission

The tutor sends verbal messages in the form of descriptions, explanations, examples and comments. She or he also sends extra-verbal messages through the use of voice, silences, non-verbal messages, gestures, audio-visual messages and so on. All these message systems can be used to carry meanings and attitudes over and above the literal or intended content of the lecture. Some of them may interfere unless the explicit messages of the lecture are structured in a way that helps the students to receive them.

Brown and Atkins (1988) identify the key skill as explanation. Explanations can be broken down into three sorts: descriptive, interpretative, and reason giving. These correspond to 'what', 'how', and 'why' questions. These modes of explanation can provide a framework for organizing the content of a lecture or talk. Content can also be organized sequentially, as in historical accounts, or around problems or the content can be divided into sections and subsections.

As well as organizing the content, the presentation has to be ordered. Four important structuring moves are identified by Brown (1982): signposting, in which the structure and direction of the lecture is made clear; frames, statements that signal a change of topic or subtopic; focus statements that highlight the key points; and links between sections. These statements link parts of the lecture together and the lecture to the previous experience of the students.

Other crucial features of lecturing are beginnings, endings, the use of rhetorical language and the maintenance of interest. A successful opening gains and holds interest, establishes a rapport with the audience and sets out the content and structure of the lecture. It will be remembered that it was suggested above that a justification for lecturing could be made out in terms of its function of stimulating students to become active learners. The rhetorical aspects, then, of a lecture are all-important on this hypothesis.

Receipt

Students' attention fluctuates. Gibbs (1992) reports that attention drops after about twenty minutes and rises again just before the end of the lecture. Changes in activity renew attention. We have already described how messages are more likely to be received if there is a break for small group discussion or problem-solving, and that, if you are to hold your students' attention, you may need to consider ways of varying your presentation. In Chapter 7 we describe how lectures can be improved by the use of audio-visual techniques.

A study (Dradi *et al.*, 1990) found that learning was more successful in lectures which used three methods of representation corresponding to Bruner's (1966) modes of representation, student activity, diagrammatic representation and oral explanation. Students who were taught entirely through the traditional oral mode did least well.

Output

Traditionally the output from a lecture has been a set of notes, which may be written up by the student at a later date. Learning is likely to be increased if these notes can be used in some way, or reordered and organized by the student as soon after the lecture as possible. If this is to be facilitated, the pace of the lecture should allow sufficient time for note taking and for thinking about the content. You will need to think about structuring follow-up activities that require students to refer to and use their notes.

It may be pertinent to put in a word of warning about student lecture notes. Gibbs (1981) reports a number of studies that show that students typically capture only a small proportion of the essential material in a lecture. He also demonstrates that there is little evidence that note taking leads to better learning than simple listening. In addition, it appears that only a tiny proportion of the notes that students take are ever referred to again for revision or any other purpose. This is a pity, since important learning opportunities are being missed.

The answer is to find ways of helping your students to create good sets of notes and to ensure that they have reasons to refer to them as soon after the lecture as possible. You may need to think about the language of the lecture and whether it is accessible to your audience and whether the level of difficulty is matched to the present understanding of the students. Evaluation techniques play a key part in determining this. You may also wish to find ways of helping students to structure their notes. The use of structured handouts is described in Chapter 7 and some methods of developing this study skill in Chapter 8.

Enquiry Task 5.7

Using the model in Figure 5.2, think of the least effective lecture you experienced as a student. Can you say which aspects were the most unsatisfactory?

Reasons for an unsatisfactory lecture

Intentions
Transmission
Receipt
Output

Is there anything in your analysis that is not captured by the model?

Alternative Methods for Teaching Large Groups

Tutors in further and higher education have become increasingly interested in exploring ways of teaching more students without an over reliance on lecturing. Some of these methods are identified briefly below.

Resource-Based Learning

One method of dealing with large numbers of students is to use a resource base to replace the lecture. This requires considerable investment and may only be introduced with the cooperation of senior management. Resources for open learning are described in more detail in Chapter 6. They may include self-instructional materials and video, audio and computer-based materials. The advantages of resource-based learning are flexibility and convenience in studying. It tends to be particularly suited to mature students who have a well developed sense of 'direction' in their learning. Wall *et al.* (1991), report that first-year students find working alone difficult. This is especially marked during a period of adjustment to the greater discretion over use of time that higher and further education may allow, but where an associated taught programme is well structured, younger students can benefit from simple resource-based learning too. For instance, one of us regularly gives students a paper to read. The taught session then consists of the students comparing their understandings gained from the paper, looking at the different ways they have organized their notes and coming up either with a list of the main points put forward by the paper (which can then be 'unpacked' and problematic issues exposed by the tutor) or a set of questions and issues that can be dealt with by the tutor.

There are more elaborate systems of resource-based learning (though these may not be more effective than low-cost simple systems). For instance, the advantages of a self-paced course can be combined with tight control over students' learning as in the 'Keller Plan'. A description and evaluation of a modified version is given in Gibbs and Jenkins (1992). In the original form students work from detailed course objectives, study guides and set texts. Surgery sessions are available for students who are having problems. These are run by graduates of the same course. Students must pass a test for each unit of the course before they are allowed to progress. The element of self-pacing is allowed for by setting the test at earlier and later dates.

Gibbs (1992) argues that dealing with large numbers requires either that you increase control over student learning or increase the degree of autonomy students have over their own learning. It is possible to combine both approaches, although you may need to be careful that you do not confuse students by sending mixed messages about what is expected of them. He gives accounts of methods that maximize tutor control over student learning and accounts of those that maximize student control.

Peer Teaching and Collaborative Group Work

Peer teaching seems an attractive way of both meeting increased demands in terms of student numbers and encouraging independence and responsibility in learning. Students either work in tutorless groups, or with a more senior student. Jackson and Prosser (1989) have shown that the use of monitored learning groups led to marked improvements in students' ability to engage in 'scholarly analysis'.

One of us worked on a first-year degree module which was focused on student control of learning and collaborative learning (Ashcroft, 1987). The aim was to foster students' open-mindedness at an early stage by exposing them to different viewpoints, to develop their sense of responsibility for their own and their peer's learning and to develop their interpersonal and communication skills. There was a lecture each week followed by a seminar session led by a small group of students. The leadership of the session rotated, so each group of students was expected to lead only one session during the term. This enabled the students to prepare very thoroughly. The tutor's role was to provide clear guidelines to the student leaders about what learning should emerge from the session, to communicate the expectation that they would explore a variety of methods to foster learning, to create a handbook of suggestions for teaching methods and to provide the essential information that should be included in each session. During the taught session, one tutor was able to tour between three seminar groups, not to 'teach', but to deal with issues that the student leaders were not able to cope with and to signal to the students that the session was taken seriously.

Learning Contracts

Learning contracts enable students to negotiate their own study with the tutor and together they reach an agreement about how and what is to be assessed. It is the tutors' role to monitor students' progress. The contract may be written on a pro forma and include objectives, resources, experiences, evidence, and criteria for the successful completion of the contract.

In our experience it is not as easy as it may seem to negotiate a contract. We have found that they seem to work better where they are formally designed as part of the course. For instance, one of us worked on a course which included an independent study unit. The process for negotiating and accrediting the contract, for its content and for the final assessment were clearly specified. In another version of the contract, the nature of part of the assessment of a course, and the criteria for marking it can be subject to negotiation between the students and the tutor. The same clarity as to ground rules need to be observed as for negotiated course content.

The advantage of learning contracts is that they enable students to follow up issues of direct interest to them in some depth; they encourage independent learning, since the student has to find their own content; they encourage students to take a real responsibility for the content and the criteria for successful learning and they may foster the students' development as a reflective practitioner of their subject. If the student works entirely alone, there is a danger that they will avoid investigations that challenge their preconceptions. The problem may be overcome if there is a facility for a group of students to negotiate a learning contract on an area where they will cooperate. One of us has had experience of this kind of learning contract, where the outcome was jointly assessed by the tutor and the groups of students, and where each of the students in the group received the same mark. She found that the process was problematic, but produced levels of reflection in some students that would have been hard to achieve in any other way (Ashcroft, 1987).

Small Group Teaching Methods

Post-Lecture Tutorials

A lecture/tutorial format is a very common way of organizing courses in higher education. The rationale is that students have the opportunity to discuss and clarify issues arising in the lecture that preceded it.

Tutorials are an expensive use of tutor time and so it is important that they are used as intensively as possible. It is generally a good idea to have a clear agenda and time frame, and to get the student to structure their thinking before the tutorial so that they receive the maximum benefit from it. For instance, you might ask a student to organize their notes (perhaps onto an overhead projector transparency). In small group teaching it is easier to achieve full participation and to keep your aims in sight. On the other hand, in some colleges and universities staff are expected to follow up lectures that they have not given, or may not have been able to attend. Often this can degenerate into the tutor trying to establish exactly what was said. In this case, you might prepare supplementary information, exercises and questions on the topics covered by the course but which are not dependent on the lectures given. Other sensible ways of organizing this event may be explored. Some of these are described in Chapter 8 in the section on educational tutoring.

Where tutorials are carefully and selectively used, they present unparalleled opportunities for you to expand your students' thinking, to challenge their ideas in a supportive environment and to help them to articulate and examine a range of possible standpoints. To realize these possibilities, tutorials require as much thought and preparation as any other teaching method. One of us heard a tutor from one of our oldest universities stating that it was sufficient for the student to be exposed to the fine minds of their tutors, and that after that it was up to the student to learn from the 'mind'. We believe that such an attitude is incompatible with the model of the reflective practitioner.

Workshop Methods

Workshop methods often involve a tight sequence of introduction and overview of the session (giving rationale), introducing a problem posing or solving activity; tutor input; problem or activity; and tutor input again. The advantages of this method are that tutor input can be closely tailored to the level of understanding the students display and students have an opportunity to discuss in groups topics in a way that does not single them out or make them feel anxious. The level of discussion and thinking encouraged is more easily controlled by the tutor and complex or controversial issues can be addressed in a way that does not seem to be allowed for by the lecture.

The important thing about a workshop is that it involves the students in active learning. They have to do something with the material to be learned. Workshops will often involve them in reorganizing material and internalizing the issues in new ways. For instance, one of us has run a session on the effects of racism on educational achievement. As part of this, students have to organize a set of statements into their order of significance. They often learn more about the issues that affect children's schooling, but more importantly, they learn that their 'common-sense' understanding of reality is not necessarily shared by others. The business of actively creating meanings in cooperation with others almost invariably leads to some students' preconceptions being challenged and fosters open-mindedness.

The tutor's role in a typical workshop approximates that of chairperson. In summarizing what has been learnt by the group, acknowledgment can be made to the contributions of each group, reinforcing the idea that knowledge acquisition is often a constructive as well as a receptive activity.

The Seminar Paper

This form of organization is most common in the older universities. It usually involves the students taking turns to read out a paper. In our experience, this usually means that discussion is confined to the student and the tutor. Other students remain silent, usually because the paper has been read so quickly, the language is generally appropriate to reading rather than listening and the ideas are usually fairly unfamiliar and difficult to follow. In this situation, you might encourage a little more active listening if you ask the student to summarize briefly the main points of the paper before they begin , and/or invite the other students to brainstorm a list of questions pertinent to the topic that the student can seek answer.

Student-Led Presentations or Seminars

Some of the advantages of the student-led seminar or presentation have been outlined above. Perhaps amongst the most important are the development of responsibility for their own and others learning and the opportunity of developing presentational skills. Unlike reading a paper, the audience is the other students. It is much more likely to be understood and to generate discussion. It should be clear to the student that part of their 'success' will be measured by their skill in getting ideas over to the audience, as well as in choosing and organizing the content appropriately. Students can be encouraged to experiment with a variety of presentational methods. These are likely to require them to reorganize and internalize the material in a new way.

If the student-led seminar or presentation is a group activity, students will be required to articulate their ideas and share understandings in order to organize material for their audience. This process is likely to create a deeper level of understanding and provide you with new insights into the students' thinking. If the student audience is encouraged to provide constructive feedback on each presentation (for instance, three things each person liked about the presentation and one suggestion for improvement), the students can be encouraged to develop a new range of communication skills that will stand them in good stead in a variety of situations that involve working with people.

One of the most effective ways of learning something is to teach it to someone else. (One of us never really understood why to divide fractions you 'turn one upside down and multiply' until she had to teach it to junior school children!)

Syndicate Groups

In the 'syndicate group' method, a topic is divided up and students are invited to work in teams on different aspects. The tutor may act in the role of the consultant during the process and at the end may do the work of summarizing. The method requires careful organization. Trouble may arise if some groups do not work well together or feel that the task is beyond their collective competence. This points to careful introduction of the method and a general valuing of cooperative ways of working in the department as a whole.

One of us worked on a first-year degree module which required students to work together in groups of about six students on a particular case study of their choice. Each group subdivided into pairs to work on particular aspects of 'the case'. Each pair had to investigate the theory behind their aspect of the case study and how it operated in practice in a workplace setting and then integrate their findings with those of the others into a coherent report which presented a structured argument. From this process, students were able to share knowledge each had acquired, but perhaps more importantly, they had learned to negotiate the focus, learned about each other's interpretation of evidence (and hence the problematic nature of 'knowledge'), agreed on a line of argument and learned from each others' approaches to presentation of that argument. The results showed more evidence of reflection than did their individual assignments (Ashcroft, 1987).

Case Studies, Simulations and Games

Case studies are based on actual practice, and are therefore more complex in nature than simulations, which are simplified versions of real life problems. Games are even more attenuated, with precise rules. Case studies and simulations are presented to students, who work in groups to come up with solutions. Sometimes students work in role. An alternative approach is to ask students to prepare their own case studies based on any work experience they may have had as part of their professional training.

Case studies, simulations and games each have the advantage of requiring students to apply what they have learned to a more or less realistic setting. It is perhaps only in this way that they can gain an insight into the effects of their values and those underpinning alternative interpretations of the material they are working with in the real world. The results can confront the students' expectations and require them to explore alternative solutions. These methods can be very useful in helping students to use their knowledge as a means of solving problems and hence to develop a deeper approach to learning.

One of us has used a simulation of a 'business' making 'rafts' from straws and Sellotape (in this case to look at learning processes in the primary classroom, although it could be used to look at the real financial problems of businesses or the application of mathematics to workplace settings). Students had to borrow 'money' (at particular rates of interest), make contracts to purchase material (with a discount for bulk buying) and make contracts for orders (with penalty clauses for late delivery). As part of the simulation, the interest rates, prices and discounts for materials changed during the manufacturing process and new attractive opportunities for bidding for new orders appeared. From this simulation of the real cash flow problems and time dilemmas businesses face, and the discussion that followed it, students found creative ways of helping children understand mathematics, learned something about active learning and the nature of problem-solving, explored some issues in practical organization, revised their opinions of the value of education–industry links, and practised a range of interpersonal skills. None of this learning could have been internalized in the same way had the students been 'told' it or had it described in a book.

Case studies, simulations and games can be used to explore controversial and difficult issues. The very engaging nature of these types of activities can lead students to become over-involved and sometimes upset. For instance, one of us has sometimes run a simulation with up to 100 people on the effects of world trade practices of the developing countries. Three groups of students have to trade counters to maximize their wealth. As part of this, one group of students is unfairly discriminated against, in that they start with a depleted bag of counters compared with the others. As the game progresses, groups who are 'winning' at various points are invited to make up a new rule. Almost invariably the 'poor' group becomes very angry and frustrated. Being part of an education course, these feelings are then applied to those of children who start out school life with an educational disadvantage, but it could equally apply to any situation where the effects of various kinds of inequality in provision or of particular kinds of international trading practices were to be explored.

Case studies, simulations and games require careful planning and very careful debriefing. The engagement of emotions may be essential if you are wishing to explore attitudes. Indeed other methods tend to lead to intellectualizing and a rationalization of existing attitudes rather than attitude change. However, it needs sensitive handling if students are to be challenged, disturbed, but not damaged by the process. This is not a reason to avoid case studies, simulations and games, since as a reflective practitioner you are likely to be interested in your students' affective as well as their intellectual development.

Enquiry Task 5.8

Tape a small group session that you have given.

Analyse the first ten minutes according to the categories below.

- overview of objectives;
- presentation of rationale;
- mention of working methods;
- setting of ground rules;
- connection with assessment requirements;
- links with previous sessions;
- domestic arrangements (e.g. room changes).

What do you actually do in the first ten minutes?

Is it a good use of time?

Summary

The competent teacher should:

- be able to use a wide range of teaching methods effectively and efficiently;
- know what the outcomes of learning should be at various stages in your students' careers;

- be versatile and flexible, matching a repertoire of methods to the complexity of students' learning needs;
- see the interdependency of factors in the learning situation and act appropriately;
- notice aspects of situations as salient;
- make judgments about the quality of the learning event.

Models of teaching include:

- teaching as transmission;
- teaching as the organization of student learning;
- teaching as an activity that enables learning to take place.

Reflective practice involves the development of situational understanding, or an intelligent skill knowledge in order to enable a response to student needs in a dynamic communicative setting. This requires you to discriminate those aspects of the situation that are salient to the students' learning.

Reflective practice involves learning from experience through an interaction of concrete experience, reflective observation, abstract conceptualization and active experimentation. It requires:

- reflection before action;
- reflection during action;
- reflection after action.

Teaching methods should be matched to the context, the students' needs and the material to be learned.

Lecturing is a common teaching method in a time of increasing staff–student ratios. It suffers from the following disadvantages:

- students may not learn from lectures or attend to what is being said;
- students may lack information about their learning and progress;
- students may lack opportunities for discussion;
- individual students' needs, level and interests cannot be catered for.

Lecturers may overcome some of these problems by:

- carefully structured assessment;
- modelling thought process required by the discipline;
- setting small group exercises and problems;
- using interactive handouts; collecting and using student responses.

Lectures can transmit non-verbal as well as the intended messages. These can get in the way of learning unless the lecture is carefully structured and ordered.

Student attention needs to be maintained, perhaps through the use of student activity, visual representation as well as oral transmission.

Students need help to produce good lecture notes. Learning will usually be increased if they are required to use their notes (preferably as soon after the lecture as possible).

Alternative methods of teaching large groups include:

- resource-based learning;
- peer teaching and collaborative group work;
- the use of learning contracts.

Small group teaching methods include tutorials. Tutorials should:

- be carefully structured;
- involve students in preparation.

Workshop methods are useful for encouraging collaboration and problem-solving. They require students to re-examine and apply their learning and may challenge their preconceptions.

Seminar papers can be dull and difficult for the student audience. Other forms of student-led presentation and syndicate group learning can encourage:

- communication skills;
- internalization of the material;
- collaboration.

Case studies, simulations and games may be the best way to explore attitudes and real life problems. They can confront deeply held feelings and need careful handling.

Entry for the Reflective Diary

Do you feel confident enough to adapt your teaching to the exigencies of life in the classroom?

Write about any change in method you have tried. Consider the following:

How did you feel?

Why did you change?

What were the gains?

Who can you talk to, apart from your mentor about your innovation?

References

ASHCROFT, K. (1987) 'The history of an innovation', *Assessment and Evaluation in Higher Education*, **12**, 1, pp. 37–45.
BAUME, C. (1992) *SCED Teacher Accreditation Year Book Vol. 1*, available from J.

Brookes, 69 Cotton Lane, Moseley, Birmingham, B13 9SE NB (Standing Conference on Educational Development (SCED)).

BLIGH, D.A. (1972) *What's the Use of Lectures?* Harmondsworth, Penguin.

BOUD, D., KEOGH, R. and WALKER, D. (1985) *Reflection: Turning Experience into Learning*, London, Kogan Page.

BROWN, G.A. (1982) 'Two days on explaining and learning', *Studies in Higher Education*, 2, pp. 93–104.

BROWN, G. and ATKINS, M. (1988) *Effective Teaching in Higher Education*, London, Methuen.

BRUNER, J.S. (1966) *Toward a Theory of Instruction*, Cambridge, MA, Harvard University Press.

CRYER, P. and ELTON, L. (1992) *Active Learning in Large Classes and with Increasing Student Numbers, Module 4, Effective Learning and Teaching in Higher Education*, Sheffield, CVCP Universities Staff Development and Training Unit.

DRADI, A., OSER, F. and PATRY, J.-L. (1990) *Efficiency of Teaching Methods According to Different Modes of Representation in Two Different Cultures. In Scientific Contributions on Education, No. 86*, University of Freibury, Pedagogical Institute.

ELLIOTT, J. (1991) *Action Research for Educational Change*, Milton Keynes, Open University Press.

ENTWISTLE, N.J. and HOUNSELL, D. (1975) 'How students learn: Complications for teaching in higher education', in ENTWISTLE, N.J. and HOUNSELL, D. (Eds) *How Students Learn*, Lancaster, University of Lancaster Press.

ENTWISTLE, N. (1992) *The Impact of Teaching on Learning Outcomes in Higher Education: A Literature Review*, Sheffield, CVCP. Universities Staff Development Unit.

GIBBS, G. (1981) 'Twenty terrible reasons for lecturing', *SCED Occasional Paper No. 8*, SCED, Birmingham.

GIBBS, G. (1992) *Teaching More Students: Problems and Course Design Strategies. No. 1: The Teaching More Students Project*, London, Polytechnics and Colleges Funding Council.

GIBBS, G., HABESHAW, S. and HABESHAW, T. (1992) *53 Interesting Things to Do in Your Lectures*, Bristol, Technical and Educational Services.

GIBBS, G. and JENKINS, A. (Eds) (1992) *Teaching Large Classes in Higher Education: How to Maintain Quality with Reduced Resources*, London, Kogan Page.

JACKSON, M.W. and PROSSER, M.T. (1989) Less lecturing, more learning, *Studies in Higher Education*, 14, pp. 56–68.

JANSSEN, P.J. (1992) 'On the construct and nomological validity of student description of studying and lecturing by means of Likert-type questionnaires: A Matrix of Neril Common Primary Factors', in CARRETERO, M., POPE, M., SIMONS, R.-J. and POZO, J.I. (Eds) *Learning and Construction European Research is an International Perspective* Vol. 3, Oxford, Pergamon Press.

KOLB, D. (1984) *Experiential Learning*, Englewood Cliffs, NJ, Prentice Hall.

MACMANAWAY, L.A. (1970) 'Teaching methods in higher education, innovation and research, *Universities Quarterly*, 2, 3, pp. 321–9.

RAMSDEN, P. (1992) *Learning to Teach in Higher Education*, London, Routledge.

SHEFFIELD, E.F. (1974) (Ed) *Teaching in the Universities: No One Way*, Montreal, Queens University Press.

SCHÖN, D.A. (1987) *Educating the Reflective Practitioner*, San Francisco, Jossey Bass.

WALL, D., MACOULEY, C., TAIT, H., ENTWISTLE, D. and ENTWISTLE, N.J. (1991) *The Transition from School to Higher Education in Scotland*, Centre for Researching on Learning and Instruction, University of Edinburgh.

WINTERS, R. and MAISCH, M. (1991) *The Development and Assessment of Competencies. Vol. 2.* available from the ASSET Programme Administrator, Anglia Polytechnic, Department of Health, Nursing, and Social Work, Victoria Road South, Chelmsford, Essex CM1 1LL.

Suggested Reading

BROWN, G. and ATKINS, M. (1988) *Effective Teaching in Higher Education*, London, Methuen.

A very good introduction, containing many useful suggestions. There is a valuable section on effective laboratory teaching, research project supervision, and study skills.

ENTWISTLE, N. (1992) *The Impact of Teaching on Learning Outcomes in Higher Education: A Literature Review*, Sheffield, Committee of Vice-Chancellors and Principals of the Universities of the United Kingdom.

A useful review of the research literature that has been carried out on the relative effectiveness of different methods of teaching.

GIBBS, G. (1981) 'Twenty terrible reasons for lecturing', *SCED Occasional Paper No. 8*, Birmingham, SCED.

A short, easy to read summary of some of the research into the effectiveness of lectures in terms of student learning, with a brief outline of some of the alternative methods.

GIBBS, G. and JENKINS, A. (Eds) (1992) *Teaching Large Classes in Higher Education: How to Maintain Quality with Reduced Resources*, London, Kogan Page.

An interesting collection of case studies where various methods have been introduced to meet the challenge of very large classes.

SCHWARTZ, P. and WEBB, G. (1993) *Case Studies on Teaching in Higher Education*, London, Kogan Page.

Excellent case studies dealing with challenges to tutor authority, credibility, student discontent and plagiarism and more. A good introduction to the idea of situational understanding.

STEPHENSON, J. and LAYCOCK, M. *Using Learning Contracts in Higher Education*, London, Kogan Page.

Contains accounts of the experience of tutors in using contracts in a range of disciplines and professions.

Chapter 6

Open and Distance Learning

Definitions of Open Learning

Bailey (1987) describes the various forms that open learning takes in the UK. These include materials production schemes, learning resource centres, practical training centres, skill centres, mobile learning centres, 'flexi study' packs, learning exchanges and circles, correspondence courses, home study, and directed or assisted private study. These forms are similar to those described in the Australian setting by Scriven and Lundin (1992). The learning context may include a company scheme or training framework, an accredited course from an educational institution or a curriculum determined wholly or in negotiation with the student ('contract learning'). The guidance provided may be directed at informing, advising, counselling, coaching, assessment or advocacy. It may be proactive, preventative, or reactive.

Open learning, in at least one of its guises, is likely to become an issue of relevance to most tutors in further or higher education as they seek to develop courses which meet the needs of new students or of their present students more effectively. The usual sense in which 'openness' is used relates to the mode of course delivery. The implication is that some of the teaching and learning takes place out of face to face contact with the teacher. In this sense, higher and further education generally involves some open learning, and therefore it is important that all of us develop skills to manage it.

The concept of 'open learning' can have various levels of meaning. 'Openness' may also relate to the teaching method. This definition was introduced in Chapter 2. In this sense, an 'open' pedagogy allows your students to interact with the question posed or the material presented. In this way they create their own learning experience through the interaction and so may reach a position you had not anticipated. Thus, 'openness' would invite the student to come back to the questioner at a stage further than they were when the question was posed. It may produce unpredicted results and therefore may create problems for you. Such a definition of 'openness' is not really compatible with a linear model of the student's learning. Materials built upon a linear model may therefore be closing opportunities for this kind of development.

'Open learning' can provide opportunities for exploration, enquiry and development. The logical extension to this kind of pedagogy is the development of forms of assessment that also invite the students to go forward and that are learning experiences in their own right. Assessment that merely tests what the student has learned, or what they can do, may not be open.

These definitions of 'openness' have clear relationships to some of the concepts contained within the reflective practitioner model and in particular to that of responsibility. If students are to become reflective 'practitioners' of their subject, definitions of 'success' must include the extent they are given and take responsibility for their own learning.

'Openness' may relate to the extent subject 'boundaries' are fixed or open to interdisciplinary influences. It is not necessary for you to abandon the discipline which the study of a particular subject brings in order to achieve 'openness' in this sense, but instead, it allows you to bring insights from other disciplines to bear on problems defined as being within the subject. An example of this is the use of ideas from psychology and sociology in understanding the relationships between humankind and spatial issues in geography.

Again clear links can be made between this kind of openness and the reflective practitioner model's emphasis on open-mindedness. Open-mindedness implies a willingness to seek out and analyse alternative viewpoints in order to examine existing assumptions. With an openness of subject boundaries, students can be exposed to the challenge to their existing definitions of problems with the new mode of thinking which other disciplines demanded. This implies that openness becomes an issue in the design of courses and in the processes involved in their delivery.

Granger (1990) summarized some of the principles which might underpin open learning. Effective open learning derives from the purposes and needs that are important to the students, rather than the institution. This implies that learning may occur in varied ways and places and that the appropriateness of styles of teaching and learning will differ significantly from person to person and from setting to setting. Bagley and Chalies (1985) point out that open learning may free the student and the course from constraints of time, place, starting date, duration, entry requirements, limits of availability and a limited range of learning methods. The syllabus may be delivered within the educational institution, but at a time and pace to suit the students; it may be part of a local system that includes study at college and at home; or it may be delivered entirely or mainly at a distance.

Enquiry Task 6.1

Find an idea with potential for development into a course or element within a course, which might be delivered through open learning. Discuss it with colleagues.

List the steps you might take in order to assess the need for such a development.

Describe the course or elements within a course:

How might the development meet (some or all) of the concepts related to open learning below:

teaching method;
student exploration and enquiry;
assessment;
interdisciplinary links;

---

setting;
student negotiation of the curriculum;
entry qualifications;
sensitivity to students' interests and needs.

List the gains and losses of this form of course delivery for the tutors, institutional management and the students.

	Gains	Losses
For the tutors		
For institutional management		
For the students		

List ways of maximizing the gains and minimizing the losses.

List issues that need further consideration.

Differences Between Open and Distance Learning

The definitions above apply to open learning. Distance learning is a variant of open learning in so far as it implies that the majority of the learning occurs at a distance (usually considerable) from the teacher and that the teacher and student seldom or never meet. Distance learning is therefore a much more limited concept than that of open learning. Other definitions of open learning may or may not apply. For instance, there may or may not be openness of entry or exit qualifications of students. Teaching methods and materials may or may not be highly prescriptive and 'close' student responses. Assessment may or may not be limited to testing understanding of the materials and content as presented; a limited range of responses therefore may or may not be acceptable. There may or may not be interdisciplinary influences, and indeed definitions of acceptable knowledge may or may not be highly prescribed and presented as unproblematic. A distance learning programme therefore may or may not include various aspects of 'openness'.

Reasons for Involvement in Open and Distance Learning

Decisions as to involvement in distance and open learning are likely to stem from a variety of sources. Probably the best reason for you to get involved is that this method is particularly appropriate to the subject matter or to the needs of your students. For instance, you may wish to produce a genuinely flexible scheme to meet your students' needs.

Demographic trends indicate that the proportion of young people in the population will continue to be at a low level compared with the past. This may encourage colleges to consider ways of attracting other student groups into further and higher education. The Manpower Services Commission (MSC, 1986) estimates that 35 per cent of the adult population within the UK want to undertake study but cannot for some reason, and that 10–12 per cent of the adult working population would benefit from open learning. Creating appropriate packages could therefore open opportunities for large numbers of people. Open learning may also enable option courses to be introduced into programmes where student numbers would otherwise make them uneconomic.

Hodgeson *et al.* (1987) report that the motivation of those responsible for the design and delivery of open and distance learning programmes may be either to disseminate knowledge or to further students' self-actualization. The first view may lead to a tendency to see knowledge as something 'given'. The second view may be riskier for you, involving as it does a sharing of control, leading to some lack of predictability of direction and development.

Open and distance learning should involve you in an open and collaborative style of working which you may find can be very enjoyable. You may be attracted to the idea of relinquishing or sharing the control over the pace of student learning. If so, you may find developing the ability to manage the help that students need a satisfying process.

From the students' point of view open learning may facilitate participation in education and extend it to new groups. It may lead to changes in the curriculum and learning methods to improve their relevance to more members of society and to an improvement in the providers' efficiency and effectiveness.

Enquiry Task 6.2

Take the idea that you discussed with colleagues for a course which might be delivered through open learning.
List the advantages and disadvantages of each of the following methods of course delivery:

	Advantages		*Disadvantages*	
	For the Student	For the Institution	For the Student	For the Institution
Face to face teaching				
Printed material with tutorial back-up				
Printed material with occasional blocks of group teaching				
Printed material with audio and videotapes				
Printed material with student-led discussion groups				
Printed material with computer assisted learning				
A combination of all of the above				

Distance Learning and the Politics of Knowledge

Distance learning is defined technically by the physical space (and to a lesser extent, time) separating you and your students. In most models of distance learning, the student rarely or never attends 'college'. At its best, it can work through the definitions of openness outlined above, although it is not necessary to run all definitions of openness at once.

Distance learning involves making a political point about education. It is about the empowering of students, since education is not 'owned' by the institution, but rather made available by it. By its nature, distance learning validates a range of different settings as appropriate contexts for learning.

If you accept this point, you may find it becomes necessary to examine the politics of knowledge within a distance learning programme. For instance, in some cases it is necessary to accept that the students for a particular course *have* to be at a distance because they are to some extent expert in 'practice'. The provision of distance education enables these people to continue their expertise on a day to day basis, rather than to become deskilled by an absence from it. Indeed, some programmes enable academic recognition of enquiry in practice as a highly valid activity (this book is based on this assumption). Such enquiry requires that the student reconcile a paradox, in that they must stand outside of their practice (or distance themselves), while continuing to act within it, in order to develop new expertise and control within that practice. The best material should open students to possibilities that they would not see without help, while they are still immersed in their situation. This is usually achieved by providing students with a new mode of discourse, or language, with which to describe and analyse practice.

Distance learning may also be usefully built into a 'ladder of opportunity'. This may be started through material that structures your student's thinking about their own starting points. Often this material is crucial to success, since entry into this type of programme may not be dependent upon the students having acquired certain entry qualifications, but rather be based on their own assessment of themselves as able to benefit from the course.

Enquiry Task 6.3

Talk to a small group of mature students. You might like to use some of the following questions as a starting point:

Why did they choose to attend college or university?
What personal qualities and qualifications did they bring to their study?
Have tutors teaching the course drawn on these?
What are the practical and intellectual difficulties they face in studying?
Did they receive any help from the institution to overcome these difficulties?
Has the organization been adapted to meet their needs?
What study skills did they lack on entry to the course?
Did they receive the help they needed to develop these skills?

How do they approach a piece of reading set for them?
What political motivation underpinned the expansion of opportunities for mature students?
Are these compatible with the students' own motivation?

Tape record the responses and analyse the tape.

What help has the institution provided that would be difficult to incorporate into a distance learning programme?

What skills do they lack for effective open learning?

How might they be helped to develop the skills they lack?

Problems and Opportunities

Distance learning programmes are often criticized because they fail to provide the kind of community of debate on which more traditional approaches are said to rely. In practice, not all traditional classes contain any real debate. Some may rely on the teacher exposition. In others there is some student–teacher interaction, but this consists of closed 'testing' questions. In others, real debate may occur, but even here a minority of students may participate. It is true that others may be involved in active listening, but active reading of a variety of viewpoints may fulfill the same function.

Nevertheless, it is important to take the question of community of debate seriously in distance learning programmes. You might solve some of the problems this poses through consideration of the meaning of 'interaction' and the advantages it brings. With careful and creative planning these advantages can be provided through various means, including occasional group meetings and correspondence. The materials themselves can encourage your students to engage in debate with non-course members. Materials that require enquiry into the perspectives of others are particularly useful for this purpose.

Your students' own imaginative powers can be brought to bear on the problem. If the imaginative powers of your students are utilized, a community of debate can be created with people from other times and places, through active reading and interaction with written material. For instance, you might encourage your students to create their own debate through interaction with readings embracing alternative viewpoints. This interaction may take the form of the students identifying or clarifying their own viewpoint after the reading. Material may encourage the students to 'create' arguments from different perspectives or to produce their own 'readings' for a variety of audiences. This approach works well with students who have an intrinsic orientation to learning as described in Chapter 2. It requires that they take a deep approach to learning. A surface approach is incompatible with this process.

Another problem which is often quoted in relation to distance learning is the difficulty of providing explanations where material proves difficult to understand. It is true that in face-to-face teaching it is easier for you to control the pace and direction of learning, but the superiority of face-to-face tuition can be exaggerated. In a lecture hall (or even seminar room) your students may feel inhibited from asking questions if the material proves hard to understand. Even if a student has the courage to ask a question, if the response still does not clear the problem, the student will be brave indeed to ask further. Your students can go over distance learning material again and again until it is fully understood. If they feel fatigued or bored by the material, they can leave it and return to it at another time when they feel refreshed.

However, you may need to provide a fall-back position if the material still is not understood. This might include core material that everyone will use and supplementary texts supplying a more extensive explanation. Many colleges and universities have come to believe that opportunities for one-to-one interaction with a tutor are crucial for some students and now provide a telephone tutorial service as part of a distance learning package.

The introduction of distance and open learning may bring you and your colleagues into new roles for which you may need preparation. If it is to be beneficial, colleagues need to be convinced of its value. The introduction may depend upon one person, perhaps you, as an enthusiast, acting as a driving force and giving great personal commitment. Other tutors may have more worries, some of which may be justified.

One concern may be the amount that is crammed into the syllabus, combined with the concern that students may not have the organizational skills for self study. These are often real problems and solutions need to be planned, for instance, keeping the size of units small and ensuring regular and frequent feedback.

Tutors may also worry that open learning will replace their jobs. Open learning must be given status and recognition by senior managers, especially in relation to staffing hours allocated. In reality, open learning is seldom a cheap option.

Tutors may also worry that they will miss the face-to-face interaction with students and that they will become more involved in administration. It is true that some may need to develop new skills. Mauger and Boucherat (1991) point out the complexity of these skills which may include skills in the arrangement of learning programmes to match student needs, organizational skills, advisory skills to help the learner obtain and maintain effective learning techniques, administrative skills, interpretive skills in order to diagnose when a student needs help, communication skills, motivational skills, and evaluative skills at all stages. Skills that are common to traditional teaching, including those involved in interaction, may need to be honed to a particular level in order to take advantage of the limited opportunities for seminar or workshop teaching with your students.

The feedback you provide from coursework may be crucial to the students' learning and development. The ways that you mark work may need to be rethought so that assessment becomes formative as well as summative. Teaching at a distance requires skills that are different from those involved in face-to-face interaction.

Open learning programmes often include small group or one-to-one tutorials. The effective and intensive use of these require particular teaching skills, for instance, counselling and facilitating. Even where students spend some of their time in college the nature of group teaching may be different than with traditional students. Face-to-face teaching may be a scarce resource in open learning programmes and its use restricted to types of learning that cannot be maintained otherwise.

Enquiry Task 6.4

Take the idea that you discussed with colleagues for a course that might be
   delivered through open learning were the conditions right in your department.
Identify the tutorial skills that would be needed to deliver the programme.
Consider which are already present in the team, which would need to be
   developed and possible ways that the skills which are lacking might be
   developed:

	Already present in the team?	*Strategy for skill development*
Tutorial skill 1		
Tutorial skill 2		
Tutorial skill 3		
Tutorial skill 4		

You may experience dilemmas associated with the self-directed nature of
distance learning, especially when that learning is embedded in the students' practice. Your students may determine the pace of study, and therefore when they
need help, but your experience may suggest that regular contact and deadlines
help reduce dropout levels and maintain academic standards. Bagley and Chalies
(1985) state that tutors find it difficult to know if certain students are 'live' or
'dead' or 'sleeping', or whether, and when, it is permissible or intrusive to 'wake'
students.

In the consideration of whether a course should include open or distance
learning, you will need to address the question of the quality of the course
materials. You should not underestimate the difficulty and cost of producing very
good quality materials. It is important to be sure that the effort is warranted and
is not duplicating the work of better resourced organizations such as the Open
University or the Open College in the UK. Colleges and universities that have
convinced themselves that this is the best method of course delivery for educational
reasons are less likely to make this mistake. The Open University and the Open
College produce content-based materials. Most colleges cannot and perhaps should
not be doing this. It may be better to use already published material to convey the
content of the course and create your own materials to convey the structure and
the modes of interaction with the material.

This approach has various advantages. The course can be updated annually
in the light of feedback and new developments in the subject. Materials can be
designed to promote more interaction, especially if they are not so 'glossy' as to
discourage the student from writing upon them.

Technological development is creating new possibilities for open learning
programmes. Recent innovations have made technology such as artificial intelligence, compact discs, electronic publishing and home computing more accessible.
Chacon (1992) describes various uses for information technology within open
learning programmes. These include information processing — especially recall-

ing — ordering, calculating, establishing the relationship between things, reading and writing. Computers can provide a means of interaction, both person-to-person and person-to-machine, through the sharing of messages. Communication may also be enhanced through encoding and transmitting information, coordinating many files and input and output devices for streamlining communication. The management of programmes of study based on information technology may be complex and the hardware is still expensive for most students to purchase for themselves. This implies that the use of information technology in open learning should probably not be an aim, but rather used as a route to an end where it is found to be the most effective method. Even where information technology is found to have a valuable role to play, Naylor *et al.* (1990) found that the human dimension of learning is still crucially important and tutors have a key role to play for most students.

The important consideration for distance learning materials is fitness for purpose. For instance, video material tends to be expensive and lengthy to produce. By the time it has been produced the course material that it accompanies may need updating. In any case, busy people may find it easier to listen to a tape while driving or occupied around the house. If good quality material has already been produced that fits the educational purposes of the course, you may be wise to purchase, or require the students to purchase it.

The effectiveness of distance learning may depend upon the nature of your outcome objectives for your students, that is, the qualities, understanding or skills that you wish the students to have developed by the end of the programme. These enable you to make 'fitness for purpose' decisions and help to provide the structure for the learning. From your students' point of view, clear outcome objectives enable them to see their successes at each stage in the learning process, and to know when they can stop. On the other hand, if they are defined in narrow terms, they can restrict the students' choices and predetermine their journey through the material and the conclusions they must reach.

Enquiry Task 6.5

Take the idea that you discussed with colleagues for a course that might be delivered through open learning.
Identify some possible *outcome* objectives for one part of the programme.
List the action that the student would take to meet the objective.
List the evidence that would enable (a) the tutor and (b) the student to know whether the objective had been achieved.

	Action to be taken to meet objective	Evidence available to the tutor that objective is met	Evidence available to student that objective is met
Objective 1			
Objective 2			
Objective 3			

Issues to Consider in the Design of Open and Distance Learning Material

Lewis (1985) indicated a number of issues that you should consider when designing open and distance learning programmes. First, you should determine who the 'client' is. The client may be the potential student, or a third party such as the employer. The requirements of an employer may be different from that of the student. For instance, the MSC (1986) reported that training managers in industry want open learning packages that are tailored to the needs of the organization. They prefer short, quality packages of six to ten hours. They may be less concerned than students as to whether there is a link to a traditional course qualification.

Issues related to effective course delivery will include an identification of the students' characteristics, their needs and the context in which they will be working. Students will have similarities and differences in their expectations, experience and needs. These should be analysed to ascertain that there is a genuine need for the course. The identification of need is not in itself sufficient. Action will be needed to turn the need into a demand for the course.

Your understanding of the students' needs should not just relate to level of knowledge and skills, but may extend to the context, including the psychological context in which the student operates. In Britain 50 per cent of adults have no post-compulsory education or training. Open and distance learning is often directed to attracting these people back into education. If you are to be successful, it is important that you understand the difficulties that have prevented these potential students from taking up education opportunities in the past. Bailey (1987) found that these difficulties may include the multiple roles many adults have to manage (for instance parent, employee and student), the learning legacies left by bad experiences of education, self-image, and vocational intentions. Blocks to learning include cost, sex stereotyping, teaching styles adopted, poor liaison between the university or college and employer, employers' attitudes, lack of information, time constraints, and unclear motivation.

Distance and open learning may be particularly appropriate for overcoming *some* of these blocks, including geography, lack of child care, timetables and terms, and a lack of a ladder or 'bridge' into study. The skills and knowledge that students bring with them may be subject related, but just as important may be other aspects of learning, such as facility with words, numbers, diagrams or information technology.

Your analysis of need should help you to work out a clearer course rationale and specific aims and objectives. Your selection of content should be related to course aims. You will need to decide its organization, for instance the course structure, the length of sections, number of levels, assessment, and sequence of presentation, with reference to the students' needs and context. You will need to make decisions about learning methods, learner activities and media. Each of these decisions may be crucial to success. For instance, we have described the importance of the balance between formative and summative assessment in Chapter 4. Within an open learning context, an appropriate balance of assessment may provide the regular contact and feedback of performance which helps to keep your students on course.

Most open learning programmes are not planned in a vacuum. Course delivery will be subject to resource constraints. The context in which the potential students operate will influence the format of course materials and their delivery. You may find that you can group students or facilities to enable some local delivery. It will be important that you consider what materials already exist within the institution, or in a format that can be purchased. The MSC (1988) found that flexibility is often highly prized by clients, but it may increase organizational and administrative costs. They found successful programmes tended to have highly efficient and centralized administration concerned with student progress, records, quality, marketing, and delivery that was decentralized or network-based, for instance through the use of libraries as information points. This form of development may become easier to arrange within the UK if the recommendations of the Follett report (1993) are accepted.

An aspect that you may overlook is the management of the programme. Management issues that need planning may include the selection of students, induction, forecasting and monitoring income and expenditure, methods of communication, setting standards, monitoring progress, marketing, distribution, evaluation, the allocation of time, subcontracting, liaisons with other organizations, staffing, revision, and review.

Enquiry Task 6.6

Take the idea that you discussed with colleagues for a course that might be delivered through open learning.

List the management and marketing actions that might be involved in undertaking each of the tasks below, during the *planning* stage.

Decide on the order in which they could be undertaken.

	Subtasks	*Priority Order*
• determining the market;		
• researching the needs and interests of potential students;		
• deciding on curriculum content;		
• deciding on methods of delivering the curriculum;		
• deciding on assessment;		
• creating learning materials;		
• decisions about selection of students;		
• setting up systems for validation/accreditation;		
• setting up systems for monitoring academic standards;		
• setting up systems for monitoring student progress;		
• advertising and marketing;		

> - creating a budget and cash
>   flow analysis for staffing,
>   non-staff costs and the
>   income.
>
> *Find out who in your institution would need progress reports on each of these management tasks.*

The Evaluation of Open and Distance Learning

In the longer term, the success of an open and distance learning programme may depend on the effectiveness of evaluation processes. Thorpe (1988) points out that the evaluation needs to be different from that for traditional courses, in as much as evaluation of the materials may be the starting point.

As with other courses, evaluation should be concerned with the improvement of learning opportunities. If your students are likely to be distant from the institution, strategies will need to be found to overcome difficulties caused to you by distance in understanding the perspectives of the students. The process of evaluation will demand planning and organization in order that you can find out the effects of action taken, and the validity of the materials and the service offered.

The aims and particular nature of distance and open learning can lead to the evaluation of particular aspects being more important than in traditional courses. Your focus for evaluation may include the quality of learners' self-evaluation, counselling and processes within the learners' progress as well as materials and tuition. Evaluation could involve many groups such as students, authors, support staff, colleagues, managers, and (perhaps) employers.

Summary

Openness should derive from the needs and purposes of the students and may relate to time, place, starting date, duration, entry requirements, and/or teaching and learning methods. It can relate to teaching method, exploration, enquiry and development, and interdisciplinary influences.

Distance learning is one form of open learning which may or may not conform to the definitions above. For instance, the aim of this approach may be either to impart a given body of knowledge or to further students' development.

Distance learning has particular problems to overcome. These include the need for a community of debate; the need for explanations when students experience difficulties with the materials; obtaining quality teaching materials; and knowing when to reactivate students who may or may not have dropped out.

Teaching materials commonly include information technology, commercial materials, video and audiotape.

Open learning usually involves changes in the roles and relationship between the student and tutor. The tutor often has to develop new skills, particularly related to collaborative working, organization and administration, counselling, interpretation and diagnosis, communication, feedback, and evaluation.

Open learning is political in as much as it challenges traditional conceptions of learning and validates alternative educational settings, definitions of teaching and learning, empowers students, builds on *students'* practice; or creates a ladder of opportunity.

The central requirement is to understand the interests of the students and their problems. These may include:

- the maintenance of multiple roles;
- learning legacies from schooling;
- self-image and career aspirations;
- sex stereotyping;
- liaison between the university or college, the student and employers;
- lack of information or time; and/or
- motivation.

Evaluation is a particular issue in open learning. The evaluation of course materials may be a starting point but it should be related to aims and the nature of the learning.

The following represents a checklist of issues you may need to address in the design of open learning programmes or materials:

- context, needs and characteristics of the client;
- rationale and definition of open learning in this context;
- objectives;
- barriers to learning as experienced by the potential students (and/or employers);
- marketing;
- resources available, constraints and costs;
- management, advice and administrative structures;
- validation, accreditation and course design systems;
- selection of students;
- assessment methods, objectives, student progress and quality control;
- teaching and learning methods;
- materials and delivery methods;
- tutor skill audit, development and training;
- evaluation methods and criteria.

Entry for the Reflective Diary

Look back at the teaching of the last week

Note the definitions of open learning implied by your methods of working (e.g. open pedagogy, exploration and enquiry, interdisciplinary work, freedom from constraints of time, place and duration, freedom from fixed entry or exit points).

Did you get the students to work at a distance from you at any point?

If not:

- Write about why you chose to make them do all their work in your presence.
- Reflect on how you might encourage them to learn in your absence in the future.

If you did:

- What methods did you use to encourage them into a 'community of debate' in your absence?
- What methods might you use next time?

References

BAGLEY, B. and CHALIES, B. (1985) *Studies in Further Education: Inside Open Learning*, Bristol, FESC.

BAILEY, D. (1987) *Guidance in Open Learning*, Hertford, NICEC/MSC.

CHACON, F. (1992) 'A taxonomy of computer media in distance education', *Journal of Open and Distance Learning*, **7**, 1, pp. 12–27.

FOLLETT, B. (1993) *Report on Libraries from the Joint Funding Council Libraries Review Group for HEFCE SHFEC, HEFCW and DENI*, Bristol, HEFCE.

GRANGER, D. (1990) 'Open learning and distance learning at Empire State College', *Journal of Open and Distance Learning*, **5**, 1, pp. 24–30.

HODGESON, V.E., MANN, S.J. and SNELL, R. (Eds) (1987) *Beyond Distance Teaching — Towards Open Learning*, Milton Keynes, SRHE/Open University Press.

LEWIS, R. (1985) *Open Learning Guide 5: How to Develop and Manage an Open Learning Scheme*, London, CET.

MANPOWER SERVICES COMMISSION (MSC) (1986) *LEA Feasibility Study: The Essence*, London, EDMU/Open Tech.

MANPOWER SERVICES COMMISSION (MSC) (1988) *Universities, Enterprise and Local Economic Development: An Exploration of Links Based on Studies in Britain and Elsewhere*, London, HMSO.

MAUGER, S. and BOUCHERAT, J. (1991) *Open Learning Tutor Skills*, Bradford Peverell, Language House Publications.

NAYLOR, P., COWIE, H. and STEVENSON, K. (1990) 'Using student and tutor perspectives in the development of open tutoring', *Journal of Open and Distance Learning*, **5**, 1, pp. 9–18.

SCRIVEN, B. and LUNDIN, R. (1992) 'Open learning centres in Queensland', *Journal of Open and Distance Learning*, **7**, 1, pp. 62–67.

THORPE, H. (1988) *Evaluating Open and Distance Learning*, Harlow, Longman.

Suggested Reading

HODGESON, V.E., MANN, S.J. and SNELL R. (Eds) (1987) *Beyond Distance Teaching — Towards Open Learning*, Milton Keynes: SRHE/Open University Press.
A series of papers which give a theoretical framework for various forms of open learning, including interactive technology.

Journal of Open and Distance Learning
This journal, published by the Open University and Longmans three times a year, contains recent research and reviews from around the world. The research is usually written in a readable and accessible style and often includes qualitative material of direct application to practical issues in open learning.

LEWIS, R. (1985) *Open Learning Guide 5: How to Develop and Manage an Open Learning Scheme*, London; CET.
A comprehensive guide to most of the issues involved in the practical implementation of an open learning programme.

MAUGER, S. and BOUCHERAT, J. (1991) *Open Learning Tutor Skills*, Bradford Peverell, Language House Publications.
A useful introduction to tutorial skill development for open learning which itself uses an open learning format.

Chapter 7

Aids to Learning

Reasons for Using Aids to Learning

We have been arguing within this book that part of your role as a tutor is to enable students to move appropriately from surface levels of learning to deeper ones. Part of that movement involves interacting with the material to be learned in order to structure and reorganize it. Audio-visual aids and information technology can be used imaginatively to assist in this process. In this chapter we will discuss their role in teaching and learning, suggest a range of uses and direct you to some which you might like to try out.

Audio, visual and technological aids to learning can be powerful tools to enrich your teaching and deepen your students' learning. They can enliven and add interest to your communication. On the other hand, they can enable you to reinforce particular learning through the use of more than one sense or through the opportunities that audio, visual and technological aids provide for your students to reorganize and represent the material with which they are working.

Some of the differences in students' learning styles have been discussed in previous chapters. These lead to differences in the ways that students use their senses in learning. Some students learn best through the process of putting their thoughts into words, others through modelling them. Some find that they learn aurally and others visually. The use of information technology and audio-visual and technological aids can bring more of the students' senses to bear upon the process of learning. They can encourage the student to learn independently of you.

Audio-visual aids are usually conceived of as a teaching tool used by the tutor. They are also useful learning tools if they are generated and used by the students. They can facilitate the internalization of syllabus material and develop the students' communication skills. Students can learn to present assessed and non-assessed material in a variety of media and consider their appropriateness for different kinds of audience. The process of thinking about communication requires the student to organize and structure their material, to sort out essential issues and to present them simply and clearly. Thus, audio-visual and technological aids can be powerful tools in the development of students' ability to organize material and thus to study effectively. Such activity, when combined with group and cooperative work also lends itself to the development of interpersonal skills and to skills in self and peer assessment.

Although audio-visual and technological aids to learning may be used to encourage passive learning, they have the potential to be employed to develop the skills and qualities students will need if they are to become reflective practitioners of their subject. These have been discussed in some detail earlier in the book and include open-mindedness and, more particularly, responsibility and communication skills.

Ideally your own use of audio-visual aids and information technology should be thoroughly professional if it is to provide a model of excellent communication. This means that where possible you should aim to use materials that bear comparisons with those commercially produced. They should be clear, well finished and used appropriately.

It seems to be a 'natural law' that technology will not work smoothly unless it is checked before a taught session. If you are lucky you will have technicians to set up and check the equipment you use. Otherwise you would be wise to set it up so that you do not have to spend a few moments rewinding or fiddling with controls and so lose the students' interest and concentration. Your use of audio-visual aids and information technology should be as slick and polished as possible. In the real world of teaching these standards may not always be achieved, but perhaps they should be aspired to as the norm.

Information Technology

There are a variety of ways that technology can be used in your teaching and it is important to be aware of the possibilities. It is not only an important aid to learning and efficient course delivery, but it is also an area that students need to know about for their future careers. Tally (1983) points out that in a technological world it is necessary to move up the technological chain to stay in business. Education tends to move more slowly than business in this respect, but here too the technological revolution has been great. In the late 1980s information technology was used in a minority of subjects in most institutions. In higher education by the mid-1990s many tutors have a computer on their desk and use it daily and many further education colleges include the permeation of information technology across the curriculum as an explicit aim. Within education, technology is moving towards a more central position within the learning process. Information technology has moved beyond mathematics and science to become an increasing feature in subjects as diverse as geography, art and design and psychology. For instance, in arts-based subjects such as English students are encouraged to use software packages for editing and revising personal writing.

Developments such as increasing student numbers may result in changes in the roles of students and tutors. For instance, you may find yourself becoming more of a resource manager. These changes are likely to affect the curriculum you have to deliver in the future. You may have to adapt to an increasing emphasis on data handling and processing. The Computers in Teaching Initiative (CTI, 1991) points out that, as access to universities is broadened, students enter with a wider variety of entrance qualifications and experience. Information technology can be used to offer a wider range of independent learning materials to meet a range of learning needs.

Information technology can be used to enable more individual learning. CD-ROMs are data banks that perform a similar function as a hard disk (except they are read-only, you cannot save new material onto them), but because they have a larger storage capacity, they can contain whole encyclopaedias, pictures, games and so on, which can be sorted, matched and interacted with. One of us has used a CD-ROM called 'Twelfth Night' to build individual skills in textual analysis on a literature course. A gloss of the meaning of each act is provided and difficult words in the text are highlighted. Students can 'click' on a word they are not sure of and a detailed explanation appears. The display is attractive with a good use of colour and students can print out any parts of the display to which they may need to refer later.

It is sometimes appropriate to use a CD-ROM for the kind of problem-focused learning which leads to a blurring of subject boundaries. Used imaginatively, it can create greater student choice as students identify their own way through the curriculum. New methods of assessment and evaluation, perhaps including the use of questionnaires, become possible. Used very selectively, these can enable instant checking and monitoring of student responses and perhaps release your time from the more mundane aspects of marking of knowledge-based assessments to undertake more useful tasks.

It may be that technology can open areas of the curriculum previously seen as 'difficult', such as the use of the statistics package 'Statview' for numerical analysis in geography, to more students. There may be an initial downside, in opening 'difficult' areas of the curriculum such as statistical analysis to students, in that you must allow time for the students to become familiar with the particular software before they can start to use it effectively. On a similar point, computer algebra packages such as 'Derive' and 'Mathematica' can now carry out many of the mundane mathematical tasks that comprise much of the technique elements of GCSE and A'level work. The debate is now on as to how this will affect mathematics in the future. Again, there are disadvantages. Ideally, to use such packages effectively, students still need to have a good grasp of the concepts and techniques involved. This implies that you can diagnose the students' individual level and provide the 'knowledge-base' they need. Once this is achieved, students can be freed from some of the onerous calculation and possibility for error to venture further and explore more realistic situations.

Because information technology is a new medium, different and creative applications are emerging all the time. Students' problem-solving abilities can be developed in a realistic setting through simulations. For instance, the 'Reiters Simulation' may enable students to set about solving a problem related to a particular discipline on limited information. This simulates a news agency producing information about a developing problem that the students are trying to solve. As the process continues, you can send new information through the 'telex' that changes and complicates the situation. Compact disk applications allow students to explore more options and the inclusion of sound and animation.

Other computer activities can develop students' abilities to think and solve problems as well as simulations and models. For example, it has been argued (Underwood and Underwood, 1990) that effective data handling and processing (i.e. information retrieval for some purpose or to answer a question) is in itself an exercise in thinking and problem-solving.

Where the hardware is available, it is now possible to use a projected computer screen instead of overhead transparencies. This will enable data to be manipulated or categories analysed in discussion with the students. They can then pull off individual hard copies of aspects that interest them.

The sheer volume of information available requires students to develop problem-solving skills that allow them to find their way round it to ask the right questions, but it also requires and develops other skills. For example, the CD-ROM of the *Times* newspapers has a selection of articles from a particular year's output of *The Times* and *The Sunday Times* — between 60,000 and 80,000 articles, depending upon the year. This is a marvellous resource for researching contemporary history or sociology, but requires skills of selection, critical analysis and synthesis to make sense of what is offered.

In the UK, the National Curriculum Document for English (NCC, 1993) suggests that students can be encouraged to use word processing at all stages of the writing process including:

- drafting (getting ideas on to paper or computer screen, regardless of form, organisation or expression);
- redrafting (shaping and structuring the raw material — either on paper or screen — to take account of purpose, audience and form);
- rereading and revising (making alterations to help the reader);
- proof reading. (NCC, 1993: 39)

The possibilities of manipulating the text using word processing are particularly well matched to point 2, deletions and amendments match point 3, and the use of a spell-checker, or even a style checker, matches point 4.

Students Learning about Information Technology

The use of information technology in as many ways as possible across the curriculum sends messages to the students about its availability and relevance to subjects apart from mathematics and science. This may help to project the many applications of technology, but it is essential to be aware that, while information technology can be useful in teaching it can, of itself, be an obstacle to learning. Enthusiasts may forget that many students start with negative attitudes. For this reason, it may sometimes be preferable for information technology to be introduced by a non-specialist.

Since students may be very nervous, free play with the technology may result in an unacceptable level of failure. A failure with a group of beginners is likely to result in the tutor being unable to keep up with their demands and with the students experiencing frustration. It may be better to ensure that the very earliest experience results in as near total success as is possible. Thus you may consider starting off in a very didactic way. As the students develop a confidence within the 'geography' of particular programs and they can find their own way around them, you may find that freer exploration becomes more appropriate.

A student's initial introduction to information technology is very important and it is necessary to identify his or her experience and allow for variation, for instance by using material that lets students progress at their own pace; having various levels of sophistication in each task; having an open-ended element in the task; and so on. Some packages, such as 'Claris Works' have a tutorial element within them which can be utilized in whole or in part for this purpose.

If your aim is to develop confidence, it may be better to focus on the applications of information technology and its implications for people, rather than on understanding machines and programs. Unfortunately, most information technology rooms make it difficult to focus on anything but the machines. Rooms where most chairs face the machines and the wall give the message to staff and students that time should be spent at the machines. If you wish to project a more human face for information technology, you may wish to reorganize the seating.

The ideal room for information technology has space for discussion away from machines. It is very human, if students are sitting at their machines, for them to be distracted by the screen and their own activities during discussion.

There is also a point about privacy. The computer screen is a very public medium, especially where chairs face the wall and tutors can look over the students' shoulders. It seems natural to 'eavesdrop' (spy?) on their work as they are doing it, but it can also be threatening. In an activity where groups of two or three students wrote a haiku together using the word processor, some of them physically hid the screen from passing viewers until they were happy with their finished product. In these circumstances you might ask the students to invite you to look at the screen when they are ready.

Gender issues in information technology have become central as computer studies has grown as a subject. Siann *et al.* (1988) found that in the UK in 1985/6 only 13 per cent of those entering information technology related courses were women compared with 28 per cent in 1978. Thus, information technology seems to have become strictly 'gendered' in a very short space of time. This may be the result of the way that 'computer studies' was conceived and taught in the early stages. It may be that traditional ways of teaching and looking at information technology have little appeal to women. Some institutions have become worried that the association of technology with male interests disadvantages women. Some now have equal opportunities policies in relation to information technology. Since only 18 per cent of higher education information technology teaching staff in Britain are women, some have included consideration of gender issues in the way the post and criteria for appointment are described.

Students in all disciplines will need to develop some understanding of information technology. Female students may experience more difficulty with this than male students. Spear (1985) suggests that girls do not get as much experience of information technology as boys. For instance, boys are up to six times as likely to be bought a home computer than girls. There is some evidence that girls' development of information technology skills may be impaired by being paired for activities with boys (Hardman and Fitzpatrick, 1994). In some colleges and universities, expensive hardware is concentrated in subjects and departments which traditionally attract more male than female students. You may wish to consider whether the design of information technology courses may influence your women students' reactions to information technology. For instance, would they prefer short, flexible, non-specialist people-centred courses?

In order to counteract the 'gendered' image of information technology, you may want to develop more appropriate teaching methods and content. For instance, you might try basing information technology on your students' personal experience, ideas and interests. You could explore whether group work with other people, rather than individual work with machines engages more of your female students' interests. Courses that introduce information technology do not have to focus on skills. You could focus more directly on the evaluation of the role of information technology in society and the critical discussion of its applications. The students do not have to be preoccupied with the artefacts of technology or take an uncritical view of it. There is a need for a moral discourse about the uses of information technology beyond issues of data protection. The uses of information technology raise important ethical and libertarian issues of the relative importance of the needs and rights of people versus the needs and interests of organizations and systems. You may have had to face some of these problems within your own institution, perhaps where the institutional needs for efficient allocation of resources (such as timetabled space) interferes with the needs and interests of your students.

Information Technology as an Aid to Teaching and Learning

Information technology can be viewed as a 'subject' in its own right which students should get to grips with in the modern world, or as an aid to teaching and learning. In this latter sense you should not restrict yourself to subject specific programs. Information technology may be of greatest help in learning when it is used to structure student activity. Generic programs can be more useful for this purpose. You could explore whether you could usefully employ information technology to generate discussion, to edit your students' conclusions, to sort ideas, to order them and pull out main points and issues. These creative uses of information technology imply an interaction with other people rather than with the machine, the machine being used purely as a tool in this discussion. One to one work on a machine of the sort common in information technology rooms and encouraged by their layout may be inimical to these uses of information technology.

A useful structuring exercise that can be used in most subjects is the group writing exercise. For instance, within a teacher training course, we sometimes give a small group of students, no more than four, a government document or a journal article and ask them to prepare a summary or a briefing document using a word processor. If this is combined with an overt requirement to use the four stages in writing outlined above, the activity not only ensures that material is discussed and internalized, but also teaches a useful study skill. The benefits of using a word processor can be illustrated if the same task is also carried out in written form. The students may find that most of the group find it hard to see what is being written on the paper but the screen should be visible to all. With the word processor handwriting problems will be eliminated; text can be reordered and modified easily and neatly; students can each receive an identical copy of the finished product quickly and easily; and the group may feel more ownership of the text on the screen than if one person has been writing it. On this last point, you will have to ensure that no single person dominates the activity by preventing access to the keyboard, and that all ideas are at least tried out.

Some types of generic programs tend to be used within a limited range of subjects. An example of this may be graphics programs which are seen as particularly relevant to design subjects. However, they can be used creatively in a wider range of subjects. Graphics programs can help students to explore the relationship between the visual dimension and a variety of other subject matter. For instance, a floor plan can be manipulated to explore the relationship between architecture and people in a religious studies programme, and enable students to explore the practical aspects of the theology of architecture. 'Mapping' and visual representation can be relevant to a variety of disciplines. Graphic programs allow students to manipulate variables and analyse the results through the principles embedded in the discipline of the subject.

The visual metaphor approach to organizing data to simplify the task of finding your way round it can be very helpful. For example, in a local history context, one can organize information about a village, its buildings and surroundings, by having a graphic of the geographical layout. Various parts of this, when activated by a mouse or concept keyboard, can reveal layers of information about the area specified.

Over recent years computer aided design (CAD) systems have become available at relatively low cost. Ingram (1989) warns against producing CAD components that are isolated from the mainstream of students' courses. CAD enables three-dimensional modelling and drafting systems, which may be used as vehicles for student-centred learning.

Data bases can be used in many subject areas to explore the effects of decisions and a range of options. Their use does not have to be confined to scientific and mathematical subjects. Word processing packages are probably the most accessible starting point for many staff and students. Ideas generated by small groups of students can be recorded on the computer and then manipulated, edited and organized in a variety of ways.

Programmes can also be used to access information for you and your students. An example of this is ERIC, a package that contains an index of educational journals that allows you to select the subject headings in which you are interested and then to access the abstracts of relevant papers. Multimedia CD-ROM information sources open up new possibilities for students. A source such as the 'Grolier Multimedia Encyclopaedia', as well as text articles, has high quality illustrations, animations and video clips. For example, in an American history course students can not only read John F. Kennedy's inaugural address, but see a clip of him delivering it and experience some of the emotion involved.

Tucker (1986) reports that the central theme of a variety of research into the use of new technology in teaching is the need for staff training. Massive expenditure on information technology resources often has had little impact on general teaching. What seems to be needed is an integration of training for audio-visual media, information technology and content and teaching method.

Enquiry Task 7.1

Find out and list the generic (non-subject specific) programs available in your college or university.

Choose up to three which you think have applications in the teaching of your subject.

- Learn how to use them.
- Find an application for each in your teaching.

- Use student feedback to evaluate the effectiveness of your use of the program.
- Improve the effectiveness of your application of one of the programs.

What did you learn about when and how to use technology in your teaching from this exercise?

Libraries as Information Providers

Libraries continue to play a central part in providing for the information needs of students. Follett (1993) reports that libraries of the future will not be single repositories, but rather systems for information access. Library staff are likely to play a more central role in student learning, and you may need to involve them to a greater extent in your teaching and planning, so that they can act as facilitators of your students' learning.

There is likely to be increasing scope for libraries to discharge their responsibilities through collaborative arrangements with other institutions or groups of institutions. This is a particularly useful development in metropolitan areas, but in other areas collaboration may also be helpful in the support of non-traditional and open learning students.

The use of information technology is likely to be an increasingly important aspect of library provision. There is already potential for electronic document and article delivery and in the near future for electronic journals.

Uses of Audio-visual Aids

Researchers and those responsible for funding or monitoring quality in higher and further education have not given the use of audio-visual aids in teaching as much time, attention and other resources as the use of information technology. Although they are used more often, there may be less help available to enable you make the most of these tools in your everyday teaching, and you may have less information about their effects on student learning.

There are a wide variety of aids to learning and each has a range of ways in which they can be employed. You may encourage students' attention if you try out a variety of teaching approaches. The use of audio-visual aids such as video can assist you by providing an opportunity to vary the pace during a taught session. Visual material can be used to illustrate an argument or focus the student on the central points. You may be able to analyse teaching and learning processes after the event only through the use of technology. For instance, you could use a small tape recorder to pick up snippets of student talk during a workshop. Playing these back may stimulate discussion of a different kind from that generated by the more traditional 'report back'. This could enable the students to learn more about group processes, or examine the categories that were focused on in group work.

Overhead Transparencies

We have found that the overhead projector has a variety of advantages over the black or white board. It enables you to face your students while you are teaching. It is hard to produce legible handwriting when you have to write in very large symbols on a vertical surface. The use of overhead transparencies can enable you to project prepared material, perhaps using computer generated images, or to write notes or diagrams to illustrate learning points in the course of a lecture. Since you can also keep them for future use, they are also a good investment of your time.

Material that is prepared in advance should be immaculately presented. Usually the best way of achieving this is to word-process the required material in large bold letters and print or photocopy it onto acetate sheets. In any case, it is essential that writing on overhead transparencies is large and well formed. The resulting overhead transparency should not be overcrowded. As a rough rule of thumb, we have found that overhead transparencies that contain more than about thirty words are seldom useful. Photocopies of tables or figures or extended quotations are much more useful to the student if they are presented in the form of handouts. In general, only the *very* simplest statistics or graphs can be usefully portrayed on overhead transparencies.

Overhead transparencies may be better used to 'map' the main points, rather than to convey information. You may find it helps your students to have the structure of a taught session explained at its start. An overhead transparency can help you to lay out the 'geography' of a session in a simple and clear way. You might then return to the overhead transparency each time you start a new phase or move on to a new issue. Mapping the students' experience in this way may help them to orientate and pace themselves.

Students are often overwhelmed by material presented in lectures. This is often because they cannot see the organizing principles behind the ideas presented and so are trying to grasp many apparently unrelated ideas. Provided they are not overused, overhead transparencies can be a useful means of encouraging the students to focus on the essential aspects of a lecture. It is seldom useful to use more than five or six overhead transparencies in a single taught session without drawing attention from central concepts. If you are using more than this number, you might consider whether you are employing them for the wrong purpose, or whether your are trying to convey too many concepts in a single session.

Overhead transparencies may be used to simplify a complex process and demonstrate the way it is built up. Overlays, placing one overhead transparency on top of another, can be a useful method of demonstrating this or for showing how component parts of an object or idea fit together. Pictures can be drawn or photocopied onto an overhead transparency to provide a visual metaphor for a concept or process. For instance, student-teachers exploring industrial awareness as a cross-curricular issue might be asked to draw a picture symbolizing their impression of 'industry' at the start of the component. At the end of the component, they may use the picture to communicate the way their image of industry has changed or developed.

You might use overhead transparencies in various ways to draw attention to points made in the course of a lecture. Coloured Perspex can be used to focus on particular aspects of the overhead transparency. Alternatively, you could mask parts of the overhead transparency, only revealing them at the appropriate moment. You could try printing ideas or concepts separately onto strips of acetate and manipulate and move them to show connections at the students' or your own suggestions. Alternatively, student ideas can be 'brainstormed' directly onto an overhead transparency and the links between them shown by lines or groupings.

Overhead transparencies can be used to draw attention to questions that you wish to answer, or wish the students to answer, in the course of a taught session. Alternatively, you could collect student questions onto a overhead transparency at the start of a session and mark each as you deal with it in your presentation.

You may find it useful to provide the students with a résumé of the central ideas or dilemmas that have been explored in the course of a taught session. An overhead transparency can provide a useful vehicle for structuring this.

As with all visual aids, overhead transparencies can be as useful for the student in their learning and assessment as for you in your teaching. Students can be encouraged to use overhead transparencies to feed back their ideas or the results of group work to the larger group. The act of creating the overhead transparency forces the student to structure and synthesize their thinking and to sort essential from peripheral issues.

Enquiry Task 7.2

Identify a central idea, concept or process within the subject you teach (for instance, the 'virtuous woman' in Victorian literature or 'sphere of influence' in geography).

Ask each group of your students to use overhead transparencies in a different way to demonstrate to the rest of the students how the concept or process is built up. For instance, by creating:

- a set of overlaid overhead transparencies;
- a pictorial metaphor;
- a diagrammatic representation;
- verbally in less than thirty words.

Assess the effectiveness of this method of reinforcing student learning and helping them to organize and structure an idea or process through:

- your own observation of the students' interaction while creating the overhead transparencies;
- the quality of the overhead transparencies produced;
- the students' own assessments of what they have learned.

Video and Audio Recording

Video and audio recording can provide examples and illustrate a variety of phenomena which would not be otherwise accessible to students. A video camera linked to a monitor is an effective method for enabling a group of students to see an artefact in close up during the course of a lecture. Alternatively, it can illustrate phenomena that are separated from the students by space or time.

The use of video and audio recording in the classroom is different from its use in the home. The point is not entertainment or relaxation, nor is it usually to provide information. Unless information is not otherwise easily accessible, other methods tend to be more effective for this purpose. Usually the point of video and audio recording is to stimulate interaction or analysis. For this reason, video and audio recording may be used most effectively if 'snippets' are carefully selected and supporting notes are provided. On some commercially produced videos, the thinking has been done for the student, rendering the tape less useful for teaching purposes. Watching the video without the commentary may enable the students to draw their own conclusions, which might later be compared with those of the programme makers.

Video and audio recording may be used to teach in your absence. For instance, a tutor in a catering department might produce a short video of how to chop various vegetables. Creating videos or audio recordings for teaching purposes can be surprisingly expensive and time consuming. Unless they are to be very simple, for instance the tutor talking directly to the camera or demonstrating a technique using one camera angle, it is often more cost effective to use commercially produced video and audio recordings.

You might explore more unconventional uses. For instance, students can create their own video or audio material from their researches. The process of communication involved in the creation of a video or audio recording encourages the students to internalize the material they are presenting. Video or audio recordings can enable cross-moderation of assessed student-led seminars or presentations.

Video and audiotape can be useful tools in the development of the students' interpersonal and management skills. For instance, aspects of interaction can be recorded during seminars or practical sessions. These can then be analysed and discussed. You might get the students to consider how they could support each other's learning differently during such sessions, perhaps by consciously varying habitual patterns of interaction. Video or audio recording of tutorials can also be used as a tool to develop study skills and to encourage students to get more out of such expensive and valuable interactions. You and your students can then analyse the learning achieved and how it might be developed.

You might record your own teaching in order to access the way you are managing the learning process. We have learned a great deal about our patterns of interaction each time we have videotaped ourselves teaching. Video and audio recording may enable you to identify communication skills that you need to develop further. Cameras are more obtrusive in the classroom than are audiotape machines. The problem can be minimized if a handheld, battery operated, self-focusing camera is used. One of us has sometimes operated the camera from her seat by holding it on her knee and turning the eye piece upwards. In this way she was able to see the picture being recorded and point the camera correctly, but the recording itself is relatively unobtrusive. Of course, ethics demand that the person or people being videotaped have given their permission.

As with all materials used in teaching and learning, video and audio images and messages can convey useful subject information, but also messages that restrict the opportunities of some students. For instance, women, members of ethnic minority groups or disabled people may be portrayed in stereotyped roles. Alternatively they, or their experience or interests may be omitted entirely. In these circumstances, you may wish to find alternative material, or to use the video or audio recording as an opportunity to explore with the students the equal opportunities issues raised by such a treatment of the subject.

Enquiry Task 7.3

Video or audiotape a tutorial discussion with a small group of students. Together analyse the interactions you have recorded. For instance:

- Who did most of the talking?
- Who did most of the thinking?
- What proportion of the talk demanded recall? reflection? analysis?
- Could/should the interactions be more equal?
- How might this be achieved?
- Did the students achieve the objectives of the session?
- What did the students learn?
- What did you learn?

Compare the students' analyses with your own.

What did you learn?

Handouts

Handouts can perform an important role in conveying information. If they are provided and read by the students in advance, the taught session can be used to explore and analyse issues rather than to inform. Many students can take in more information from reading than from a lecture. They can reread sections they find difficult to understand or remember and have the handout to refer to at a later date.

Handouts can help to structure the students' thinking and note taking during a taught session. Morgan *et al.* (1988) report research showing that students given skeletal handouts perform better in examinations than those who take all their own notes. These handouts can be in the form of a set of main headings with spaces for the student's own notes, or a matrix in which the student makes notes against two sets of headings. Alternatively the handout may take the form of a set of questions to be addressed. The amount of detail provided seems to be important to this. Information in handouts may facilitate recall, but if there is too much detail, it may inhibit the 'encoding' involved in the student taking some of their own notes. In addition, consulting handouts during lectures may interfere with the student's ability to attend to what you are saying unless time is taken from the lecture to enable the students to read. Thus, in some circumstances, handouts containing nothing but headings may be more helpful to students than those with the fuller text.

Students seem to be programmed to take down verbatim information presented on overhead transparencies. It can save time, and perhaps enable students to record their queries and reactions to the material presented, if they are provided with photocopies of the overhead transparencies at the start of the session.

The effectiveness of a handout seems to be affected by how soon after a lecture the student makes use of the material. Learning will be maximized if this happens immediately after the lecture, for instance, when students have to draw on the material in a practical class or seminar following a lecture. Where there is not a follow up session, a *very* full handout given at the end of the session may improve results.

Time can be given in class for students to read a handout. This has the advantage of providing a change of pace and presenting material in a form that is easily absorbed and ensuring that it is actually referred to by the students. It also prevents students from being distracted by trying to read the handout at the same time as they should be listening to you or to each other.

Handouts can be improved by the use of newer technologies. For instance, images can be reduced, enlarged or superimposed using a photocopier. Most colleges and universities now have photocopiers that can reproduce in colour and collate documents. Desk-top publishing programs are becoming more user-friendly. They enable you to reproduce top quality graphics and text for handouts or overhead transparencies. Simple word processing packages can enable you to experiment with different sizes of texts and various fonts and styles. It is becoming more important for handouts to look professional. Poorly reproduced typewritten material is off-putting for the students who, rightly, expect higher standards. Most tutors have some access to a laser printer, even if they have to go to a learning or resource centre to use it. A laser printed handout, with well laid out text and graphics and plenty of space around it, is much more likely to be used by the student than an overcrowded handout with small, poorly produced lettering.

Enquiry Task 7.4

Create a summary covering the main points you wish to convey during a taught session. Do not give it to the students at this stage.

At the end of the session ask small groups of students to:

- discuss the notes they had taken during a session;
- come up with an agreed version.

Discuss with the students:

- which main points have been conveyed;
- the differences in the way they have been absorbed and ordered;
- what they have learned about note taking.

Think about the differences between the students' and your version of the main points.

What did you learn from this exercise?

Slides and Photographs

Slides and photographic material can be useful as part of the teaching and learning process. They can illustrate ideas that are not otherwise accessible. Alternatively they can act as a stimulus for discussion or to encourage observation skills in the student. They can encourage the student to learn in your absence, perhaps by providing an illustrated record of some of the main ideas or processes presented in a taught session. Carefully selected slides and open questions can force the student to think and empathize. Alternatively, a slide sequence can be used as a didactic tool, perhaps to demonstrate a particular manual skill or the correct way to operate a piece of equipment.

As with the use of video or audio recording, the careful selection of images and consideration of equal opportunities messages included or excluded by the material should be considered. Because visual images tend to be dense and complex, selection is also important if students are not to become bored or overwhelmed by the material. A small number of slides, carefully analysed, may be more effective than a slide-based lecture where one image after another is presented.

As with other visual materials, the use of slides and photographic images can be as useful for the student in their learning as it is for you in your teaching. For instance they could use photographic images to demonstrate an idea or its development or they could modify them in various ways to convey new meaning and highlight issues. Such a use of images forces the student to develop that sense of audience that is central to communication skills. The selection of images is likely to require them to internalize the main issues and to consider their effects upon the audience.

Flip Charts and Posters

The use of posters raises some of the same issues as the use of slides. The images used can be very potent and should be selected with care, not just for their relevance to the subject, but also for their social significance. Carefully selected or created posters can be enjoyable and humorous but at the same time relevant. They can encourage you and your students to reconceptualize material in visual form and thus enable a deeper understanding.

Requiring students to produce posters or organize their ideas onto a flip chart often forces them to order and prioritize the material presented. The process of creating a poster or recording the main points of a discussion onto a flip chart will tend to foster group coherence and can be used to promote discussion, reflection and synthesis. If changes in attitudes or understandings are recorded over time, the poster or flip chart can be a dynamic illustration of the students' learning process and serve to reinforce that process. Interactive posters can serve the same purpose. Alternatively, groups of students can present particular views on a controversial issue to encourage empathy and an understanding of the problematic nature of much 'knowledge'. As with other visual aids, the creation of a poster or the organization of ideas onto a flip chart requires the student to develop a sense of audience and an awareness of issues in communication.

Enquiry Task 7.5

Ask small groups of students to create a poster that captures the essence of a controversial issue within the subject or a component you teach.

How have different groups approached the tasks?
What does this tell you about:

- their grasp of the dilemmas inherent in the controversy;
- their feelings about the issue;
- the interpersonal skills they have or have not developed;
- the communication skills they have or have not developed?

How can you incorporate what you have learned about the students' thinking and skill development into your curriculum planning?

Summary

A combination of teaching methods, incorporating the use of information technology and audio-visual aids, enables students to learn through the senses that best suit their learning style. Information technology and audio-visual aids may be used creatively in order to maximize active learning. Students develop communication skills and internalize and structure their understanding of the syllabus by creating their own aids. You can use information technology and audio-visual aids to structure your teaching or as an aid to non-traditional assessment. Ideally, your use should be highly professional and provide a model of good communication and presentation.

The increasing use of information technology is likely to lead to changes in the role of the tutor, including more resource management and an emphasis on data handling, reading skills, individualized learning and student choice. It may provide opportunities for more problem centred and cross-curricular teaching and learning, new methods of assessment, and more students enabled to tackle 'difficult' subject areas.

Students fearful of technology may cope better if they are introduced to the technology in a highly structured way so that failure and frustration can be avoided and if applications and interaction are stressed rather than programs and machines. Fewer women study or teach information technology. The problem may reside in the way information technology is conceived and taught, not in women's abilities or interests.

Information technology may be better conceived as a tool for learning rather than as a subject. The range of generic programs that may be used in teaching across the curriculum includes graphics packages, data bases and word processing. Successful permeation of information technology across the curriculum seems to depend less on the purchase of hardware than on staff training.

The model of communication provided by your own audio-visual aids to learning should be excellent and bear comparison with commercially produced material. It is important to consider equal opportunities issues in the images and material selected. The creation of their own audio and visual aids can help students to develop their communication skill and force them to internalize, prioritize and structure their learning.

Audio-visual aids may be used to:

- teach in your absence;
- demonstrate the structure of a taught session;
- lay out the principles linking the ideas discussed;
- focus students' attention on essential aspects;
- show how a concept or process may be built up;
- collect and order students' ideas;
- list questions to be addressed;
- provide a résumé of the main issues;
- illustrate or examine phenomena not otherwise accessible;
- monitor group work and interaction;
- cross-moderate practical assessments;
- enable you to monitor your own teaching.

Overhead transparencies should be professionally presented. You may find it best to use no more than five or six transparencies, each with no more than thirty words.

Generally, video and audio recording used in teaching should be of professional quality. Carefully selected snippets, used in moderation, tend to be the most useful.

Handouts are often the most effective of the aids to learning for conveying straightforward information. They should be well produced, well laid out and not overcrowded. Formats for handouts include headings with spaces for student notes, a matrix with spaces for student notes as well as full supporting notes. They may be used before, during or after a session. Learning is increased if they are referred to soon after or during a session.

Slides and photographs can be used to illustrate phenomena that are not otherwise accessible. They may be used to encourage student discussion and analysis or as a didactic tool. A small number of slides or photographs are usually more effective in any one session, since visual material tends to be complex.

Posters can provide potent images that can reinforce learning. Students may be encouraged to create posters in order to reconceptualize and prioritize the issues. The process of creating a group poster can encourage reflection, discussion and empathy and promote group coherence.

Entry for the Reflective Diary

Make a pictorial or diagrammatic representation of your concept of effective teaching and learning.

Think about the ways that audio, visual or technological aids fit into this conception.

Write about the ways that you use audio, visual or technological aids to learning at the moment, the problems with your present use, and the ways in which you might adapt your use of these aids to make it more congruent with your model of teaching and learning.

References

COMPUTERS IN TEACHING INITIATIVE (CTI) (1991) *Computers in Teaching Initiative Annual Report*, Oxford, CTISS Publications.

FOLLETT, B. (1993) *Report on Libraries from the Joint Funding Council Libraries Review Group for HEFCE SHFEC, HEFCW and DENI*, Bristol, HEFCE.

HARDMAN, M.A. and FITZPATRICK, H. (1994) 'Effects of social interaction and the social context on social and cognitive development', Bolton Institute of Education, listed in *Current Research in Britain*, p. 328.

HOLDSWORTH, N. (1994) 'Early salvoes in the sex war', *Times Educational Supplement*, 8 October.

INGRAM, P. (Ed) (1989) *Computer Aided Design in Further Education*, London: FEU.

MORGAN, C.H., LILLEY, J.D. and BOREHAM, N.C. (1988) 'Learning from lectures: The effect of varying the detail in lecture handouts on note taking and recall', *Applied Cognitive Psychology*, **2**, 2.

NATIONAL CURRICULUM COUNCIL (NCC) (1993) *English*, London, HMSO.

SIANN, G., DURNDELL, A., MACLEOD, H. and GLISSOV P. (1988) 'Stereotyping in relation to the gender gap in participation in computing', *Educational Research*, **30**, 2, pp. 98–103.

SPEAR, M.G. (1985) 'Teachers' attitudes towards girls and technology' in WHYTE, J., DEEM, R., KANT, L. and CRUICKSHANK, M. (Eds) *Girl Friendly Schooling*, London, Routledge.

TALLY, G. (1983) 'What will the world of work demand from education and training in the future?' in TUCKER, J. (Ed) *Education, Training and the New Technologies: SCETT Conference Look Out for Learners*, London, Kogan Page.

TUCKER, R.N. (1986) *The Integration of Media into the Curriculum*, London, Kogan.

UNDERWOOD, J. and UNDERWOOD, G. (1990) *Computers and Learning*, London, Blackwell.

Suggested Reading

ASHCROFT, K. *et al.* (1989) 'Using Audio-Visual Aids Creatively' in RUST, C. (Ed) *Teaching in Higher Education: An Induction Pack for New Staff*, Birmingham, SCED.

This pack of materials provides advice and support for lecturers who are new to teaching in colleges and universities. It does not go deeply into the issues, but may be useful for the tutor who wishes to experiment with practical classroom applications.

Computers in Teaching Initiative Annual Report, Oxford: CTISS Publications.

The Computers in Teaching Initiative covers 90 per cent of subjects taught at undergraduate level in universities. The subjects covered include physical sciences, human sciences, social sciences, humanities, accounting, land sciences, languages, law, music, textual studies, and medicine as well as computer studies. It promotes the effective use of computers in teaching. The annual report provides a listing of the CTI centres for each subject, the contact name and the kinds of help, publications and training available.

INGRAM, P. (Ed) (1989) *Computer Aided Design in Further Education*, London, FEU.
This booklet is free from the Further Education Unit. It provides an overview of the basic features of CAD and suggests application in the teaching of electronic engineering, built environment course, art and design and fine arts.

Counselling and Student Support

Introduction

This chapter deals with student support and the role of the personal tutor. Counselling and student support will be important issues for you if you believe that part of your job as a tutor is to be concerned with your students' welfare as well as their intellectual progress. Student support can be a problematic business which, like many aspects of teaching, is perhaps best achieved through skills built upon a body of knowledge about counselling and student development.

In this chapter we have made a distinction between educational tutoring and educational counselling, although in practice, it is not always possible to distinguish between the two forms of student support. Educational tutoring used in this context to refer to a programme of regular events that are directed to such matters as developing study skills, interpersonal skills and encouraging students' development as autonomous learners, which fall under the umbrella of 'personal and social education'. In many institutions, this takes the form of a carefully planned and monitored programme.

Personal and social education relates to a number of aspects of learning that are dealt with elsewhere in this book, in particular the management of self and others, assessment and student learning, and monitoring student progress. The curriculum as it relates to personal and social education is both overt (i.e. planned and implemented in a structured way) and hidden. You contribute to the hidden curriculum through expectations and behaviours that may be largely unconscious, but which provide messages to your students about what is valued and accepted by you and the institution.

The ideas in this chapter include the notion that the planned curriculum as it relates to personal and social education should support the student's movement towards independence and self-sustained learning. We place a particular value on students' development as autonomous learners. This implies that the content can be renegotiated, at least to some extent, to meet student needs.

Educational counselling on the other hand, is a process that may be applied in crisis situations, or situations that your students perceive as crises. These may include the need for emergency 'repair' work on defective study skills, help with conflict or bullying in groups, help for students who lose confidence or have to deal with emotional events that interfere with learning. There are many styles of counselling which originate from different theoretical models of the therapeutic process, including gestalt, rational emotional and neurolinguistics. The ideas within this chapter are mainly based on the non-directive counselling style by Carl Rogers (1983). We have found this style to be the safest for non-experts, as it allows the student to explore issues at their own pace and at the depth where they are able to cope.

Institutional Frameworks for Educational Tutoring

Wells (1983) suggests that educational tutoring requires a clarity and agreement amongst the teaching staff about the types of behaviour which indicate a sound pastoral care programme and some evaluation or assessment of this behaviour. This may be harder than it appears at first sight. For instance, it implies that objectives of the pastoral programme should be clearly stated and achievable at different levels. Objectives could refer to group or to individual performance. In either case you would need to keep them under review in a variety of situations. This will only be possible if they are unambiguous and if they were accessible to a monitoring process without an invasion of the students' privacy.

We believe that the starting point for a sound pastoral programme may be found within the business of knowing oneself. You could try to use a variety of techniques to help the student to understand aspects of their study and other behaviour. For instance, you might use questionnaires to introduce a 'language' for talking about aspects of personality and patterns of interaction and their effect on managing teaching and learning. Where these techniques are used, you may need to help your students see the results not as the 'truth', but rather as a starting point for thinking about aspects of 'self' and how this might impinge on their action and reaction to study and other students. It may be important for you to help students to understand that learning style is not 'fixed'. The students know a great deal about themselves and for this reason they should be allowed to come back with objections.

Educational tutoring is increasingly becoming a structured activity. Within the reflective practitioner model, it might focus particularly upon the student's growing understanding of aspects of their values, study and other behaviour and their movement towards independence and self-sustained learning. This growing understanding should be accompanied by a critical consideration of the consequences of their behaviour and values for the student themselves and for others. These ideas relate closely to the qualities prerequisite for reflective practice outlined in earlier chapters, especially open-mindedness and responsibility.

Many institutions are developing policies and objectives about educational tutoring. In some there is a carefully organized programme often associated with records of progress and achievement. The programme may include group and individual sessions. The individual session may closely resemble a staff development appraisal interview, with a set agenda, based on the student's own assessment of their achievements and problems, and finishing with the identification of agreed goals to be reviewed at a specified time. An important aspect of a programme of personal development in further or higher education is that it should be based on the student's *self*-assessment.

Educational Tutoring

Some tutors equate personal tutoring with vague ideas of 'welfare' support, rather than with a developed programme of personal development. In this section we are assuming that the main focus of educational tutoring is the systematic development of study skills. This often begins with the student's self-assessment of their strengths and weaknesses, supported by the tutor. Wells (1983) suggests that at an early stage this might include an assessment of the student's ability to pick out key points in study material or taught sessions and to identify key questions. Part of the programme for personal development may be concerned with the student's developing ability to separate peripheral issues from salient points.

Another basic study skill is the ability to plan and organize written work. You may be able to help the student to formulate decisions about the main headings within a piece of work or conceptualize it in diagrammatic form. Your students may need to develop the ability to identify logical connections between ideas and structure their written work so that a reasoned coherent argument is apparent.

Students' development of the ability to use tutor comments on their work to set targets for themselves and to monitor their own progress towards their target is likely to be an unsystematic process without a well-developed institutional, course or departmental marking scheme. The creation of such a scheme may be problematic where there is a lack of trust, cooperation and goodwill amongst the tutorial team. Nevertheless such a scheme should help the student separate those comments relating to particular aspects of a piece of work and those of more general significance. They also need to recognize when comments which at first sight seem particular, taken together with other comments start to form a pattern.

Some students need to learn how to be good time managers and people with tidy and systematic study habits. You may be able to help them to develop a study retrieval system that works for them, but which contains all the information required to make it useful. They may need to develop methods for organizing their time and ordering of their study. They may need to learn how to take notes from reading and lectures so that they can both attend to the material and retrieve it at a later date.

Such a programme should leave space for the student to bring their own issues and concerns but is also likely to include work towards key objectives identified by the institution as essential. In an educational context, these key objectives are likely to include the development of a range of interpersonal skills. These may include skills and qualities of leadership, cooperation and empathy. In certain contexts, you may be interested in helping students to develop an understanding of social issues, for instance, issues of race and gender. In particular, if you are interested in helping your students develop themselves as reflective practitioners, you may be interested in helping them to explore systematic methods of developing as open-minded learners who are willing to take responsibility for their own actions and to support others in their learning.

Enquiry Task 8.1

Consider one group of students that you teach.

List steps that might be taken to help students develop a limited range of study skills (e.g. the students' ability to: pick out key points from study material; plan and formulate written work; use tutor comments to set targets;

---

manage their study time) and the criteria they might use to determine whether they had succeeded.

Action Plan   *Criteria for Success*
Step 1
Step 2
Step 3

Discuss with an experienced colleague the extent to which they could use this model to define students' learning needs.

Educational Counselling

In the next few sections, we explore the ways that counselling may be used as one way of tackling some common problems, such as the student with a worrying study skill problem, the student who is conforming to peer pressure at the expense of their work or the student who has to make a difficult choice and needs help to sort out the options. It will not be sufficient to enable you to tackle deep-seated emotional or very delicate problems. These usually require outside help and advice, or at the minimum, time to think and discuss, before they can be dealt with by the non-specialist. One of the most important counselling skills to develop is the ability to recognize your own limitations and to see when a problem is too great for you to manage unaided.

Counselling as a mode of interaction can be useful to help a student overcome a deep-seated problem in their study or to help them overcome a lack of responsibility, open-mindedness or empathy with others. At other times, you may be able to use some of the techniques to encourage the student or a group of students to explore issues and problems using their own resources, rather than relying on you to do their thinking and feeling for them. Thus, counselling within the learning process should be primarily directed at helping the student learn to become more self-sufficient and helping them to deal with ongoing situations. It is a powerful tool if employed skilfully and sensitively in making the student think for themselves and rise to the emotional and cognitive challenge of further or higher education.

Differences between Educational and Therapeutic Counselling

The educational counselling interview between tutor and student is one method for fostering personal development. Other than in a few well resourced universities, it is not commonly used as part of the normal learning process. More often the educational counselling session is a one-off event to solve a particular problem. It may be more useful to think of the interview as part of a process that involves the student in preparation, review and action. The interview part of the process is an expensive use of tutor time. It therefore needs to be used as effectively and skilfully as possible. In many circumstances, tutors can usefully draw on techniques developed in therapeutic counselling to structure one-to-one interviews.

Counselling in an educational context has aspects in common with counselling in a therapeutic context. The aim of both kinds of counselling is usually to encourage the 'client' in independent action and to make decisions for themselves which facilitate their progress. There are, however, important differences. In particular counselling as part of the educational process is usually directed towards goals that are determined, at least in part, by the tutor.

Therapeutic counselling is often a comparatively long process, usually involving a minimum of several sessions and sometimes lasting months or years. You may have a very limited amount of time and attention allocated to educational counselling. You may need to set goals within the first or second interview and leave the student to monitor his or her own progress. Occasionally, you may need to spend longer than this on educational counselling or progress may need to be monitored by you. However, in most institutions, time constraints mean that this has to be the exception rather than the norm. In some circumstances, you may find that it is most useful to use counselling as just one phase of a one-to-one tutorial or seminar session to explore issues, before moving on to a more 'teacherly' mode of discourse.

Therapeutic counselling requires the counsellor to take a totally non-judgmental approach, even where the client is revealing socially unacceptable behaviour and attitudes. Education involves informal and formal assessment. Students are expected to make progress towards externally defined goals. These goals may include the development of identified attitudes as well as skills and understandings. Therefore, in practice, counselling cannot always be non-judgmental in the educational context. For instance, a goal of teacher education may be to counter racist stereotypes. You may view racism amongst student-teachers as an attitude to be eliminated rather than explored. Nevertheless, you may find that exploration can reveal to the student the 'unreasonableness' of the feelings and the unacceptable consequences of acting on them.

It is important to be aware that your goals may well conflict with the student's. A student may be more concerned to get to a solution with minimum time and effort or to access the tutor's knowledge and understanding. They may feel frustration when they are made to do the thinking and the work themselves.

Therapeutic counselling is usually centrally concerned with the exploration of emotions as an aid to personal and interpersonal development or to deal with an emotional crisis. You may need to refer those students who experience the kind of excessive stress that justifies therapeutic counselling to more expert services. Because much of education is primarily concerned with thinking and learning, educational counselling is often concerned with the exploration of feelings as they enhance or inhibit learning. You may want to focus more on skill development, the development of conceptual frameworks or patterns of behaviour likely to enhance learning. The material for discussion is less commonly threatening to the students' sense of self. Therefore you may find that it is appropriate to confront the evasion of problems or issues directly. You should be aware that such direct confrontation may not be as unproblematic as it seems at first sight. For instance, for a minority of students, failure may be or may appear to be a real possibility. For some of these students, the costs of failure can be very high indeed in terms of loss of self-esteem, loss of career prospects or humiliation in front of peers or significant others.

Finally, therapeutic counselling is almost always sought by the client. It is seldom imposed by the counsellor. Students do not always come to the tutor asking for counselling. When a student comes for 'advice', you may decide that counselling is a more appropriate method for tackling the student's problem. The student may not be aware that you have made this decision on their behalf. In a minority of extreme cases, you may decide to force compliance by an actual or implied threat of failure if your invitation to 'help' is ignored. Thus educational counselling may not be totally voluntary. This lack of choice may be the most fundamental difference between counselling as part of the normal learning process and within a therapeutic context.

Enquiry Task 8.2

1 Prepare a simple questionnaire to discover from a small group of students what study skills they feel they lack, for instance, the ability to:
   • identify key points or issues within their reading;
   • prepare headings or diagrams to structure essays;
   • identification of logical connections between one item and the next;
   • develop reasoned arguments;
   • organize their own study retrieval system;
   • use tutor comments on essays to set and monitor targets for themselves;
   • organize their time; or
   • take notes from reading.
2 Ask them to write about the most significant of these 'lacks' and how it affects them.
3 Decide whether educational counselling would be of benefit to any of the students.

How will you help the others?

Setting Ground Rules for Educational Counselling

In order for counselling to be successful, you need to be clear why the student needs your help and what desired outcomes may be assisted by it. It is important that you clarify for yourself and the student the limits to the help you are offering. In particular, the student must know that you cannot 'solve' their problem for them. People tend to be resistant to advice, and so 'telling' a student how to solve any but the most straightforward problem is unlikely to help. In any case, if the student does take your advice and it works, you may find that you have encouraged them to become dependent on you. If your advice does not work, the student may be harmed. One aim of education is to encourage the student to think and learn. If you solve the student's problem for them, you will have done the thinking and learning rather than the student. This does not mean that you never give advice, but rather that it may be more effective to get the student to make his or her own diagnosis of the action they need to take.

Skills and Qualities in Counselling

Rogers (1983) stressed that successful counselling depended upon three qualities in the counsellor. The first of these is *congruence*. This implies that everything about you should ring true and that you should strive to be genuine and not to restrict yourself to a 'tutor' or 'counsellor' role. In practice, there must be limits to this in educational settings. You have the right to keep parts of yourself separate from your students and the duty to put your students' needs above your own self-expression.

The second quality described by Rogers is *empathy*. This implies that you should creatively imagine yourself in your student's shoes, so that you can think the way the student thinks and experience the world the way they do. Again, in the educational setting, you may find the opportunities for this may be distinctly limited. Nevertheless, you may be able to listen to your students actively and with imagination.

The final quality Rogers described is *unconditional positive regard*. This implies a non-judgmental acceptance of the student and the ability to value them as a person. It suggests that where you do not agree with the student, or share their values, nevertheless you do not offer criticism. If you are in any way involved with assessment, you may find this difficult. Indeed, in the case of certain attitudes such as sexism or racism, you may decide that unconditional positive regard is undesirable. On the other hand, the ability to 'see' the world that the student inhabits can be of help in enabling one to respect and like a student while dis-approving of and seeking to change some of their attitudes.

This is of course an ideal that you are unlikely to be able always to achieve. A psychotherapist does not have to 'do business' with their client. You have to deal with your students on a regular basis outside of the counselling context. You may have to deal with behaviour that is absolutely inappropriate in an educational context and that you cannot accept. Sometimes this behaviour is linked to some fundamental defect of character in the student which you cannot like or respect. Perhaps the best you can do in these circumstances is to try to understand the origins of the behaviour and to find a way of dealing with it that makes clear its unacceptable nature, but protects the interests of the student, to the extent that they are compatible with those of the other students and the institution, and the dignity of the person.

Geldard (1989) outlined a number of skills that the counsellor should develop to enable their clients to make therapeutic progress. Many of these may be ap-propriate within the learning process. Perhaps the most important is the ability really to attend to what your students are saying. If you wish to help the student to explore issues and dilemmas and move their thinking on, it is important to remember the details of what you are told. You may need to find ways to convey that you are listening, such as mirroring the student's posture and the speed and volume of speech. In the early stages of a counselling interview this mirroring may be exact. Once rapport has been established, you may want to encourage the student to relax or unwind. You could try gradually moving to a more relaxed posture. This sometimes results in the student copying the non-verbal behaviour and also becoming less tense. Intermittent eye contact, but not staring may also help to communicate to the student that you are listening carefully to what they have to say.

It is important to avoid thinking about how you will respond while the student is talking. You need not be afraid of leaving gaps in the conversation while you think about a reply. The way you respond to what the student is saying may affect the extent to which you are able to help them sort through the issues.

Paraphrasing is a useful technique which can enable the student to recognize the most important content by expressing it clearly and briefly. Where you are dealing with a student who is experiencing some distress that is hindering their learning, it can be useful to listen for the particular feelings that are expressed and to reflect it back. Statements such as 'you are anxious' can help the student to discuss the real problem. Sometimes a student may need permission for their feelings. You may find that simple statements such as 'It's OK to cry' can help in some circumstances.

On some occasions you may experience situations which are too emotionally charged for you to deal with. This may be a particular problem if you are a male tutor dealing with a female student in crisis. Where this is the case, you owe it to yourself to seek help at an early stage. It is important not to bite off more than you can chew or to try to resolve every difficult situation on your own.

Questioning is an important skill in counselling. Too many questions can be threatening and interrogative. Closed questions can encourage a limited response (although they may be useful in focusing a vague statement made by the student). 'Why' questions are more likely to elicit an intellectual response, which is fine if this is what you are after. However, they may encourage answers focused 'out there', rationalization and excuses rather than encouraging the student to face difficult issues within themselves or their behaviour.

Summarizing is a useful skill which enables the main points to be drawn together, clarified and organized. Similarly, reframing the problem can be helpful if the student is looking at a problem from a narrow perspective. You could try to restate the issues, giving them a different emphasis.

Confrontation may lead to aggression and denial if used in unskilled hands and in situations which the student finds threatening. You may find that it helps to reflect back what the student has said, to state what you have noted (particularly any contradictions) so as to enable the student to draw their own conclusions. However, on other occasions you may find confrontation has value in the learning process, especially where you want to draw attention to basic issues that the student is evading. For instance, it may be the only way to stop the student going over the same ground again and again and to make them look at their problem squarely.

It may be necessary to confront potentially destructive behaviour and to explore its origins and consequences. In particular, you may find it is necessary to challenge self-destructive beliefs. Beliefs about what the student 'should' or 'ought' to do, think or achieve, can get in the way of them making progress in their learning. One of us has known a student from a high achieving family who believed she 'must' achieve a first class honours degree. This led her to consider dropping out of a course when she found her best efforts led to average achievement. She has also known a male student to persist in 'laddish' behaviour, at the expense of his studies. Confronting his beliefs about gender appropriate behaviour, and the ways that this was restricting his opportunities led to progress. Exposing contradictory statements embedded within what the student has been saying can sometimes help them start to sort through which are the real issues and which are rationalizations.

One of the important skills in counselling, whether for therapeutic or educational purposes, is the ability to time and effect the ending of an interview. Termination of an interview can be a difficult matter. You may feel you owe it to your students to give them as much time as they think they need. If you are an approachable person this will lead you to devote many hours to counselling individual students. There is an 'opportunity cost' to using time in this way. You may end up overstretched and unable to keep to deadlines. You may neglect other aspects of your job. You may be comforted by the knowledge that important issues tend to be dealt with early in any interview. If the student knows at the start how much time they have been allotted, they may be more likely to be content to fit the discussion into the time available.

You might consider preparing the student for the end of the discussion by telling them that they are getting towards the end of the time available. You might try signalling the final stage of the interview by summarizing the main points and stating agreed goals. The important thing is to avoid giving a contradictory signal towards the end of a session, perhaps by asking questions or reflecting back on content or feelings. This kind of interaction invites response from the student and is likely to prolong the interview.

In the final analysis, it is OK to be assertive and to say clearly that the discussion must end. When you have seen a student regularly, you may need to take steps to break dependency. It may be helpful to bring the issue into the open and agree that this session ought to be the last. It is always possible for the student to make another appointment if they really feel they need it. The next interview may be more productive if you make it clear what work or thinking the student should have completed by then.

The boundaries between counselling and leadership are not always clearly drawn. For instance, one of us had a head of department who followed all the precepts of counselling outlined above, but left her frustrated. She analysed the problem and realized that she already had a very good grasp, both intellectually and emotionally, of the problems she was experiencing. What she really wanted was *direction*. The tutor is also in the position of a leader in some circumstances. One of the more important counselling skills for you to develop is the ability to recognize when a counselling mode of discourse is inappropriate.

Enquiry Task 8.3

Undertake the following tasks related to the key skills in counselling. Get a trusted colleague to undertake them independently:

Rapport:
List ways to establish rapport in a one-to-one interview.
List those kinds of non-verbal behaviour that might be 'matched'.

Active listening:
List dos and don'ts of active listening.

Clarifying:
List questions or key phrases which help to clarify a student's meaning.

Summarizing:
List what behaviours would constitute poor summarizing.

Contracting:
List questions to stimulate the student to define action they might agree to try out.

Discuss your list with your colleague. Did you agree with their perception of these key skills? Were you surprised by the similarities or differences between your list and theirs? Would you want to add to your lists in the light of your discussion?

Record Keeping and Confidentiality

It is never possible to be certain as to which students are going to develop the kind of problems that involve a degree of complexity. When these cases arise, it is usually helpful to have a clear summary of the history of the problems and the help the student has received so that this can be looked at holistically and patterns explored. A minority of students who experience problems can project them onto those tutors who have done most to help them. This can be damaging to you unless you have kept a clear account of the precise nature of the help you provided. For this reason, it is sensible to keep brief records of every substantive interview you have with any student. Such records might include:

- the date;
- the student's name;
- factual information provided by the student;
- description of the problem;
- factual account of what was said and agreed in the interview;
- note of any follow-up action taken by you; and
- date and time of next session (if any).

Students may pressurize you into promising confidentiality, for instance by saying 'I don't want anyone else to know this'. This will put you in a difficult position, and you may need to devise strategies for dealing with these kinds of situations such as telling her or him that you will not tell anyone unless it becomes absolutely necessary, or you would always tell the student first if you felt you had to break a confidence, or you would never break a confidence lightly. Although confidentiality is the preferred option, you might be wise to avoid promising it to the student at any stage.

It can be difficult not to agree to confidentiality if the student says that they do not want others to know what they are about to divulge, but to make promises of confidentiality could put you in a vulnerable position should the situation change. In any case, you may need to divulge your records to protect the student, yourself and others. Any situation may escalate. An apparently simple problem could develop into an issue where you are obliged to seek help, such as an allegation of sexual harrassment against another tutor or student. You may need to take action to protect other people or contact other professionals for help with a problem beyond your competence. At the most extreme, a situation may develop where the law requires disclosure. If you have assured the student of confidentiality, you may find yourself confronting an ethical dilemma if it becomes in the student's or in someone else's overwhelming interest to break that confidentiality.

Support for the Tutor

It may be important that, if you become involved in counselling students, you make opportunities to talk to others about the problems you have to deal with and your own feelings. A good tutor will be empathetic and therefore they will 'feel' the problems the students bring to them, at least to some extent. At the end of a stressful session it may be important for you to 'debrief' yourself, especially if you are the sort of person who finds it hard to switch off at the end of the day. The simplest way to do this is to remind yourself of your name, some of your roles and about some of the more mundane aspects of your life. This can seem a pointless exercise, but it could help you to ground yourself after you have been in an empathetic role.

It is often difficult, but necessary, to refocus energy from obsessive thoughts about student problems back to the here and now. Techniques for doing this include making an 'appointment' with yourself to think about the student's problem at a more appropriate time. This may provide the permission you need to think and do pleasant things until then. Some stress may be avoided if you have realistic expectations of yourself, peers and employers and recognize the limits on the help you can realistically provide for students.

The work of tutors in further and higher education is becoming increasingly varied and skilled. It requires much flexibility and a range of problem-solving abilities. The demands of your work may result in stress and a fall in your effectiveness unless you receive adequate support from within the institution. Stibbs (1987) suggests certain conditions that promote effective staff care. These include the encouragement of innovation and creativity and genuine delegation and shared responsibility. If these are lacking in your workplace, you may be able take comfort from the idea that the stress you experience probably results from your situation and is not attributable to your personality.

Lodge and McLaughlin (1992) stress that tutors have needs as teachers and as people. You have the right to ask for the support you need. The support you receive should be matched to these two sets of needs. Since the 'cocktail' of needs is different for each person, there should be a range of support offered. Ideally, your managers should spend time assessing the problems of each staff member and how they relate to that person's needs as a staff member and as an individual. This may not be possible in your institution, but you have a right to regular appraisal and guidance and to expect managers in the institution to provide support for you if you tell them that you are under stress.

Brockie (1992) points to the importance of interpersonal processes in promoting a supportive climate. However, team building is not automatically a 'good thing'. Teams based on feelings of exclusivity and superiority can lead to the formation of cliques within the workplace. An emphasis on competition will increase this tendency. Cooperative working across teams will make for a more supportive atmosphere. You can then make a contribution to cooperative or competitive working. You may be able to bring the issue of mutual and institutional support to the forefront, for instance by asking that a staff meeting consider staff needs rather than focusing on student or curriculum issues.

Of course there are needs in common among most tutors. In a supportive institution there are likely to be induction systems with preparation before arrival to a post and an ongoing induction programme and a user friendly handbook. There should be good channels of communication and the support available for different types of problems should be clearly stated. It is critically important that you have access to personal support, whether for critical incidents or for dealing with ongoing problems.

Enquiry Task 8.4

Consider how good you are at asking colleagues and managers for the support you need at work.
How often in the past term have you:

- felt stressed as a result of helping a student;
- told others how you felt;
- asked for feedback on the way you dealt with the problem;
- asked for help?

Consider how supportive you are of other colleagues.
How good are you at:

- noting tensions in your colleagues;
- showing interest in their problems;
- expressing praise or appreciation; or
- asking about their feelings?

Can you change your behaviour so that you give and receive more support?

Stress and Transactional Analysis

Stress is an important aspect of people's working lives. It is has important effects of performance. Too low a level of stress can be dysfunctional and lead to 'rustout'. In our experience this does not seem to be the most common problem among tutors in further and higher education. It seems to be more common for levels of stress in these contexts to be too high. This may result in the kind of pressure that leads to 'burnout' if it continues for a sufficient length of time. Stress can be extremely damaging to your health and work. Teaching can be a highly stressed activity. You are quite likely to find that there is no training available routinely within your institution on ways of managing stress. This implies that you may need to develop your own methods. This section outlines some of the techniques which might be of help. Because factors outside of the control of the individual tend to contribute to stress, it is likely that no technique will solve all your problems, but consideration of techniques and issues can help to make stress manageable.

Stress is a problem that is likely to be shared by tutors and students. Tutors who have found ways of understanding and managing their own stress may be in a better position to help students. Financial worries and other 'objective' problems can contribute, but perhaps the biggest cause of stress for people employed in education is dealing with other people. It can be helpful in those circumstances to have a language to analyse what is happening within the stressful interpersonal relationships.

Transactional analysis (TA) provides one such language. It is founded on a number of basic concepts originated by Berne (1964) and developed by Harris (1970). The first of these concepts is the notions of OK and not-OK. The assumption is that people are always in one state or another and that they spend too much of their time feeling not-OK to a greater or lesser extent. One of the purposes of transactional analysis is to move us from a not-OK to an OK state. When we are feeling not-OK in our relationship with another person it is likely that the other person will be feeling not-OK as well. It also seems that people who are feeling not-OK set up situations that perpetuate that feeling and that we each have a 'favourite' not-OK feeling. Thus people will habitually react to a range of situations with a particular emotion such as guilt or anger or anxiety. These reactions may have been learned in childhood by imitation because they were acceptable to the person's family. Thus the same stimulus will set off different not-OK feelings in different people and people may then set up situations to reinforce these feelings.

Transactional analysis aims to enable us to see what is happening and to explore alternative ways of being. This is achieved in part by recognizing the 'ego states' contained within each of us, and those of others. This can help us analyse what is going wrong when our interactions with others are experienced as unsatisfactory and to decide on strategies to improve them. The ego states are contained within each of us, although we will be exhibiting only one at a time. Many of us have a 'favourite' ego state, which we may fall into on occasions when it is inappropriate. The ego states include the 'Parent', the 'Adult' and the 'Child'. When we are in the Parent state we feel and behave in ways learned from adults in childhood. It concerns taking responsibility or charge of others. Thus we may be nurturing and look after others. In other words we may be 'motherly' or 'fatherly'. On the other hand, we may communicate disapproval in our parent role or try to control the actions of others. When in the Adult state we act 'objectively'. This might involve asking for factual information, collecting evidence, exploring alternative courses of action and so on. When in the Child state we feel as we habitually did when a child. We experience strong feelings, pleasant or unpleasant. For instance, we may feel resentful about the demands made by more powerful people. Where such 'childish' behaviour is inappropriate to the situation we now find ourselves, we will be in an 'Adapted Child' ego state. Such behaviour may be whining or unduly submissive. We may also act as the 'Rebellious Child'. On the other hand, a reaction to an event may be an uncomplicated and spontaneous emotion, for instance gaiety or anger. This kind of reaction is likely to indicate a 'Free Child' ego state.

In their Parent state an individual will tend to talk in terms of 'ought', 'must' or be giving care or praise. When someone reacts to us in their Parent state when we want factual information, this is an example of a crossed transaction. Crossed transactions generally lead to an experience frustration, unless we can analyse what is going on. In this transaction, one party is in the Adult state and expecting an adult reply in the form of information. The Caring Parent response is perceived as irrelevant or perverse. Crossed transactions tend not to be sustained. On the other hand, if we are in a Parent state (caring or controlling) and interact with someone in a Child (emotional or resentful) we will tend to sustain the interaction (perhaps to the detriment of progress), because our state feeds off of and into the other person's. This is called a complementary transaction. Complementary transactions also exist where both parties are in the same ego state.

The point of transactional analysis is to examine what is going on in relationships that are not proving fruitful in order to decide whether the typical mode of interaction is helpful or not. If it is not, the person can force a change, for instance by refusing to enter complementary modes of transaction. Transactional analysis also enables us to look at whether we tend to operate in one ego state and need to broaden our repertoire in order to meet our own needs and goals or facilitate those of others.

OK feelings will be enhanced in us and in others by recognizing and supplying the needs implied by each of these states. For instance, the Child in us requires physical affection, the Adult requires congratulations about our work and the Parent requires thanks for caring. The actions that supply these needs are termed 'positive strokes'. If we are lacking positive strokes in a particular area, we may need to ask for them from others. We also need to accept positive strokes when they are supplied. There is a tendency among people with a low self-esteem to reject positive strokes, for instance by deflecting the reward onto others or rejecting or ignoring it.

'Negative strokes' reinforce the negative feelings we have about ourselves. Unfortunately, most of us have also learned to seek and give negative strokes, at least in some circumstances. We learn this by observing and experiencing those given and received during our childhood. We need to examine our own stroke patterns so that we do not give and seek out negative strokes, but rather maximize our opportunities to give and accept positive ones.

We have found transactional analysis to be particularly helpful in analysis face-to-face interactions and one-to-one relationships where these have gone wrong in some way. It may be less useful where the dysfunction results from things that go on behind your back (assertiveness may be more useful here, see below), or for dysfunctional group interactions. Because we each have the capacity to act within our Parent, Child, or Adult, depending on the circumstances, someone can act within their Child with one person and within their Parent with another in a bewilderingly short period of time. Transactional analysis may illuminate certain problematic group relationships, but it may not be possible to use it directly to alter the situation.

Enquiry Task 8.5

List the things that cause you to feel stressed.

List the ways you cope with stress.

What are the costs and benefits of each of these methods?

Costs   *Benefits*

Consider whether any of those things that cause you stress result from your inter-actions with particular people.
If they do, work out what is the habitual ego state of each of you during those interactions.
Identify ways that you could change the nature of these interactions.

Assertiveness

Stress may be caused by the inability of the individual to communicate their wants and needs. This can be as true of the tutor as of the student. The expression of wants and needs is particularly difficult where there is a power differential, for instance, a student dealing with a tutor or a tutor dealing with their head of department. This difficulty can result in the person either submitting to a situation that they find uncomfortable, or, if the situation becomes too stressful, becoming aggressive. Aggressive or submissive reactions are not likely to improve matters. On the other hand, assertiveness techniques can enable the person to state their needs and feelings unambiguously so that the problem can be addressed and constructive action taken.

In a learning context, it is particularly important that the student is empowered to act assertively. Submissive behaviour is likely to result in learning needs not being met. Submissive students may not gain their fair share of teacher attention. On the other hand, aggressive behaviour may result in hostility and disadvantage the student in the long-term. Many people have been taught as children not to make demands. Others may have experienced levels of frustration that they can only deal with with aggression. Both of these responses tend to be maladaptive in a learning situation. There are skills and techniques which the tutor can learn, and later teach, to help them and their students to handle difficult situations in a way that will not cause damage.

Assertive behaviour depends upon a recognition of our own rights, but not at the expense of those of others. It is important not merely to assert these rights, but to *believe* in them as valid in our own case. This does not mean that a person should always be on the look out for opportunities to exercise these rights, but that they feel justified and able to do so when it really matters.

Assertiveness also depends upon a willingness to take responsibility for our reactions and feelings, rather than to impute blame to others. Assertiveness is not a method of 'dumping' bad feelings and uncertainty on other people (as the person in an Adapted Child ego state might), but rather accepting and 'naming' our own feelings and needs. For this reason assertive statements often start with phrases such as 'I feel . . .', 'I find . . .', 'I am not . . .' or are expressed as statements of fact such as 'This meal is cold.' Assertive statements do not complain about others. They state the situation and state what needs to be done.

This does not mean that the assertive person fails to recognize the other's needs or reactions. On the contrary, very often it is useful to recognize and 'name' the person's reaction, but this will not deflect the assertive person from also making the points or demands that they have decided are necessary: 'I realize that this will be inconvenient for you, but I need you to take action by Friday'. When dealing with conflicting points of view it can be important to keep track of both sides of the issues: 'I hear your point, but here is mine', in order to avoid the perception that one person's viewpoint has been negated by that of the other.

Assertiveness is about having choices. One of these choices is the ability to act assertively, rather than aggressively or submissively. This choice does not have to be exercised at all times. Indeed, it might be exhausting to a person and to those around them if they never accepted minor inconveniences for a quiet life or always expressed negative emotions in a calm and reasonable way. However, within an educational context there will be occasions when aspects of another person's behaviour are important to the tutor or student or their work or when they will wish to negotiate a change in the relationship. On those occasions, having the option to act assertively can help. This is because assertiveness enables the person to be open and honest about wants and needs in a way that provides the maximum opportunity for the other to react in a way that is not defensive or dismissive.

Specific techniques have been outlined in more detail by writers such as Dickson (1982) and are summarized below. An important aspect to bear in mind is the role of body language and the small phrases that pepper our everyday language. These have to match the assertive message. If assertiveness is contrary to submissiveness, apologetic body language will not be appropriate. Neither will phrases such as 'I'm sorry but . . .'. Similarly, threatening body language and phrases that impute personal motives or unfavourable judgments about the other person should be avoided. It is important throughout to focus on behaviour rather than personal characteristics and to protect the other person's right to their personal dignity. Using the language of transactional analysis, assertiveness usually employs our Adult, rather than our Adapted Child or Controlling Parent.

One assertiveness technique is often referred to as the 'broken record' and involves a simple repetition of the point to be made or the action that should be taken. The refusal to respond to excuses or complaints while at the same time remaining uncritical avoids the possibility of being drawn into dialogue and side-tracked. It makes it difficult for the other person to do other than to comply or refuse, accept or reject. This forced choice will be uncomfortable for the other person, so you should be aware that the technique carries the risk of damage to your relationship with the other person.

The importance of recognizing and disarming feelings such as anger that the other person may be experiencing has been referred to above. In this way it is possible to acknowledge others' feelings and their right to them *but* also to state clearly their effects on you. The advantage of this technique is that it avoids a spiral of accusation and counter-accusation.

For assertiveness techniques to be effective, it is sometimes important to reflect carefully on the real situation and on the meanings underlying your own and other people's actions. This may enable you to 'cut through the crud' and analyse the real issues, rather than allowing yourself to get stuck in repeated arguments.

There is a skill in giving criticism or compliments. This skill involves being direct, specific, prompt and positive. Giving criticism is uncomfortable for both parties and it is unreasonable to expect the other person to feel comfortable about it. When giving criticism, it is important to acknowledge all sides of an issue. Making value judgments about the person's motives or behaviour or 'labelling' the other person is likely to be counter-productive. It is unfair to give criticism about an aspect of behaviour that the person cannot control or about many aspects of the person's behaviour so that it becomes overwhelming. Thus the aim of the criticism should not be to get things off your chest, but rather to enable the relationship to be improved. By focusing on this, it may be possible to have a conversation that is constructive in its approach. The important thing is to recognize the other person's position, to give them specific information, such as the effects of their behaviour on you or your own emotions or feelings about the situation, and come to an agreed outcome. Criticism is often difficult to give and the 'interview' may need preparation. It may be useful to take advice from others about the approach that you should take. Criticism is usually better given in privacy.

When receiving aggressive criticism, you do not have to accept that you have caused the person's anger, nor to respond to it directly or confront the injustice. If you do wish to confront the situation, Dickson (1982) suggests that the first step is to gain the person's attention by repeating a phrase in a calm voice such as 'Please listen to me', then to catch the person's eye and make a statement that recognizes the person's anger, expresses your reaction to it and willingness to help them look for a solution. The next step is to seat the person and allow them to become calmer. At that stage it is important to listen, perhaps employing the counselling skills outlined above, before finally moving towards joint problem-solving, if this is appropriate. Of course, the person may not react according to Dickson's script. In these circumstances, it may be help diffuse the aggression to admit a contribution to the problem, however slight.

In any case, it may help to remember that you have the right to decide not to confront the situation. There are techniques that may help you to deflect the attack. These include acknowledging the truth of any factual statement made while ignoring the implied value judgments; acknowledging there may be a *possible or general* truth in the statement made, while not ignoring the implication that it applies in these circumstances; or acknowledging that the other person has a perception that what they are saying is true. Alternatively, you can ask the person for more information about their reaction to the behaviour being criticized or about the nature of the behaviour itself. This final technique may lead to a position where the real motive that underlies the attack becomes clearer and can be dealt with in a way that respects dignity of both individuals. All these techniques make it difficult for the person to continue the attack. Unfortunately, common human responses such as defending yourself, denying the criticism or counter-attacking tend to prolong the incident.

With informed or well intended criticism, the situation is different. Time may be needed to evaluate the points made. However, it is important that the person being criticized consciously decides *for themselves* whether to accept the validity of the criticism or to reject it. We each have the right to be the ultimate judge of ourselves. Accepting your right to make mistakes makes it easier and less painful to assess accurately the validity of criticism. When accepting a criticism, you do not also have to accept guilt. When rejecting well intentioned criticism, it is not necessary to experience rejection, but rather to acknowledge it as an opinion held by the other person.

In these and other circumstances where you do not wish to make an instant response, it is acceptable and right to ask for time to think. This will enable you to consider how and what you feel and what you wish to do about it. You may need more information, in which case, ask for it. In many circumstances you may wish to 'write your script' before further discussion. This may enable you to state your position and feelings clearly. You may then be in a position to specify what you would like (and what the benefits will be). The ability to express the desired outcome from a meeting and to specify the preferred future action is an important assertiveness technique.

Some people seem to be unable to take a compliment at its face value. The result is to throw the compliment back in the face of the giver. It is more rewarding to the compliment giver if the person accepts it with thanks. There is also a skill in giving compliments. Compliments are more satisfactory and easier to accept if they are related to a specific event or behaviour, rather than general. A 'good' compliment may indicate the effect of the behaviour on you and will include a statement of positive feelings about the other person.

Saying 'No' Assertively

The ability to say 'no' is an important assertiveness skill. It may be difficult, especially for tutors who are frequently self-motivated people and for students who are relatively powerless. People generally do not like to hurt or offend others or to appear to be selfish. It is human to wish to be liked. Because saying 'no' to others is likely to be inconvenient for the person making the request, they are unlikely to feel as positive about the person refusing afterwards. In saying 'no' people can fear being seen as inflexible or rude. Saying 'no' makes us feel guilty because we have not internalized the fact that we have a right to do so, or the fact that our rights are as important as those of other people. Unfortunately, the effect of always saying 'yes' can be exhaustion and inefficiency.

You may find that you are more able to say 'no' assertively if you model your behaviour on someone who exhibits this skill. The broken record technique described earlier can be useful. It may help to keep the refusal of a request short and to avoid elaborated excuses or much in the way of reasons. For instance a statement such as 'I must say no to that extra marking. I have other priorities just now', rather than using phrases such as 'I can't', shows that you are taking responsibility for the refusal. It is usually helpful to acknowledge the person making the request, for instance by acknowledging that your reply will cause them difficulties. Once the request has been turned down, it may be better to move away. Remaining on the scene is tempting, as one may wish to rebuild bridges, but it provides opportunities for negotiations to reopen.

There are occasions when you may not wish to say 'no', but rather 'yes if . . .' On these occasions it is important to state your needs or conditions clearly. On the other hand, you may want more time to consider or prepare a response. You are entitled to ask for time and to be firm about not being pressurized to give an immediate response. You are also entitled to ask for more information before making a decision.

Enquiry Task 8.6

With a group of students:

1 Brainstorm a list of 'rights' which an individual has in their relationships with other individuals in the workplace:
for example,
the right to make mistakes;
the right to say 'no' etc.

2 Design assertive responses to any of the following situations that have relevance for you:
a colleague who is always late and leaves you to pick up the pieces;
a tutor or manager who habitually makes decisions and then rescinds them;
a student who has a responsibility for part of a joint project you are involved with, but who does the job badly;
a colleague who does not respect your personal boundaries;
a student who hogs a disproportionate amount of seminar time;
a colleague who makes sexist remarks;
a student who talks through others' presentations;
a relation who phones up for a long chat just as you are going to watch a favourite TV programme.

Write notes of what you learned from these exercises about your own attitudes and those of the students to assertive behaviour.

Summary

There are a range of skills that a tutor needs to develop if they are to be successful in using counselling as part of the learning process. These include:

- attending to what the student is saying;
- paraphrasing;
- reflecting back feelings;
- matching non-verbal behaviour and speech patterns;
- questioning;
- summarizing;
- reframing the student's problem;
- confronting destructive beliefs and behaviour;
- exploring options with the student;
- finishing the interview;

- encouraging independence;
- keeping careful records; and
- catering for the tutor's own needs.

It is usually sufficient to ask the student themselves to list their options, but the tutor may need to include tentative suggestions of their own. When exploring options with a student it can be helpful to:

- summarize the student's general conclusions about options open to them;
- talk about positive and negative aspects of each option, starting with that least preferred;
- describe the student's dilemmas to them and ask the student to expand each part; and
- ask the student to identify goals for themselves and them help them break down the steps towards those goals.

When the tutor and the student seem to be reaching an impasse, it is usually better to stop the discussion and make a new appointment to explore it further.

Dealing with stress and conflict can be made easier by:

- analysing interactions with others to see whether they habitually include crossed or complimentary transactions;
- recognizing the human need for positive strokes and the effect of negative ones;
- practising assertiveness techniques when these are appropriate including:
  broken record,
  disarming anger,
  accepting your own emotions,
  cutting through irrelevant issues,
  giving criticism or compliments,
  being direct,
  asking for time,
  writing a script before a meeting,
  using someone else as a model,
  recognizing others' point of view, but keeping track of your own,
  receiving criticism and evaluating it,
  saying 'no' assertively.

Entry for the Reflective Diary

Write about situations where your skills in each of the following were important to your word as a tutor:

- communication skills;
- observation skills;
- morale building skills;
- skills in expressing emotion;

- skills in maintaining social relationships; and
- assertiveness skills.

Decide which of these skills you should target for further development.

Write about how you might monitor your progress in developing these skills.

References

BERNE, E. (1964) *Games People Play: The Psychology of Human Relationships*, Harmondsworth, Penguin.

BROCKIE, D. (1992) 'Learning to look after ourselves: Experiencing pastoral care for pastoral carers', *Pastoral Care in Education*, **10**, 2, pp. 3–6.

DICKSON, A. (1982) *A Woman in Your Own Right*, London, Quartet.

GELDARD, D. (1989) *Basic Professional Counselling: A Training Manual for Counsellors*, New York, Prentice Hall.

HARRIS, T.A. (1970) *I'm OK — You're OK*, London, Pan.

LODGE, C. and McLAUGHLIN, C. (1992) 'Organising pastoral support for teachers: Some comments and a model', *Pastoral Care in Education*, **10**, 2, pp. 7–12.

ROGERS, C. (1983) *Freedom to Learn for the 80's*; 2nd edn, Columbus, OH, Charles E. Merrill.

STIBBS, J. (1987) 'Staff care and development', *Pastoral Care in Education*, **5**, 1, pp. 36–39.

WELLS, H. (1983) *Active Tutorial Work*, Worcester, Blackwell.

Suggested Reading

BERNE, E. (1964) *Games People Play: The Psychology of Human Relationships*, Harmondsworth: Penguin.

This is a useful guide to transactional analysis and its application in everyday life.

GELDARD, D. (1989) *Basic Professional Counselling: A Training Manual for Counsellors*, New York, Prentice Hall.

A simple, easy to read guide to basic counselling skills in the therapeutic setting. Teachers in higher and further education will need to adapt the principles to their own context.

NORTHEDGE, A. (1990) *The Good Study Guide*, Milton Keynes, Open University Press.

This is a detailed and thorough guide, of use and interest to tutors and students alike. It breaks down individual study problems, such as coping with examinations and suggests strategies for improving individual performance.

Pastoral Care in Education.

This is a useful journal for tutors interested in issues in pastoral care. It specializes in fairly short, easy to read articles. They tend to be school, rather than further or higher education, focused but issues are considered that apply to a variety of age groups and levels. Volume 10, Number 2, published in 1992, has a useful series of articles on support for the personal tutor.

Chapter 9

Equal Opportunities

Definitions of Equal Opportunities

Equal opportunity is centrally important to the lives of many students. Sensitive awareness and action enriches the educational experience of men and women, members of the majority and of the minority communities, able bodied and disabled people and people from all social groups and localities. Equal opportunity is about inclusion, justice, fairness and learning from and about the rich experience of many people and groups. In this chapter we argue that the principles of equal opportunities are those that underpin most models of good practice.

Equal opportunities may be defined in various ways. One model takes the view that true equal opportunities require that all members of society are entitled to the same provision. This notion underpins the national curriculum that now applies in all schools in Great Britain. Only in very exceptional cases may particular children be excluded from parts of the national curriculum. The aim is for as many children as possible to benefit from the same curriculum.

This model may lead to problems of match between the curriculum and the individual needs of students or their experiences. In Britain, the Department for Education and Science (DES, 1989) implicitly recognizes this problem in its statement of principle that every pupil should have a broad and balanced curriculum but that this curriculum should also be relevant to their particular needs. The model may also neglect the values and experiences of particular groups. This last dilemma was central to the controversy about political interference in the English and history curriculum. Objections centred upon the invalidation of the experience and culture of working-class children and those from ethnic minorities in favour of that of the white middle class.

Another model of equal opportunities is based on the view that differences in attainment are due to attitudes, and not to biological differences (Bigger *et al.*, 1990). This implies that problems lie not in the individual or group which is experiencing disadvantage, but in their treatment by individuals, such as tutors, colleges and universities, or society. It requires that efforts should be made to root out intentional and unintentional discrimination. In this model, equal opportunities are about minimizing barriers to achievement, particularly individual and institutionalized discrimination. Such barriers include underlying attitudes of those with power; curricula that exclude the experiences and culture of all but the most dominant group; and simplified, stereotyped and uninformed opinions about the abilities, interests, attitudes and experiences of particular groups of people.

The starting point for equal opportunities may therefore be the elimination of prejudiced attitudes within individuals. Prejudice is a favourable or unfavourable feeling towards an individual (or group). This feeling exists prior to and is not based on first-hand experience of that person. Prejudice often involves stereotyping. This is a simplified and rigid view of a person which results from preconceived ideas about people belonging to particular groups and thereafter filtering one's experience of individuals through that view. People belonging to particular groups are thus seen as conforming to a standardized pattern or picture. This picture will tend to be reinforced by others who hold similar stereotyped views and by the uncritical interpretation of judgments made about the stereotyped person or group. Stereotypes are often, but not always, negative and lead to discrimination within our society.

Another view takes tackling of institutional discrimination as the starting point. Discrimination involves making distinctions, especially on the grounds of race, sex, class or disability, which lead to unfavourable treatment. Distinctions can be reinforced by the practices of powerful groups or individuals within an organization or society, and can lead to institutional discrimination. Long established practices and procedures within education can act in a discriminatory way. These practices are not usually discriminary in intention. More often they are the result of sloppiness or inertia and a lack of awareness about their effect.

At its most basic level, equal opportunities imply that all students and staff in an institution have the right to freedom from discrimination. In practice, this ideal is seldom realized. In most cases, institutional discrimination is unintentional and unconscious. Education often perpetuates inequality of opportunity through various mechanisms such as the use of language, students' own tendency to stereotype themselves and each other and the 'hidden curriculum'. Often it is a result of institutional structures, set up for other times and for institutional convenience, that act in a discriminatory way against certain groups and individuals.

Equal opportunities in institutional terms has a number of possible components. These include issues of access for all students, such as: access to a broad and balanced curriculum; access to a common educational experience and opportunities to fulfil potential; access to teacher expertise; and access to choice. Questions of access become more central and critical in further and higher education because entry is usually selective in some way. The process of selection denies entry to some individuals, and thus mitigates absolutely against equality of opportunity. It is therefore essential to ensure that the processes of selection focus on *relevant* experience and ability. It is necessary to monitor outcomes to ensure that certain groups are not disadvantaged and that, once on the course, all students have an equal chance of success.

Other institutional aspects of equality of opportunity include issues of respect and value for individual students within the institution and courses. Many universities and colleges have higher status subjects and courses. The status of these courses may transfer to the respect accorded to individual students. For instance, a student on a subdegree course in a university may be treated with less courtesy by administrative staff than a student of a post-graduate management programme.

Equal opportunities in education is increasingly becoming a concern for colleges and universities. This is in part because they recognize the necessity of meeting the needs of new client groups. This may be a response to worries during the late 1980s and early 1990s about a decreasing cohort of 16–19-year-olds and to political pressure. In the UK, the National Advisory Body for Public Sector Higher Education (NAB, 1988) encouraged higher education to widen access. This led to a review of the participation of people from ethnic minorities, disabled people and other groups such as mature people in higher education. The Department for Education (DES, 1991) is still committed to increasing participation.

Some tutors and institutions are less than wholehearted about the provision of equal opportunities. This may result from a fear of adverse effects on traditional standards of excellence. Much of the data available (Smithers and Robinson, 1989; Adelman 1991; Ashcroft and Peacock, 1993) indicate that, far from creating a problem, increased access leads to more people achieving a rising standard. The creation of equal opportunities may be seen as involving the use of scarce resources. It is true that tackling deep-seated issues involves an opportunity cost, but it is also true that the promotion of equal opportunities generates behaviour which represents the best general management and teaching practice. Thus effective action to promote equal opportunities at the individual and the institutional level may lead to higher standards of success in other aspects of the institution. The effectiveness of such action depends less on the direct allocation of large amounts of resources than on will and organization. What is required is an open-minded enquiry into evidence as to the effects of practices and attitudes, a consideration of the long-term consequences of actions taken and a wholehearted search for solutions and improved systems and relationships.

Language and Equal Opportunities

There is a growing tendency to accuse those tutors who support the right of various groups in society to express a preference as to the words that are used to refer to them, and to respect these rights in their own use of language, of 'political correctness'. Ironically, it is now almost politically dangerous to seek to persuade colleagues to respect the feelings of particular groups about the labels and titles that are used to describe them. Those seeking to use 'traditional' labels do not admit that their own action is essentially political. A willingness to offend the less powerful sections in our society, to tolerate the fact that your language leads to groups feeling excluded, patronized or stereotyped, is a political act. It is a short step from this to institutional actions that may exclude, disadvantage or make unwarranted assumptions about less powerful groups in society. The implication of some arguments of those who advocate 'political incorrectness' is that this possibility is not worth investigating or remedying.

The language that we use is a means to define the agreed limit to the behaviour of individuals in society. For instance, while watching an old BBC drama production, it was interesting to note the phrase 'mutton dressed as lamb' being employed in the play to 'police' the acceptable range of dress (and by implication, behaviour) allowed for women over a certain age. This is a phrase that is less commonly used today. Perhaps partly as a consequence, women who twenty years ago would have looked middle aged in their 30s and 40s, nowadays can dress fashionably and remain feeling young and attractive. Even today we retain phrases such as 'old dear', which limit our expectations of older people, and their expectations of themselves. Fortunately, people are more unwilling to accept this kind of labelling, and are forcing even the most reactionary to change their ways. It is now unacceptable to call a black person working in a restaurant 'boy'. Let us hope that soon it will be equally unacceptable to call mature women working in offices 'girls'.

The Open University (1993) points out that there is usually a suitable alternative for a word or phrase that excludes and stereotypes a group in society. Examples of this include 'police officer' instead of 'policeman'; 'black people' instead of 'blacks'; 'school meal supervisor' instead of 'dinner lady'; and 'older people' instead of 'old folk'. Most of these more sensitive descriptions convey a human dignity that was lacking in the more traditional label. It is true that some descriptions can appear ugly or clumsy, for instance 'chair' or 'convener' instead of 'chairman'; 'human being' instead of 'man'; 'they' or 's/he' instead of 'he'. A sensitive tutor, who cares about the opportunities, dignity and feelings of their colleagues and students, may feel that this is a small price to pay. Those who reject more sensitive descriptions are making a political statement that the traditional foundations of the language matter more than the cultural sensitivities and opportunities of other people. We believe that it is part of the role of the educator to extend opportunities and to open possibilities that might not even have occurred to their students otherwise. It is anomalous for the tutor in these circumstances to use language that implies exclusion and limits for particular groups.

Enquiry Task 9.1

With a mixed-sex group of colleagues (students or tutors) make a list of words or phrases that any member considers sexist.

Discuss how each word or phrase sounds if applied to both sexes.

Decide on non-sexist alternatives for each word or phrase.

Reflect on what you learnt from this exercise about your own attitudes to gender and language.
How do your attitudes differ from those of other members of the group?

Look at a selection of recent government publications.

Do the images, examples and language used apply equally to the sexes?

Age

For many years, most of further and higher education catered primarily for the needs of young people. It was not just the old who were unintentionally excluded by some institutional expectations and processes, but also the majority of adults over the age of 25. More recently, most universities and colleges have become interested in meeting the needs of the mature student group. A few have also started to consider age as a factor in their employment policies for staff.

Age is an equality issue that eventually applies to everyone, so everyone has a vested interest in addressing it. Demographic trends and trends in patterns of employment suggest that more mature people will wish to undertake study within further and higher education. Therefore, it is also in the interests of institutions to consider equal opportunities for mature people. Research conducted by Ashcroft and Peacock (1993) with mature students on a four-year teaching degree course indicates that analysing the study needs of mature students benefits all students, since the needs of younger and older students are often in common. In addition, the mature student group has particular needs. While some of these needs had cost implications, most were a matter of will and organization. The tutors' attitudes to mature students and their willingness to adapt organizational arrangements to meet their needs were crucial to their success. Tutors who understood mature students' anxieties about assessed work, enquired about their study skill needs and capitalized upon the experiences that mature students had brought with them were able to contribute to their success.

Ashcroft and Peacock found that mature students, including those with non-traditional entry qualifications, achieved at least as well as the younger students from the first year onwards. This ran counter to tutor expectations. While most tutors felt that mature students did well by the end of the course, they tended to believe that the mature students found the first year a struggle. It is possible that the mature students are more likely to express their worries and to ask for the help they need at an early stage than are younger students or that they lack confidence that their non-traditional qualifications could provide as secure a skill and knowledge base as A levels. Smithers and Robinson (1989) also found that mature non-standard entry students at three selected universities did slightly better than their younger counterparts, although the authors point out that selection had been particularly thorough.

Enquiry Task 9.2

List the ways *you* adapt your practice or the curriculum so as to support the learning of mature students.

Design a simple questionnaire aimed at finding out what practices and procedures would facilitate their study.

- at an institutional level (e.g. social and practical networking support structures);
- at course or programme level (e.g. advanced planning of timetables and work flow).

Which of these might be achieved within limited resources?
How might you use your evidence to influence policy and practice?
Design an action plan to improve your own support for the mature students you teach.

Gender

Gender stereotyping is pervasive in society. Gender refers to socially ascribed feminine or masculine characteristics learned and reinforced by society. The term is a useful one and should not be used as a 'polite' term for sex. Each society polices the gender roles considered suitable for males and females and thus these roles vary between cultures. The effect is to attribute fixed traits on the basis of biological sex and ignore individuals' preferences and abilities in favour of these assumptions. This leads to a failure to encourage individual interests and talents and disadvantages both sexes. For instance, boys and young men are more often alienated from school and education sufficiently to play truant, they are overrepresented in remedial groups of various kinds and they are more often criminalized than are girls and young women. Something appears to be happening that is restricting the social development of these young people. Perhaps the opportunities of some young men are restricted by their own gender expectations or those of others. Gender stereotyping will restrict the roles, careers and study opportunities of a significant number of people of both sexes. The policing of gender roles by peers, the family and educational institutions may be fiercer for young men than young women. This may be because the traditionally female roles have lower status. Gender expectations can lead to people embarking on lifelong careers to which they are unsuited. The full range of careers or subjects to study may not be considered, if some are traditionally associated with the other sex.

Sexism is the belief that one sex, female or male, is inherently superior. This belief restricts the choices and opportunities of one sex. Where this belief is widely held by those with power, whether consciously or unconsciously, it will have real effects on people's life chances. World statistics show that women make up 54 per cent of the population, are responsible for 64 per cent of the total hours worked, earn 10 per cent of the total income and own 1 per cent of the world's property. If education is about opening opportunities, it seems that, as far as gender issues are concerned, positive action is needed.

The problems that women face in education and employment in society and the waste that this leads to are well documented (Mackay, 1991). Hurdles include being the 'right' age, having a continuous work or study record or being geographically mobile. Female mature students may thus face multiple discrimination. The experience documented by studies such as Ashcroft and Peacock (1993) indicates that employers may be missing opportunities to employ exceptionally able people. A study in the USA by Adelman (1991) found that women's performance in higher education was generally better than men's and that they had a better attitude to education than men did. Despite this many women failed to find rewards in the labour market. Their educational experience was discounted.

Equal opportunities does not imply that the sexes are the same. The differential experience of males and females leads to significant differences in attitudes and career orientations. The important thing is to find ways to broaden the options available to individuals, through changing institutional and individual practice and by providing members of disadvantaged groups with opportunities to develop the skills and understanding that will enable them to compete on equal terms with others. Part of the role of further and higher education may be to encourage employers to value the qualities disadvantaged groups (such as women) bring and to the individual to recognize and market those qualities.

Studies such as that by McCrum (1994) show that women obtain fewer first class and third class honours degrees than men have been used to justify theories that women are in some way more 'average' than men. Alternative explanations are not difficult to find. For instance, women are underrepresented in subjects such as mathematics and science, which traditionally produce more extreme scores in assessment, and concentrated in the humanities where fewer students overall are awarded first class honours. Women also tend to prefer courses offering continuous assessment rather than assessment through final examinations. Continuous assessment implies a number of assessment points that are aggregated. This process will generate a tendency towards regression to the mean in the final scoring.

Discrimination in education on the grounds of gender is perpetuated in various ways. These include the use of language that assumes the world is male unless otherwise stated. However, confronting sexism in education involves more than the avoidance of exclusive language. It also involves looking for positive ways to include women and men on equal terms and to broaden the range of possibilities for men as well as for women.

There is evidence that females have a different experience of education from males and that they achieve differently. For instance, girls and women tend to underachieve in technology and science. They tend to receive a much smaller proportion of tutor attention than males, and so end up being taught less (Delamont, 1990; Kelly, 1981; Deem, 1984). It is interesting that the schools that girls or boys attend seem to make a difference as to the extent of these sex differences. This indicates that differences in attainment can be created, at least in part, by institutional practices and attitudes, rather than biological differences. Some schools or colleges seem to police students' conformity to gender roles more than others. Students attending these institutions will suffer reduced options and informal sanctions if they do not conform closely to gender stereotypes. Thus colleges, universities and individual tutors make a difference, through their policies and behaviour, to the range of opportunities offered to their students.

The individual tutor may improve the range of opportunities for their female and male students by acquainting themselves with the circumstances that underlie the differential achievement. For instance, if you are involved with introducing women students to an aspect of science, you might bear in mind the need for appropriate role models in the choice of visiting speakers and suitable examples and applications. Kelly (1984) found that girls were interested in the social and human applications of subjects including science. You might therefore ensure that this aspect is fully discussed. Expensive technology may be concentrated within subjects that tend to attract more men than women. If this is the case in your institution, you may be able to argue for the purchase and use of new technology within those subjects that attract more women than men. Deem (1984) found that women tend to react less favourably to competition than men. If you wish to be fair to both sexes, you may decide to employ a range of teaching methods, including cooperative working. You might even monitor your own behaviour to ensure that you are allowing women as much time as men to solve a problem before you 'help'.

Colleges and universities do not appear to be doing enough to promote equal opportunities for women and men within their own organizations. For instance, the Equal Opportunities Commission (1985) reports that women in Britain are grossly underrepresented in senior posts within further and higher education. Acker and Piper (1984) suggests that this kind of underrepresentation leads to an ethos which perpetuates inequality for staff and students. However, it appears that policy statements and their implementation can have an effect. In the UK, local education authorities have often taken a leading role in supporting such policies. The different policies of different authorities may have contributed to the noticeable and consistent differences in patterns between areas in the promotion of men and women. The Further Education Staff College (FESC, 1987) notes this difference within public sector further and higher education colleges. For instance, within the Inner London Education Authority in 1985 9.3 per cent of principals of further and higher education colleges, 49 per cent of vice principals, 23.7 per cent of heads of department, 9.1 per cent of readers and 12.4 per cent of principal lecturers were women. In Merseyside only 5 per cent of principals, 19 per cent of vice principals, 6.9 per cent of heads of department, 2 per cent of readers and 6.7 per cent of principal lecturers were women.

Enquiry Task 9.3

Design one or more simple checklists to monitor your interactions with male and female students over ten-minute periods during various practical sessions or seminars using the following starting points:

- What proportion of the demands on your attention are made by male and female students?
- What proportion of the time are you doing the talking?
- What proportion of the time are male students doing the talking?
- What proportion of the time are female students doing the talking?

Design a strategy for ensuring you give equal attention and teaching to the male and female students you teach.

How would you justify the use of this strategy to an interested colleague?

Consider the following questions:

- who sits where;
- how are small groups selected;
- are there any criteria for selecting small groups;
- how are group leaders elected/selected; and
- what is the 'division of labour' in group work?

Do you need an equal opportunities strategy to deal with any of them?

Race

Discrimination on the basis of race is a common experience for students from ethnic minorities in Britain today. Colleges and universities have a responsibility to ensure that all students have the opportunity to develop their full potential. This requires that we eliminate racist practices, whether conscious or unconscious, and that we confront racist attitudes held by students. The challenging of prejudice and ignorance should be a fundamental part of each student's education. Bigger *et al.* (1990) suggests that tutors should go further than this by developing their own and the students' knowledge of minority cultures, and especially how the experiences of other cultures relate to the subject taught and the way that each subject has traditionally been perceived within Eurocentric cultures. Central to this process is uncovering and exploring omissions and exclusions within what has been traditionally considered the body of subject matter 'worth' teaching. We believe that the consideration of inclusion should be a factor in the choice of curriculum and the design of teaching materials. For instance, on an English course you might include some literature from India or Africa.

Racism seems embedded in British history and society. The link remains between imperialism and racism. Black people find themselves referred to as immigrants in their own country, they find authority is less often willing to believe black witnesses and they find themselves the butt of harassment and name calling. Racism operates at a variety of conscious and unconscious levels. For instance, the Swann Report (1985) found that throughout the UK education system black people, especially Afro-Caribbean males, are more likely to be defined as having behavioural problems. At another level, members of minority ethnic cultures may find that their names are altered or mispronounced. One's name is a fundamental aspect of one's self. Each of us has the right to the dignity of being called by the name we own.

The Swann Report found that racism is extensive within the British education system and that it is responsible for much underachievement. Interestingly, it asserts that racism is a white problem that is predominant in all-white schools. Much of this racism seems to be the unintended result of the continuation of practices and assumptions carried over from a time when Britain was a largely homogeneous society. Today some of these practices deprive minority groups of access to a range of opportunities. The report states unequivocally that educational institutions must counter the insidious evil of racism and emphasizes the importance of institutions in predominantly white and rural areas, as well as urban multicultural areas, in preparing students for a pluralistic society. This implies that every college and university should have a policy for multicultural understanding and equal opportunities that permeates all aspects of the institution's work and that such a policy cannot be welded on to existing practices.

By creating disharmony and by preventing certain groups from fulfilling their potential, racism has an effect on the whole of society. If we are to make a positive contribution, we need to face up to and eradicate our own prejudices. Few tutors would admit to beliefs that particular ethnic groups are inclined to crime or to be lazy, but some may feel uncomfortable about particular aspects of a particular culture, for example, the role of women in Islam. This issue is very problematic. You may not be able to value practices that are anti-equal opportunities. Tutors cannot combat racism by asserting that minority cultures are perfect in every respect. On the other hand, feelings of unease should not lead white tutors to assume that Asian people invariably hold sexist views, or that practices that we assume to be based on oppression necessarily are so.

The view that private culture can be multicultural provided that the public culture remains white and traditionally 'British' has profound negative effects of the opportunities and feelings of self-worth and pride available to members of ethnic minorities. 'Colour blindness' denies the rich cultural resources now available in Britain. Life is easier for white people to cope with if it is treated as 'mono-chrome', since they can ignore the influence of slavery, immigration policies, suppression of religious beliefs and territorial robbery on British history, geography and modern economics, but it makes it much harder for black and Asian people to locate their own experiences within a wider perspective. The omission of black culture and experience from our recording of history has the effect of invalidating that experience.

Racism can also start through the low expectations some tutors have of members of particular groups. All stereotypes are damaging and misleading, including 'positive' ones, such as the supposed capacity for hard work of all Asian people. It is part of the tutor's role to ensure that cultures are represented as accurately as possible, and from the point of view of that culture, rather than a Eurocentric interpretation.

It may be necessary to rehearse situations that may come about. For instance, you may need to decide about how you will deal with racism in the classroom, whether it is intentional or unintentional. In addition, you may need to develop a strategy to enable all the students to participate fully. This may include the examination of teaching materials and curriculum for racist messages.

Enquiry Task 9.4

List examples of institutional racism that you have noticed within your college.

Discuss the issue with a small group of students and at least one tutor who belongs to an ethnic minority group from within your college.

Were they able to suggest more examples?

Design a set of actions you could take to start to counter racism within your institution. For example:

Action	*Target date for implementation*
Find out the range of languages spoken by students in the college;	
Develop an understanding of some of the religious beliefs held by Pentecostalists, Rastafarians or Sikhs;	
Examine resource material and examples used in your lectures for bias;	
Put a paper to your departmental committee outlining equal opportunities issues in the admissions process etc.	

Social Class

Social class reflects the pattern of divisions that exist within a society on the basis of factors such as rank and economic status. Groups of people with similar social, economic and political positions tend to promote and favour people who share those positions. This may be partly because successful people tend to have high self-esteem and therefore like and value people they perceive as being like themselves. Alternatively, it may be because values and experiences that do not conform to those commonly held by such groups are not recognized or held to be relevant. In this way the life chances of the most and least privileged tend to be perpetuated.

Localism is a variant of social discrimination. It is a form of prejudice that assigns certain characteristics to people from particular localities. Thus certain voices, such as English West Country accents, are not associated with intelligence. Prejudice may exist against people from particular types of location (rural, inner-city, suburban), or types of housing area (public sector or private), or geographical areas such as the north or south of Britain. Much of this prejudice is associated with class, and especially the use of accent as an indicator of class.

The tripartite system of education in the UK was designed to provide 'different but equal' education depending upon the child's level of ability. This assumed that ability was a unitary concept, that it was a 'fixed' commodity uninfluenced by educational experience and measurable in an objective way. Experience later indicated that each of these assumptions could be challenged. Worries about the fairness of selection systems, especially the effects of social class upon the results, led to the development of comprehensive schooling.

The influence of social class on educational opportunity appears to have fallen out of fashion as an area of enquiry in recent years. There are signs that interest is again reviving since the evidence of the widening social differentials has emerged during the 1980s and early 1990s. In addition, it has become recognized that at least some of the barriers to opportunity which members of ethnic minorities face may be issues of class. These problems often include a lack of financial resources to support continued study and conflicting values and attitudes between the home and school/college cultures regarding appropriate teaching methods and curriculum content.

Douglas (1967) found a variety of class factors that affected educational achievement. These factors included space to study, provision of books, visits, family size, parents' experience of and attitudes to education, parental language, and parents' aspirations for their children. These factors combined to create the 'educational environment' of the home, which in turn was related to the resources of the community where the home was located.

Special Needs

Some definitions of 'special needs' refer to a deficit in the student that requires 'remediation'. Others refer to an institutional or interactive model, implying that the institution should be doing things differently if all students are to reach their full potential. Terms such as sensory disability, intellectual disability, intellectual handicap, emotional difficulties, behavioural difficulties, and English as a second language imply the first, deficit in the student, model. Descriptions such as 'students we find difficult to teach', 'students we find difficult to control', 'students who have lost motivation through failure', 'students who struggle with inappropriate provision', or 'students who need more than we can routinely give' imply the second, institutional or interactive model. The second model requires that you and your institution examine all the factors contributing to learning difficulties experienced by some students. These difficulties may include factors within your or the institution's control, such as the match of demands made to student abilities and experience, the quality of teaching, resources for teaching, physical conditions, staffing level and the 'ethos' of the institution.

Difficulties created by the institution may interact with those created by the student's experience or ability, such as social disadvantage, health, anxiety, attendance problems and fatigue as well as the speed and efficiency of intellectual functioning.

It is not always clear what our duty should be towards students in the post-compulsory education sector who have special needs. Most institutions will have the provision of equal opportunities as an objective. Most, however, actively discriminate against students with special educational needs, especially those that result in the student experiencing learning difficulties.

Further and higher education is not required to provide education of any kind for all students who could benefit. It is simpler and more cost effective to concentrate resources upon traditional students who have needs in common rather than particular to each individual. Some might say that resources used this way would provide society with a better return. Fortunately, since learning difficulties are common (Warnock, 1978, suggests one in five of children and young people in the UK have special educational needs and the Open University, 1993, states that 14.2 per cent of the population is disabled), most colleges and universities do not operate in a moral vacuum and questions of justice and fairness do impinge. In addition, Further Education Funding Council 'weightings' provide attractive unit resources for those further education colleges that provide programmes for students with special educational needs.

The first barriers to equal opportunities that disabled students face are usually presented at the admissions stage. Certain kinds of intellectual disabilities may be of a nature to preclude a student from benefiting from advanced courses in further education or from higher education. However, there are a number of students who might benefit if suitable provision was available. Too often, admissions tutors assess an applicant's needs without reference to the student's own assessment of their needs and their strategies for solving remaining problems. This can deny certain groups of students the opportunity others have of trying and risking failure. Fortunately, colleges and universities in Britain are being made increasingly aware of the self-advocacy movement (Further Education Unit, 1990). This movement empowers disabled people by taking account of their own assessment of their needs and abilities.

A degree of flexibility and planning can enable groups of students to participate in further and higher education. Some universities provide literacy and numeracy support for their students. Tutors and students should be working together to find ways of ensuring that as many groups as possible can benefit from the full curriculum, interact with peers and experience success and independence. Entering into a dialogue will broaden the range of solutions considered. After all most disabled people have many years' experience of solving the difficulties they face.

Some colleges cater for students with special educational needs, both as a matter of benevolent humanitarianism and expediency. Additional funds are often available to assist in meeting specific needs from governments and from organizations such as the European Union. Since the early 1990s there has been a growth in special needs provision. This growth has been accompanied by a debate about integrated and segregated learning, which focuses sharply upon whether deficits implied in the term 'special education needs' reside in the student or in the student's interaction with the educational settings they have experienced. Although integration has become a goal of most special needs provision, segregation may be achieved in various ways. These include withdrawal from normal lessons and restrictions upon the student's timetable and subject choices.

Catering for students with special educational needs is likely to require much preparation and management. For instance, students may experience learning difficulties as a result of their experiences of schooling. Providing more of the same is not likely to be of help. New and more appropriate curricula and teaching methods will have to be developed. This may be easier to achieve in a segregated setting. The question is then raised as to whether such a context mitigates against the definitions of equality of opportunity in the definitions in the first section of this chapter. If the answer to the question is affirmative, and if equal opportunities in education is a right or an ideal to be aspired to, segregated provision for students with special educational needs would raise many dilemmas.

The research into schooling and special educational needs points to various problems with segregation. Children in segregated classes do not always have access to specialist subject teaching. This would also be true of students in many further education colleges in the UK. Their teachers tend to specialize in 'special needs' teaching, rather than in the subject being taught. Students in such settings may experience the same kinds of restricted opportunity as children in special schools. In addition, more able students may lose out on the social learning which would be achieved by more heterogeneous groupings.

There are some six million disabled people in Britain today. The Open University (1993) has 4000 disabled students and the numbers are growing at a rate of 10 per cent a year. Institutions which make provision for their needs find that there is a steady demand for their services. The Open University issues guidelines to assist tutors in dealing with disabled students without marginalizing or patronizing them. They remind tutors not to assume in their use of examples that everyone can walk down the street or drive down the motorway. The role of language is emphasized. For instance, labelling people with their disability through the use of terms such as 'epileptics' rather than 'people with epilepsy', can suggest that epilepsy is the only or most important part of that person's identity. Omissions are as important for disabled people as for people from ethnic minorities. You might consider using images of disability as illustration where the disability is incidental to the activity being described.

Interestingly, groups representing people with special educational needs now prefer the term 'disabled people', rather than 'people with disability'. This is because it implies that people are disabled by society, rather than owning the disability themselves. This is an important point of principle for disabled people. Well meaning efforts to 'help', such as using pathetic images, or describing people as 'victims' or heroic to raise funds or praise their efforts are as disabling as more physical barriers.

Enquiry Task 9.5

Do you know your institution's policy with regard to:

- how to go about assessing a students' special needs;
- referral to medical/social records;
- discussion with teachers from a student's previous school or college?

Do you know what sources of funds are available to support a student with specific learning needs such as dyslexia who is following a mainstream course:

- from within the institution;
- from outside?

Find out the answers where you are unsure.

With a colleague, brainstorm strategies you might adopt to encourage:

- a student you teach to maximize their potential; and
- your department to improve their practice with respect to students with a particular learning disability (e.g. hearing loss).

How do political and economic priorities encourage and/or discourage you from catering for students with special educational needs?

Exceptional Ability

The aim of equal opportunities policies is to enable all students to reach their full potential. It is often assumed, without there being much evidence that this is the case, that the needs of very able students are met by their own efforts. Ability does not seem to be entirely innate and therefore the teaching students receive will make a difference as to whether exceptional potential is nurtured. Some very able students do not do well out of our system. 'Performers' who are well motivated do well, but others may not. In classes taught as a whole, they may spend too long on 'hold'.

You may recognize many able students who are not obviously 'academic' or who have not chosen to study academic subjects. Sometimes the abilities of this kind of student may not be recognized unless you are on the look-out for exceptional ability. These students are especially likely to be missed if they are female, black or working-class. (More teachers nominate boys than girls for enrichment and black and working-class students are underrepresented in academic areas.)

Recognizing exceptional ability and catering for it is not easy. Even within the university system, the talents of these students will not be developed properly unless they are recognized and efforts are made to provide the challenges required for real development. This becomes particularly apparent when the various types of ability are examined. The 'good all-rounder' is probably the easiest to recognize and cater for. Some students have exceptional ability in one area. These students may find it difficult to ask for the help they need in interdisciplinary work and may therefore underachieve. Some students may have underdeveloped written skills. Their exceptional ability may not be recognized in a system that relies on measuring ability through written examinations. Other students may have high ability, but low motivation. Some of these students may find themselves on unsuitable courses, where they experience frustration. Some may find it difficult to keep on task and may need short-term goals if they are to fulfil their potential. Some students' exceptional ability may be masked by poor social skills. These students may have been 'misfits' throughout their schooling, partly as a result of their exceptional ability. They may benefit from help, even at this late stage, to enable them to empathize with the group. Commonly, high ability in areas that are not valued by the institution go unrecognized. Unfortunately, this tends to happen if the ability is in areas, such as leadership, that are needed in society as a whole. If you wish to lead a class, you may find students with leadership potential can be threatening and come to regard them as a nuisance.

If the system is to nurture all the talents of students, provision and planning must be devoted to the needs of exceptionally able students. Ogilvie (1973) defined the top 10 per cent of pupils in schools as more able and the top 2 per cent as 'gifted'. He found that students may be talented in a variety of areas. These include physical talent, artistic talent, mechanical ingenuity, leadership, high intelligence and creativity. Dinton and Postlethwaite (1985) found that about 10 per cent of students in each subject area would benefit from an enriched curriculum to develop their special talent. HMI reports (e.g. HMI, 1989; 1990; 1991 and 1992) show that the talents of the most able in the UK were not well matched to the tasks that they were given.

What Can Be Done About Equal Opportunities?

You may be able to make a positive contribution to the creation of more equal opportunities through various types of action. You might decide to contribute to whole college and departmental policies, for instance by suggesting that appraisal might be focused on equal opportunities issues. You might ask your course team to discuss organizational issues, such as staffing, visiting speakers, lists, task distribution amongst students and choices offered (including what choices are set against each other). You might look at your own teaching and try out strategies to ensure equal opportunities. You could think about the choice of resources and illustrations used in your teaching. Other issues worth exploring include ways of eliminating bias in the materials, marking, and in self-assessment. An important aspect of teaching is the allocation of your time and the quality of your attention to various groups of students. Mutual classroom observation with a trusted colleague can be very useful here. Alternatively, it may be useful to look for support and ideas from outside the college, for instance through courses and conferences on equal opportunities.

Strategies for Action on Equal Opportunities

A number of publications provide more or less detailed guidelines for action that might be taken by individuals and institutions to promote equal opportunities (ILEA, 1985; Equal Opportunities Commission, 1985; Open University, 1993). Each set of guidelines needs to be interpreted within the context of the particular institution. One of the most important first tasks is to ascertain where the priorities for action lie, since it is unlikely that all can usefully be dealt with at once.

It is important to develop agreed criteria and definitions of equal opportunities, ascertain responsibilities for policy implementation and strategies for evaluation and monitoring progress. A sound equal opportunities policy will embrace staff, students, curriculum and institutional ethos. It should include selection and recruitment. A comprehensive policy for staff and students would include monitoring of appointments, including the placing of advertisements, the images used in publicity material, selection processes, and the composition of selection panels. Aspects which might be acted upon include explicit, inclusive statements on publicity materials and the training of all staff involved in contacts with staff and students, including support staff. The monitoring of selection criteria and elimination of unnecessary criteria (such as age) and the accreditation and valuing of prior experience, such as parenting, for both staff and students will increase opportunities for groups traditionally underrepresented. Students from groups underrepresented may be encouraged by links forged between colleges, universities and particular schools. Strategies may include 'taster' courses and events, bridging courses that include recognized methods of recording progress and achievement, and special enrichment classes. Once on the course, students from underrepresented groups may find themselves isolated unless steps are taken to provide suitable support. For instance, you might be able to persuade a course team to group female students in a traditionally male subject so that they are not in a small minority in classes.

You may wish to review the curriculum you offer to ensure that it is not discriminatory by omission. You could suggest that equal opportunities should be a regular item of course planning meeting agendas. Constant efforts may be needed to reorientate the curriculum to the needs, interests and experience of all students. Formal action may be needed as a starting point, such as an audit of women's experience as reflected in the curriculum you offer. You may seek to monitor the language and materials that you use for the messages implied by the images included and excluded. It may be useful for the institution to build non-discriminatory, non-racist and non-sexist resource banks of materials. You can make some impact by the maintenance of the spaces where you teach, the images you use in display material, and the quality of the displays themselves.

You may feel relatively powerless to influence policy creation, but policy can sometimes be created and implemented from the bottom up as effectively as from the top down. Important starting points include the recognition of achievements already attained, the identification of the key points for change and strategies that influence these. Committees such as academic or departmental boards, course team meetings, student or staff union meetings or governors may represent the key points at which you may be able to initiate change. You may have to identify the groups or individuals who could be the focal point for change and who might resist it. The widest policy discussion slows the process, but enables sound policy to be created and makes it more likely that it will be accepted and implemented. You and your colleagues can support each other in the development of good practice, for instance by mutual classroom observation of a structured or un-structured (perhaps with fly-on-the-wall notes) kind. You can discuss aggressive or dominant students or promoting learner control of study as equal opportunity issues. Areas that lend themselves to collaborative development with colleagues include the development of a variety of forms of teaching and assessment (such as negotiated assessment, oral assessment, collaborative learning and collective writ-ing) so that all students experience a style that suits them. You may also discuss ways of recognizing and building on skills and experiences that traditionally go unrecognized (for instance, technological skills in managing and maintaining a home).

It is in the area of the institutional ethos where you as an individual tutor may find most difficulty in initiating 'bottom up' change. The ethos of the institution tends to reflect the allocation of resources and the will and direction set by senior staff. The development of systems for complaints and grievances are essential elements of an effective equal opportunities policy. In order for these to be effective, discriminatory behaviour and incidents (such as harassment), procedures for deal-ing with them and a range of consequences will have to be defined. Priority in resource allocation should reflect the policy, for instance in the creation of a wel-coming environment reflecting to some extent a feminine ethos, adequate clean toilets and rest rooms for all groups. Sensitivity in timetabling of classes and key meetings for staff and students with dependents can open up opportunities for them. You may be assisted in realizing your full potential if assertiveness train-ing, career counselling and support groups of various kinds are offered. It may be important that training and other events, which raise awareness and understanding of equal opportunity issues, are put on for staff and students and that informal and formal opportunities for demonstrating organizational and managerial abilities (such as the chairing of committees) are monitored.

Quiz: Are the following true or false?*

(With grateful thanks to Giti Paulin of Oxfordshire Equal Opportunities Unit)

1   Forty-six per cent of the black population was born in Britain.
2   Six per cent of senior managers are women.
3   The average woman is economically inactive for only seven years of her adult life.
4   There are thirteen minority languages in Britain which have at least 100,000 speakers.
5   The first Race Relations Act in Britain was passed in 1965.
6   Black people first settled in Britain in the sixteenth century.
7   Only 5 per cent of households are made up of a working husband, economically inactive wife and two dependent children.
8   Males receive more attention in class than females.
9   The Sex Discrimination Act 1975 applies to both men and women.

10 Asian people are 50 times and Afro-Caribbean people 36 times more likely to be racially attacked than white people.
11 One-third of women teachers are unmarried.
12 There are only 800 black teachers nationwide.
13 Fifty per cent of male graduates and 24 per cent of female graduates gain degrees in science.
14 The Irish are the largest single immigrant group to enter Britain in modern times.
15 Men talk and interrupt more than women in mixed sex conversations.

* *Answers are at the end of this chapter.*

Summary

Prejudice and stereotyping result from preconceived, inaccurate and simplistic views of other people. These views are reinforced by society and by sloppiness and inertia within management practices.

Equal opportunity involves the identification and removal of barriers to achievement. People may be denied the right of opportunity to a broad and balanced curriculum, common educational experiences, teacher expertise and choice through inappropriate institutional processes, poor attitudes of teaching staff or a lack of value and respect for some types of courses and students. A sound equal opportunities policy tends to promote higher standards for more students and improved institutional management.

Various forms of discrimination may be alleviated by:

- sensitive and inclusive use of language and images;
- thoughtful allocation of teacher time;
- provision of appropriate role models;
- inclusion of the aspects of a subject relevant to various groups within its teaching;
- the thoughtful allocation of technological resources;
- use of varied teaching and learning methods, including cooperative methods;
- examining all factors that contribute to the difficulties students face;
- extending students' personal knowledge of the issues of relevance to various groups (e.g. principles of self-advocacy, particular cultures);
- enabling students to assess their needs and strategies to solve problems they face;
- exploring their own negative and positive stereotypes.

More mature people are wishing to study within further and higher education in Britain. They can be supported by recognition of the skills that they have acquired, a willingness to adapt organizational arrangements and the provision of study skill support.

Gender refers to socially ascribed sex roles. These can be influenced by educational institutions. Stereotyping disadvantages women and men by restricting their choices and limiting their repertoire for action. Women face a variety of hurdles within education and society, including notions of the 'right' age, having a career break and a lack of geographical mobility. Women are underrepresented in senior posts within further and higher education.

Discrimination on the basis of race is common within education. It is as much an issue in mainly white colleges and universities as in more urban multiracial situations. Institutional racism is usually the result of management practices suitable for a homogeneous society remaining unexamined. Institutions should have policies which permeate all aspects of their work.

People are disabled by society, rather than by their condition. Universities and colleges routinely discriminate against people with special educational needs. Those such as the Open University who make efforts to meet their needs find there is a steady and increasing demand. The debate today is about segregated versus integrated provision. Integrated provision creates management problems, but enables students to experience full curriculum choices, specialized subject teaching and social experience.

Exceptional ability is relatively common and must be recognized and nurtured by good teaching. It will be found in many aspects and subjects, in courses at all levels and among groups traditionally disadvantaged by education. Students with exceptional ability in a particular area may find it difficult to ask for and accept help in other areas. Tutors should develop skills in recognizing exceptional ability.

Equal opportunities policies should encompass students, staff, the curriculum and institutional ethos. The ethos of an institution is a matter of will and direction as much as resources.

Entry for the Reflective Diary

Write about the aspects of equal opportunities with which you feel most and least comfortable.

What are the sources of your comfort or discomfort?
Discuss these with a trusted colleague who has some knowledge and expertise in the areas identified.

Write about your reflections on this conversation.

Identify what skills, attitudes or knowledge you need to develop in order to improve your practice in relation to equal opportunities.
Draw up an action plan to develop these skills, attitudes or knowledge.

References

ACKER, S. and PIPER, D.W. (1984) *Is Higher Education Fair to Women?* Guildford, SHRE and NFER–Nelson.

ADELMAN, C. (1991) *Women at Thirtysomething: Paradoxes of Attainment*, Office of Research, Washington DC, US Department of Education.

ASHCROFT, K. and PEACOCK, E. (1993) 'An evaluation of the progress, experience and employability of mature students on the BEd course at Westminster College, Oxford', *Assessment and Evaluation in Higher Education*, **18**, 1, pp. 57–70.

BIGGER, S., ASHCROFT, K., GIBB, M. and PAULIN, G. (1990) *A Fair Deal for All: Equal Opportunities in School*, Oxford, Westminster College and Oxfordshire LEA.

DES (1989) *The National Curriculum: From Policy to Practice*, London, DES.

DES (1991) *Higher Education: A New Framework*, London, HMSO.

DEEM, R. (1984) 'Block 6', *Gender, Race and Education: Unit 26*, E205, Milton Keynes, Open University Press.

DELAMONT, S. (1990) *Sex Roles and the Schools*, 2nd Edn, London, Routledge.

DINTON, C. and POSTLETHWAITE, K. (1985) *Able Children: Identifying Them in the Classroom*, Windsor, NFER–Nelson.

DOUGLAS, J.W.B. (1967) *The Home and the School: A Study of Ability and Attainment in the Primary School*, St Albans, Panther.

EQUAL OPPORTUNITIES COMMISSION (1985) *Equal Opportunities in Post-School Education: Guidelines for the Elimination of Sex Discrimination and the Promotion of Equal Opportunities in Further and Higher Education*, Manchester, EOC.

FURTHER EDUCATION STAFF COLLEGE (FESC) (1987) *Coombe Lodge Report: Women in Further and Higher Education Management*, Bristol, FESC.

FURTHER EDUCATION UNIT (1990) *Developing Self-Advocacy Skills with People with Disabilities and Learning Difficulties*, London, FEU.

HMI (1989) *A Survey of Prevocational and Non General Certificate of Secondary Education Provision 14–16 Year Olds in Five Schools in Leicestershire and Lincolnshire*, Stanford, DES.

HMI (1990) *Modern Lanuages in Business and Management Courses in Further Education*, Stanford, DES.

HMI (1991) *Higher Education in Further Education Colleges*, Stanford, DES.

HMI (1992) *Aspects of Community Education in the London Borough of Hammersmith and Fullan*, Stanford, DES.

INNER LONDON EDUCATION AUTHORITY (ILEA) (1985) *Implementing the ILEA's Anti-Sexist Policy*, London, ILEA.

KELLY, A. (1984) *Girls into Science: Final Report*, Manchester, Manchester University Press.

KELLY, A. (1981) *The Missing Half: Girls and Science Education*, Manchester, Manchester University Press.

MacKAY, R. (1991) *Woman Managers: The Untapped Resource*, London, Kogan Paul.

McCRUM, N.G. (1994) 'The academic gender difference at Oxford and Cambridge', *Oxford Review of Education*, **20**, 1, pp. 3–26.

NATIONAL ADVISORY GROUP FOR PUBLIC SECTOR HIGHER EDUCATION (NAB) (1988) *Action for Access, Equal Opportunities Group*, London, NAB.

OGILVIE, E. (1973) *Gifted Children in Primary Schools: The Report of the Schools Council Enquiry into the Teaching of Gifted Children of Primary Age*, London, Macmillan.

OPEN UNIVERSITY (1993) *An Equal Opportunities Guide to Language and Image*, Buckingham, Open University Press.

SMITHERS, A. and ROBINSON, P. (1989) *Increasing Partnership in Higher Education*, London, BP Education Service.

THE SWANN REPORT (1985) *Education for All: The Report of the Committee of Enquiry into the Education of Children from Ethnic Minority Groups*, London, HMSO.

WARNOCK, H.M. (1978) *Special Educational Needs: Report of the Committee of Enquiry into the Education of Handicapped Children and Young People*, London, HMSO.

Suggested Reading

FURTHER EDUCATION UNIT (1993) *Planning FE: Equal Opportunities for People with Disabilities or Special Educational Needs: A Handbook*, London, FEU.
A summary of the key issues which create or hinder opportunities and the steps a college could take to respond to new opportunities for meeting the needs of people with a range of disabilities.
FURTHER EDUCATION UNIT (1993) *Implementing Multicultural and Anti-Racist Education in Mainly White Colleges*, London, FEU.
A report of a project exploring ways in which multicultural and anti-racist curriculum changes might be put into action in colleges with few students and staff from ethnic minorities.
LEWIS, V. and HABESHAW, S. (1990) *53 Interesting Ways to Promote Equal Opportunities in Education*, Bristol, Technical and Educational Services.
This contains a list of practical, simple steps a tutor can take to promote equal opportunities in their own teaching. It is fine if you want a list of things to do, but limited if you are interested in exploring the underlying issues a little further. The effects of each of the ideas could be usefully monitored in conjunction with the research instruments contained in Kate Myres book *Genderwatch*.
MYRES, K. (1992) *Genderwatch: After the Educational Reform Act*, Cambridge, Cambridge University Press.
This is a short readable guide. It takes as its starting point the notion that tutors can develop their own practice by collecting evidence as to the effects of their strategies and actions and reflecting upon it before embarking on a new round of action and monitoring. It contains a number of very simple instruments for collecting action research data on your own practice, which could be adapted to apply to equal opportunities in relation to race, disability and age as well as gender.
OPEN UNIVERSITY (1993) *An Equal Opportunities Guide to Language and Image*, Buckingham, Open University Press.
This is a short leaflet (19 pages), which is useful as an introduction to the main issues involved in the role of language in equal opportunities. It covers age, cultural diversity, disability, gender and sexual orientation. It has an excellent reading list for those who wish to follow up this aspect.

The answer to all the questions in the quiz is TRUE.

Chapter 10

The Evaluation of the Teaching and Learning Process

Introduction

Evaluation is one the most important tools available to you in the development of your teaching and your ability to facilitate your students' learning. Good quality evaluation requires that you develop and practice a range of techniques. Evaluation is a dynamic process, by which you exercise and develop skills and qualities of reflective teaching and in doing so perhaps come to define them differently.

The reflective practitioner model is evaluation led. It has been stated earlier in the book that reflective practice is much more than a process of 'thinking about', that it involves the systematic collection of evidence and the seeking out of alternative perspectives on that evidence. Evaluation is therefore the starting point for reflective action. It is the process by which you review the field of action for your planning, including your analysis of the students' interests and needs; the resources available to meet those needs; and the alternative teaching and learning methods that you might employ. As a reflective practitioner, evaluation should also be incorporated into the action phase of your teaching. As you teach and as the students learn, you will be collecting evidence as to the effects and effectiveness of your and their approaches. Ideally this data should be recorded and ordered, so that it can form a basis for reflection and further planning. In order to ensure that your planning and action are as informed as possible it is likely that periodically you will wish to collect data in a more systematic way.

Thus evaluation should be formative and summative. It includes the collection of data in 'quick and dirty' ways and also more focused, ordered and systematic collection. The important thing is that this data can best become 'evidence' through a process of ordering, organization, discussion and reflection with colleagues.

The processes of deep and thorough evaluation and its honest interpretation almost inevitably leads to pain. You are likely to find aspects of your teaching and your students' reaction to it which challenge your assumptions about the kind of teacher and person you are. You are likely to be disappointed and disheartened on occasions. On the other hand, we have found that there are compensations, for instance when evaluation has pointed the way to a redefinition of a particular problem that enabled us to transform it into an opportunity.

In any case, as a reflective teacher you will be committed to evaluation, since evaluation, based on real data, is central to open-mindedness. It gives you access to the perspectives and viewpoints of others, so that you can re-examine your own actions, values and understanding. In addition, it provides the means by which you can look at the long and short-term consequences of your actions. If you are to develop the quality of responsibility, you will need to focus your evaluation beyond the notion of 'what works' to questions of worthwhileness.

Perhaps above all, evaluation enables you to develop the quality of wholeheartedness. It is the means by which you can continue your search for better practice and for more appropriate definitions of best practice.

Enquiry Task 10.1

Do you know:

- what internal or external requirements exist for evaluation of courses you teach;
- how teaching quality is assessed in your department;
- the departmental 'norms' as to frequency and thoroughness of evaluation;
- whether there are particular groups whose interests it is important you meet in the future (e.g. women students, employers)?

Find out the answers to any questions where you are unsure.

Purposes of Evaluation

There has been a shift in responsibility for quality assurance from the mid-1980s in Britain, for instance, from local education authorities and the Council for National Academic Awards, to institutions themselves. Tutors in universities and colleges, unlike those in schools, have not been shorn of their traditional curriculum and pedagogic autonomy. Even where outside bodies specify outcomes, such as the National Council for Vocational Qualifications and the Council for the Accreditation for Teacher Education, it is increasingly the case that the curriculum and its management are left to institutions to determine. This has led to evaluation at institutional and tutor level becoming more central to the quality of student experience.

With the introduction of student charters, students' expectations of evaluation as it relates to their particular needs and interests are likely to be raised. This is not a new phenomenon. Silver (1992) points out that the British government's policy since the 1980s has been to redefine students as consumers or clients and therefore to increase interest in ascertaining their views.

Evaluation can fulfil a variety of purposes. Student and other feedback may be collected for different purposes: accountability, to provide information on institutional performance indicators, to enhance students' self-assessment, professional development and so on. There is some overlap between these purposes. For instance, the tutor, the institution and the students' purposes may be served by evaluation that refers to course objectives and institutional mission. On other occasions they conflict, however. For instance, evaluation focused on the professional development of the tutor may not yield information of use to the institution in its relationship with the funding body.

Commonly, evaluation is used to provide the tutor with more or less instant feedback on how a course is being received by the students. This might include particular aspects of a course, such as individual modules or work experience elements, or the course as a whole. On the other hand you may be interested in exploring your teaching and the students' learning at a different level. For instance, you may be interested in discovering your students' approaches to learning and the appropriateness of these approaches, or you may wish to use self-evaluation as an aid to your students' thinking.

Thus you may be interested in assessing the general effectiveness of a course or you may wish to evaluate a specific issue. Some departments now specify focuses for evaluation (for example, the use of information technology or equal opportunities), and require all courses to look at those aspects over a particular year. Where this is not the case, you may yourself decide to focus on particular aspects of your teaching such as: its relationship to the course objectives, the appropriateness of the content, comparisons of the value of particular elements, aspects that are of importance to your students, or you may wish to check a particular hypothesis or collect data about a particular problem.

Nixon (1992, p. 4) points out that evaluation can take a variety of forms on a continuum from 'measurable quantifiable data at one extreme, to a naturalistic description of complex social settings at the other'. He defines some of the purposes of evaluation in rather different terms. He suggests that evaluation may be about sharing understandings with colleagues and students, alerting the team to potential problems, challenging the accepted practice or dominant hegemony, or stabilizing development and confirming insights gained. It may be directed at influencing practice in terms of teaching quality, policy making or student achievement. Evaluation directed at one of the aspects above is quite likely to produce data which requires action in another. Individuals may use evaluative data for their personal development or for micropolitical purposes directed at change within the institution, such as informing, explaining or persuading.

McCormick and James (1988) point out that evaluation may be carried out by 'insiders' or 'outsiders' depending upon its scope and purpose. Outsiders may be specially commissioned or imposed (e.g. OFSTED (Office for Standards in Education) inspections in the UK). Insiders can include teaching team members or institutional managers. In this chapter we will focus on insider evaluation, mainly conducted at the tutor level.

Central to many evaluation issues is the notion of 'fitness for purpose'. Evaluation systems should fit the various purposes intended for them. The evaluation methods and instruments you choose should yield the information you need and the evaluation itself should reveal the extent to which the teaching and learning process fits the purposes of the various interest groups and your own theories of teaching. The final aim of evaluation should be to make this 'fit' more exact.

Enquiry Task 10.2

With what evaluation have you been involved?

Can you match its purposes and the methods employed?

Purpose   *Method*
Purpose 1
Purpose 2
Purpose 3
. . .

How might the evaluation been improved?

Models of Evaluation

Lloyd-Jones *et al.* (1985) describe a model involving the identification of actual and anticipated outcomes, but also the nature, value and desirability of these outcomes. This model of evaluation is highly compatible with the reflective practitioner model with its emphasis on education as a moral enterprise.

Heathcote *et al.* (1982) describes educational evaluation as a process that relates to the identification, description and appraisal of the effects and effectiveness of all aspects of teaching. It should therefore include all educational strategies, approaches and content, not merely those which have undergone recent change. They point to two focuses of evaluation: the student and their learning; and the wider context of education. This context includes the teachers, the teaching methods and the learning environment. The learning environment will include the immediate institutional setting and its available resources, but also those of the local community and the economic and political climate as it affects education. Thus evaluation may be concerned with the appraisal of the whole learning situation. It differs from assessment, which concerns only the assessment of the students' learning performance. Assessment results are only one aspect of evaluation.

This is an important point to keep in mind if you are working in one of the areas that are increasingly focused on 'learning outcomes'. A competency-based approach can lead to the evaluation being entirely focused upon the question of whether the students performed in particular ways, Questions such as whether that performance is worthwhile, whether the definitions of 'competence' are accurate, whether the defined competences are adequate for a course at that level, whether the particular competency approach is meeting student needs, whether there have been fortunate or unfortunate unanticipated inputs, processes or outcomes may not be explored. In particular, it can be tempting in these circumstances to focus on what is taught, rather than what ought to be taught. The National Institute of Adult Continuing Education (1991) points out that the values and ethos implied by particular competences, and the extent that these are compatible with the ethos of a subject or a profession provide an appropriate starting point for evaluation.

When you evaluate a course, you may need to consider aspects of the delivery that may have turned out differently from that which you anticipated. In particular, you may need to think about and perhaps assess what you anticipated and what actually happened before the course started (such things as resources allocated, student qualification and so on), what happened during the course and what outcomes there were. Where there are differences between what you anticipated and what actually happened, you may need to assess whether these differences are desirable or undesirable.

The first of these issues, the anticipated and unanticipated antecedents to a course, is often ignored, but can raise important issues. For instance, McDowell (1991) points out that students do not come to a course as 'blank slates' but arrive with their own expectations, motives and intentions. These may well be modified by later experiences, but nevertheless they provide a framework from which students make judgments when asked to evaluate your teaching. Second, many have a strong 'vocational' orientation, but have different interpretations of this. Students are thus likely to be influenced by their own definitions in the ways that they view the relevance of aspects of the content of courses (such as theories of practice in professional courses). In addition, students come with their own experiences, self-images, anxieties and feelings about the course. For instance, if the course was a second choice, or if they have arrived by an unconventional route students may place particular value and status on the course and this may influence their evaluation.

In considering evaluation, it is often desirable to identify the groups who are to benefit from evaluation and to recognize that their interests may sometimes conflict. One group who will have a strong interest in the education you provide are the consumers. In most cases these will be your students, but in the longer term, they may include employers. For the student, the benefits associated with studying a course may cover a much wider range than that encapsulated in the teaching. Additional benefits may include aspects such as social possibilities, which may be facilitated, or not, by the course and your teaching.

The second interest group are the providers of education. This includes yourself as a teacher, but also those in the establishment hierarchy. There may be some overlap of interests, for instance the desirability of a 'good' reputation, meeting the aims of the course or professionalism. However, there may also be substantial differences in priorities. For example, you may wish to maximize the resources allocated to your course but your managers may wish you to economize. Alternatively, you may be particularly interested in helping weaker students to develop to their full potential, while institutional managers see success in terms of tangible performance indicators that can be publicized. There are likely to be substantial differences when it comes to more subjective matters, such as task satisfaction. Teachers and students may also have hidden and individual priorities, many of which may be related to the preservation of 'self'. These differences may give rise to dilemmas, and the way that these are recognized and resolved will have effects on how each evaluates the 'success' of the course.

Some people may wish to use the evaluative data for a variety of political purposes. Some of these may be legitimate (but not unproblematic), such as reassuring funding bodies that their money is well spent. Other political purposes may be less legitimate, for instance, a manager may use evaluative data as a way of comparing one tutor's performance with that of another. This point is dealt with in more detail below.

Amongst the more overtly political purposes of evaluation is demonstrating that quality assurance systems are operating. This aspect is receiving more attention in the recent literature. For instance, Pollitt (1990) criticizes much practice in evaluation because it emphasizes professional development at the expense of wider public accountability. Despite much of the rhetoric surrounding quality assurance, it may be that political purposes encourage the evaluator to seek out data that indicates that the present practice is appropriate. Thus, political purposes may be inimical to developmental purposes. If you genuinely wish to improve your own and your students' performance, you will try and seek out weaknesses as well as strengths. You are more likely to feel secure in this process if you can be sure that this information will be used for its intended, formative purpose and not used in evidence to form a summative judgment against you or your institution.

Enquiry Task 10.3

What performance indicators could be used to judge the quality of courses, teaching and departments?

Performance Indicators

A course you teach
Performance indicator 1
Performance indicator 2
Performance indicator 3
. . .

Your teaching
Performance indicator 1
Performance indicator 2
Performance indicator 3
. . .

Your department
Performance indicator 1
Performance indicator 2
Performance indicator 3
. . .

Which of these performance indicators might be of interest to:

the funding council;
employers;
institutional managers;
other tutors;
you;
your student?

Issues in Evaluation

Gibbs *et al.* (1988) points out that the results of any evaluation will be influenced by its setting. Large group teaching will generally produce lower ratings for 'teaching effectiveness' than small group settings. Optional courses will tend to be better received than compulsory elements. Students' ratings of the same quality of teaching may be lower at the start of their course, when they are feeling insecure and perhaps confused. Later in the course, those who were totally unable to cope have left, and those that remain are likely to have got to grips with studying at that level.

The effect of context upon student ratings require that results are carefully interpreted. This makes it vital that the purpose and audience of the results of a survey are clear. If senior managers have access to the results of student evaluation of your teaching, and if they fail to take into account the context, you may find yourself unfairly advantaged or disadvantaged. This problem will be compounded in systems that use the results of student feedback to make formal or informal comparisons of tutors. There is increasing pressure on institutional managers to use these kinds of ratings in the allocation of performance related pay. They may be loath to add an interpretation in the light of contextual factors, fearing that this may be seen as 'subjective'. Unfortunately, some may prefer 'objective' data that they know to be structurally flawed.

One of the centrally important issues in evaluation is the extent that students are able to express their views with privacy. Some tutors delude themselves into believing that their relationships with students are so strong that the students will not mind telling them uncomfortable truths. Perhaps they forget how difficult most of us find it to tell anyone, even a close friend, that there is an aspect of their behaviour which we would like changed. The power differential between the students and the tutor can cause students additional problems. Should a tutor not accept a criticism, she or he may have real opportunities to do the student harm. At the most basic level, students may be very dependent upon the tutor liking them.

Evaluation should involve you in triangulation, in checking your impressions of student wants and needs against other sets of data. If you evaluate with no outside or anonymous voice, you will probably end up checking your impressions against your impressions, and find, inevitably, that the data supports your impressions!

There are particular problems using student feedback collected incidentally in the course of your teaching as your only evaluative data. In particular, students may not be aware that they are giving feedback, rather than just having a conversation, and so may not make considered responses. Any responses that they do make are liable to be socially acceptable, rather than painfully honest. In this situation, the tutor is totally in control of what feedback they consider 'relevant'. Data is collected when it arises. This may lead to unconscious selection.

Some of the problems outlined above can also apply to more systematic methods of data collection, where the student is not able to provide the data anonymously, or at least without fear of being identified by the tutor whose work they are evaluating.

When embarking on evaluation there are a variety of practical considerations to take into account. These include decisions as to the scope of the evaluation and the amount of data to be collected. Evaluation may be focused on a smaller or greater number of people and on a smaller or greater number of issues. With regard to the latter, you may need to decide whether to study a limited number of specifically intended goals, or try to encompass all goals without preconceived ideas about which ones were intended or not. You may have a hypothesis you wish to test. Alternatively it is sometimes very useful to undertake 'goal free' evaluation to look at 'what is'. On occasions, this is likely to surprise you.

You will need to decide what exactly you are evaluating. You may be concerned with processes or products: that is, with transactions that take place during teaching or with the products at the end of teaching. (Products might include the type of student learning identified or more specific things such as the quality of essays or examination scripts.) This may influence whether the evaluation should be concurrent to provide feedback on a project as it is in action, or summative.

You will need to make choices as to who will provide feedback. You may wish to involve students, tutors teaching with you, institutional managers or employers.

Enquiry Task 10.4

You may have a hunch that something is working well or badly on your course. In order to check out whether you are right:

- brainstorm a list of brief statements that describe the situation (or its opposite) from the students' point of view;
- list them on a questionnaire;
- create a rating scale for your students to complete.

For example:

		Strongly Agree	Agree	Neutral	Disagree	Strongly Disagree
1	I find the reading for the course too easy.					
2	The course is sufficiently challenging.					
3	etc.					

Evaluation Methods

If you believe that evaluation should yield data that you can count, tabulate and compare, you will have to face all the shortcomings and problems of quantitative research in education. Variables can seldom be isolated, the situation is dynamic and subjectivity must enter into decisions about categories or questions. You might seek to collect data in the form of 'stories' that describe what is going on in the participants' own words. This qualitative approach allows the complexity of the teaching and learning situation to be described, but leaves even more room for interpretation and self-deception. Perhaps you should not expect evaluation data to reveal 'the truth' but rather to indicate areas upon which you should focus, reflect, and perhaps change.

Gibbs *et al.* (1988) describe many of the methods available to evaluate your teaching and the students' learning. Each has its strengths and weaknesses. For instance, the questionnaire may be useful as a quick check on how you and the students are doing. They can get at at perceptions of behaviour but not at the behaviour itself. In addition, they have the added problem of giving the impression of some sort of 'objectivity'. In practice, a questionnaire seldom produces objective data. Generally, the questions are chosen and formulated in the light of the values of the person who devised them. Gibbs *et al.* assume that this is a bad thing. On the other hand, if you are interested in exploring the relationship between your espoused values and those that are actualized in your teaching, provided it is recognized, this subjectivity may not be a real obstacle to you improving your teaching.

Questionnaires may incorporate scales that demonstrate the subjective importance of the item or the strength of feeling about it. They can contain open or closed questions, depending on your purpose, the depth of your investigation and the number of student responses you wish to analyse. Closed questions have a limited range of information, but the data is easy to access and so, perhaps, less subject to bias. Open questionnaires can get at shades of opinion, but the sheer volume of data yielded may make analysis overly time consuming.

The anonymous questionnaire can enable students to react reasonably honestly, but questionnaires and interviews share many of the the same problems of interpretation. In particular, the students' answers will be filtered through their value system and the meanings that they ascribe to your questions. These meanings may be at a variety of levels from the direct decoding of the words on the page, through to an interpretation of the model of teaching and learning which they imply.

Interviews may be used for a variety of purposes. They can be used to collect the main data for the evaluation. Alternatively they can be used to help you to identify issues for inclusion in a questionnaire, they may be a useful preliminary to a group discussion or they may be necessary to clarify the results. They tend to be time consuming to undertake, so it is as well to be sure that the interview is the only way to collect the data, and that you (rather than perhaps the students) are the best person to undertake the interview.

Interviews and discussion can take place with individuals or with groups. Group discussion can be helpful in enabling you to gain a large quantity of qualitative feedback from a number of students in a relatively short time. It is possible to use group discussion in quite large groups. You can get students to discuss particular issues in small groups and to report back to larger groups. The larger group may then be required to identify the most central issues to be reported to the whole group. The difficulty with this method, and with most group methods, is that the results may reflect the views of the vocal members of the group. Strong feelings held by less assertive students may be missed.

Nominal group technique (NGT) can help to overcome this problem and create a feeling of commitment and ownership of the evaluation among the students. In addition, questionnaire and interview agendas set by the tutor may well fail to get at student concerns. Nominal group technique is just one method that gets the students themselves to set the agenda without dominant students intimidating the rest.

In NGT, the tutor sets very general questions for the students to consider, such as 'What helped me to learn from the course?' and 'What hindered my learning from the course?' Students spend a few minutes individually brainstorming the answers to these questions. Each student's complete list of 'helpful' and 'unhelpful' factors is read out and the tutor records them onto a flip chart. Duplicated items are crossed out at the end of this process. The tutor asks for clarification of ambiguous factors, so that the meaning is clear to all. Each factor is numbered, and each student individually ranks them in order of importance. From an analysis of the replies, you can discover the issues that are significant to many students. For instance, if 100 per cent of the students rank 'clashing hand-in dates for assignments' first, you can have confidence that this is a real issue for the course and not just a problem for a few disorganized individuals. There are a number of variants of this technique (see Gibbs *et al.*, 1988, pp. 77–79).

The ground rules for NGT are important. For instance, no other student may speak apart from the student being addressed by the tutor; the tutor will not evaluate ideas that emerge, but merely record them and ask for clarification as to their meaning where there is ambiguity; and no tutor or student must be named. We have found that with a group of about thirty students, the process takes about one hour.

Because the agenda is so open. NGT is like goal-free evaluation in that any item that is of concern for students is legitimate. The results can be quite surprising, interesting, useful and in some cases, upsetting. It is important, therefore, to use the results as a basis for further discussion with students to find out if criticisms are due to temporary or localized events, rather than anything fundamental. An important aspect of NGT is that, if legitimate problems are unearthed, action of some sort should be taken.

Enquiry Task 10.5

With reference to a course you are teaching, brainstorm your own answers to the general questions, based on your knowledge of a particular student group. For example:

'What do my students find straightforward on the course?'
'What do my students find difficult on the course?'
'What ought to be changed on the course?'
'What ought to stay unchanged on the course?'
'What is valuable on the course?'
'What is least valuable on the course?'

Use NGT to find out if your hunches about student opinion were right.

There are a variety of less elaborate and quicker student centred techniques, which provide a useful alternative to the usual tutor centred evaluation. For instance, you could prepare large sheets of paper to pin on the wall with a main heading on each (e.g. 'About the teaching', 'About the content', 'About the assessment') and columns down the right hand side headed by a three or five point rating scale (e.g. Strongly Agree, Agree, Neutral, Disagree, Strongly Disagree). Groups of five or six students can each be given one of the main headings and be asked to design unambiguous statements. It is as well to ask them to make the statements positive. For instance, they may want to indicate that the session or course was rather boring, in which case they might include a statement such as 'I found the course very interesting'. You can explain that, when it comes to the rating, they can indicate their feelings by strongly disagreeing with it. When each group have created three or four statements, they can be written on appropriate sheets. These then are pinned on the wall and the students move around the room ticking the column that most accurately reflects their feelings about each statement.

The beauty of this technique is that you end up with ready tabulated results and it can be used with almost any number of students. One of us has managed a group of over 100 students in a one hour session, by dividing the main group into twenty-one subgroups and providing each subgroup with their own headed piece of large paper. She managed to find seven issues worth exploring, and so three groups worked on each of them. After these groups had formulated their questions, each set of three groups got together to amalgamate questions with major overlaps, before the questions were written on the master sheets. This 'pyramid' technique can be adapted to other forms of group feedback. However, like most group methods, it is open to some degree to domination by more vocal group members.

Whether you use student centred or tutor centred evaluation may depend to some extent on whether the course you wish to evaluate has a fixed syllabus and predetermined competences or whether it is designed to be responsive to students' needs and levels. Increasingly, institutions are experimenting with responsive courses. Some of these have a negotiated syllabus, which depends upon an evaluation of the students' interests and needs. If this is not undertaken carefully there is a danger that the dominant students' interests are met at the expense of those of the others.

Teaching and learning logs can be a useful starting point to evaluation. If you have been undertaking the enquiry tasks and reflective diary entries in this book, you will have been completing one of the more elaborate forms of learning log. Student learning logs can be useful for both you and the student to access the quality of the learning and your facilitation of that learning. You may ask students to interact with the course material and their feelings about it in various ways. Alternatively, you may wish to focus on the students' use of time or other study habits.

Some institutions believe that student representation on key committees or the creation of a consultative committee can be an alternative to other forms of student feedback (Silver, 1992). While this representation and consultation may be useful for other purposes, or good in its own right, it suffers from inherent weaknesses as a means of evaluation. The student members are unlikely to be numerous enough to reflect accurately the views of the student body as a whole. Representatives may try to collect feedback themselves, but are unlikely to have the resources, opportunity or skill to do so in a systematic way. Thus, the feedback obtained is likely to be very partial and to reflect the views of a vocal minority.

With samples of less than twenty students, whatever the method you use to evaluate your teaching, results may be valid for the group but difficult to generalize from. Whatever method you use you may bias student response by the way it is administered. Perhaps the best method is to triangulate with more than one method. For this reason, it may be useful to collect your own responses and those of colleagues involved in the course in a systematic way, and give them due weight. We have found that systematic collection of tutor views is often ignored because 'we know what the other tutors think'.

There is no point in collecting data unless you intend acting on them and unless the data are accurate and accessible. Generally you will get a more accurate and representative set of data if those from whom you have collected it (especially the students) believe you will act on it. It is worthwhile taking trouble over this aspect. For example, we usually tell our students that they will have access to the published results of their evaluation and the action plan that results from the full evaluation.

McCormick and James (1988) describe other rather ingenious ways of collecting evidence about teaching and learning. These include looking for physical traces of learning, such as wear in particular books or library records of their use. The unintended curriculum can be explored through content analysis of student work, course documents and curriculum materials. We have never explored this method, mainly because it looks rather time-consuming relative to the amount of data it might yield and compared with more direct ways of collecting evidence.

Ex-students can have a particular perspective on the courses they have experienced. If your teaching is designed in some way to prepare your students for the world of work or for further study, it is possible that the best way to assess its efficacy is to question them after they have left. In addition, you may have introduced students to complex or challenging ideas, which they found difficult at the time, in the hope that they will provide a sound basis for later development. On the other hand, you may be more interested in following up students who have dropped out of the course. In each of these cases, many of the techniques outlined above may be used. Silver (1992) found that exit surveys and telephone interviews could be particularly valuable.

Finally, as reflective tutors, we believe that it is valuable to discuss the results of any evaluation exercise with colleagues.

Enquiry Task 10.6

List methods you might use to collect data on your teaching and on the students' responses to it.

What are the advantages and disadvantages of each method?

	Advantages	*Disadvantages*
Yes/no questionnaire		
Questionnaire with 1 to 5 rating scale		
Open-ended questionnaire		
Structured interview		
etc.		

Add to your list in the light of a discussion with an experienced colleague.

Observation of Teaching

You may wish to have your teaching observed for a variety of reasons. For instance, you may need a second opinion on a problem. Alternatively, you may want general feedback on your effectiveness. The observation of teaching involves many issues. You may be happy for a peer to observe your teaching, provided you like that person and you trust them to share their results only with you, but be less happy about observation that is a compulsory part of an appraisal process.

Whether observation of teaching is voluntary or not, you may be able to impose a structure on it, to make it meet your purposes and enable you to use it as an aid to the development of your teaching. If the observation is imposed centrally, you may be able to suggest an observer you could trust and a focus you would find helpful.

Your teaching can be observed by a peer, by a superior, by a student or by yourself. One of the easiest ways to observe yourself is to set up a video camera or an audiotape recorder. One of us has found video to be the most useful and now aims to video her teaching at least once a year. Viewed privately or with a colleague (and sometimes with huge embarrassment), she has always learnt something new about her teaching. She asked a colleague or student to hold a small hand-held, self-focusing camera on their knee with the eye piece upwards so that they can check that it remains pointing in the right direction.

Observation of teaching can be undertaken in various ways. Fly on the wall observation can be very revealing. This is the technique where everything seen is noted in an uncritical stream of consciousness which can be interpreted later. On the other hand, more structured schedules can help you to focus on particular issues, such as the amount of attention you give to particular students, the quality of your questioning or the amount that you dominate and initiate ideas.

Enquiry Task 10.7

List the ground rules that are necessary to make the observation and appraisal of your teaching acceptable in the following circumstances:

                             Ground Rules

Peer appraisal:
Ground rule 1   eg: I decide on who may appraise me.
Ground rule 2
Ground rule 3
. . .

'Top down' appraisal
Ground rule 1   eg: I know and agree with the criteria which
                                    will be used to appraise me.
Ground rule 2
Ground rule 3
. . .

The Design of Evaluation Instruments

There are a wide variety of questions that may be addressed before any research instrument is designed. Most importantly, you will need to identify precisely the areas you intend to be addressed by the evaluation. These areas may include aspects such as learning outcomes, assessment, teaching materials and documentation, teacher guidance, relevance of content and so on. For instance, the Council for National Academic Awards (1992) suggests that if you take a holistic view of education, you should be interested in evaluating the profiling system for your students.

Once the main areas are established, specific questions will be formulated. For instance, if you wish to investigate the assessment scheme, you might ask whether your students share the same understandings of the meanings and purposes of the learning outcomes, whether the assessments meet these purposes, whether the students are clear as to the criteria, whether the criteria are relevant to their needs and stage of development, and so on.

Schratz (1992) points out a range of possible research instruments, from the 'quick and dirty' (e.g. asking students to give quick written feedback to one or two verbal questions), to unsophisticated but useful methods (e.g. asking an outsider to discuss with groups of your students their impressions of the taught course) to more elaborate ideas but which still require limited research skills (e.g. asking students to keep a personal journal, or keeping one yourself) to instruments that require some expertise in their design such as questionnaires.

Questionnaires may include specific questions, requiring focused or multiple choice responses, or open responses. Sentence completion is one way of providing for a more open response that can protect you from being overwhelmed with data.

Silver (1992) found that questionnaires are the most commonly used of the formal methods for collecting student feedback. The successful use of questionnaires depends upon the ability to ask appropriate questions that will yield reliable and usable answers.

We have found that specific questions or statements tend to yield data that is more useful and usable in course and personal development. For instance, questions such as 'Do you think the course was worthwhile?' are unlikely to lead to specific indicators for action. A question such as 'What aspects should be retained in next year's course?' may be more helpful. Questions should be direct and simple, with no more than one thought or issue per question. It is generally a good idea to avoid conditional clauses or negative questions. Students are generally quick to spot and respond poorly to value-laden questions or those that have socially acceptable answers. On the whole, you may get a more representative sample if questionnaires are issued and collected in the course of a single timetabled session.

You do not have to make up questionnaires from scratch. Indeed if you are inexperienced in this kind of research, it may be better to use or adapt one of the published questionnaires on the market. Gibbs *et al.* (1988) provide a fair selection that you can copy or use as models for your own purposes.

Interviews may be structured, semi-structured or unstructured. If unstructured interviews are conducted as an everyday conversation, they are likely to yield fairly random data. The 'feel' needs to be conversational, but the planning should be very thorough. You may need to plan open questions, clarifying questions and questions that lead to precise definitions of meaning. Strategies to keep the conversation 'on task' will be needed. Unstructured interviews can be useful as a first step to narrowing down on particular issues of interest to your students. You might consider interviewing students in groups for this purpose or interviewing course representatives. (Although, by their very nature, course representatives may not actually be representative of the views of the quieter students, unless *they* have collected views systematically.)

Structured interviews also need careful preparation. Many of the features of 'good' interview questions are in common with those of questionnaires. For instance, on the whole good questions contain only one idea, are clear, simple, neutral and non-judgmental. Semi-structured interviews allow follow-up and probing questions. These need particular care, in case they suggest criticism or an 'accepted' answer. Where you wish to touch on controversial issues, you may be successful if you start with a few 'warm up' questions of a non-controversial, descriptive kind.

The interview can be recorded in various ways. The simplest method is to take down the main points in note form and then read back your interpretation of what they have said to the interviewee. This is perfectly adequate for most purposes. Tape recording (provided there are no technical problems and it does not inhibit the interviewee) produces the most accurate record, but transcribing tapes is enormously time consuming, and then you are likely to have to summarize what was said in your own words in order to make the data manageable.

Observation of teaching involves decisions about the purpose of the study and the focus: student, tutor, or the interaction between the two. McCormick and James (1988) point out that if the observation is structured, the number and type of category will need to be decided as well as the frequency of recording, the period of observation and the number and selection of people to be observed.

Evaluation instruments should have some reliability and validity; that is they should be designed to measure or elicit what you claim they do. For instance, an interview schedule should be designed to reflect the respondent's views accurately, rather than to lead them to particular responses. Equally, you cannot claim that an interview with a small sample of students on a course represents the views of all the course members, nor can you claim that your observations of a teaching event are valid if the meanings of the observational categories are ambiguous. In addition, you should be careful not to claim more about your findings than they actually show. For instance, you cannot tell from a chat with a course representative that all the students on this course are discontented.

Structured observation schedules are difficult to devise and subject to a number of threats to their validity. Amongst these are problems of ensuring that the definitions of categories of behaviour remain stable during the observation (this is called construct validity), and of ensuring that the instrument measures what you intended it to (content validity). Structured observation is most likely to be of use where you have a highly specific question to ask or problem to solve, such as: 'Am I involving all members in the group in discussion?' 'Am I asking higher order questions of male and female students equally?' 'Am I distributing my time fairly?' If you are using the schedule as an aid to your thinking and reflection, and if you can discuss the difficulties of categorization and so on with the observer, these threats to validity should not detract too much from the learning you achieve. In any case, the amount of time you take in designing and validating any research instrument should be in proportion to its value to you in improving your teaching.

Enquiry Task 10.8

Design a questionnaire for collecting student feedback on a session or course you teach.

Look at the questions. Have you:

- included just one thought or idea in each question;
- avoided negatives;
- kept your sentences to fewer than twenty words;
- avoided value-laden questions;
- used any jargon or acronyms;
- kept the number of questions to a minimum;
- checked your questions with an experienced colleague to ensure they are unambiguous;
- a clear idea of how you will analyse your results?

The Organizational Framework for Evaluation

It seems that evaluation based on evidence, especially the systematic collection of student feedback on all courses, is increasingly becoming an institutional expectation (Silver, 1992). In some cases, institutions or departments have created centrally administered questionnaires. Some of these are directed at the needs of course evaluation, and some probe the students' views of the institution or department as a whole. In other cases there is a recommended 'model', but responsibility for modifying and conducting the evaluation is devolved to a greater or lesser extent.

If you have to operate a centrally determined evaluation, you may have suspicions as to its purposes and relevance. The format of the research instrument is likely to create difficulties in particular contexts and with particular students. In most institutions, students are taught in varying ways according to their needs, subject and level. To evaluate the experience of students with severe learning difficulties, those on a degree course, those on a lecture-based course and those on a workshop-based course using the same instrument may not be appropriate.

Where you and the students have some 'ownership' of the form and the focus of evaluation, you are more likely to see value in it. Evaluation can be time consuming and unless you see it as having relative value, compared with other demands on your time, you may be tempted to go through the motions.

The extent and frequency of any prescribed evaluation may affect tutors' perception of its relative value. Your feelings may be influenced by the balance you perceive between your own and your colleagues' control over a course, as against that of the department or the institution. The gradual elaboration of quality assurance mechanisms within institutions has led to a shift in that control towards the institution. The decisions about the focus and form of evaluation may be taken more or less close to the point of course delivery. Where these decisions are remote, they may sit uneasily beside the machinery for planning, implementation and monitoring of student learning at the course level. The degree of freedom over course content, methods and evaluation has important implications for reflective practitioners.

Summary

Evaluation is central to the reflective practitioner model. It may be summative or formative and more or less elaborate. The results of honest evaluation are likely to challenge your assumptions and lead to a development of your theories of teaching.

Evaluation may serve various purposes: accountability, information provision for managers, the enhancement of student self-assessment, and professional and course development. It may serve the interests of various groups: students, tutors, institutional managers, and employers. These interests and purposes sometimes conflict. Evaluation may be undertaken by insiders or outsiders.

Whatever the interests, purposes or method chosen, the important criterion is fitness for purpose.

All aspects of education and its context should be subject to evaluation. Evaluation may involve investigation into the anticipated and actual inputs, processes and outcomes of teaching and learning. Competency-based approaches to learning may encourage an exclusive focus on learning outcomes.

The results of any evaluation depend in part upon its context. This means that they should be interpreted with care. Particular problems will arise where such results are used to compare tutor with tutor. Exclusive reliance on data collected incidentally during teaching poses particular problems. Evaluation involving triangulation tends to be most useful.

Evaluation methods include individual and group techniques, student and tutor generated instruments, questionnaires, interviews, observation, teaching and learning logs, student representation on committees, and the analysis of students' work, course documents and materials. Each method has its advantages and disadvantages.

Ex-students can provide valuable data through telephone surveys and exit interviews.

The observation of teaching provides particular problems and opportunities. Professional development is more likely to be enhanced if such observation is voluntary. Observation may be structured or unstructured.

The design of an evaluation instrument demands more or less skill depending on how focused and elaborate it is. In general, questions or categories in evaluation instruments should be focused, unambiguous, clear, non-judgmental, non-value-laden and focus on the intended issues. It is vital to provide anonymity for students providing feedback.

The organizational framework for evaluation may determine the focus and type of evaluation. Where tutor and students have ownership of evaluation, educational and developmental purposes may be served better.

Entry for the Reflective Diary

Are you clear about these dichotomies?

Quantitative	——	Qualitative data collection methods
Hypothesis testing	——	Goal free evaluation
Tutor centred	——	Student centred evaluation
Bureaucratic	——	Developmental functions
Outcome focused	——	Process focused evaluation

Discuss any that you are unclear about with a colleague experienced in evaluation of educational research.

Write about how some of these dichotomies relate to your developing theory of teaching and learning.

References

COUNCIL FOR NATIONAL ACADEMIC AWARDS (1992) *Profiling in Higher Education: An Interim Report*, London, CNAA/DE.

GIBBS, G., HABESHAW, S. and HABESHAW T. (1988) *53 Interesting Ways to Appraise Your Teaching*, Bristol, Technical and Educational Services.

HEATHCOTE, G., KEMPA, R. and ROBERTS, I. (1982) *Curriculum Styles and Strategies*, London, FEU.

LLOYD-JONES, R., BRAY, E., JOHNSON, G. and CURRIES R. (Eds) (1985) *Assessment — From Principles to Action*, London, Macmillan.

MCCORMICK, R. and JAMES, M. (1988) *Curriculum Evaluation in Schools*, 2nd Edn London, Croom Helm.

MCDOWELL, L. (Ed) (1991) *Course Evaluation: Using Students' Experiences of Learning and Teaching*, Newcastle: Newcastle Polytechnic Marcet.

NATIONAL INSTITUTE OF ADULT CONTINUING EDUCATION (1991) *What Can Graduates Do: A Consultative Paper for the Unit of Adult Continuing Education*, Leicester, UDACE/ National Institute of Adult Continuing Education.

NIXON, J. (1992) *Evaluating the Whole Curriculum*, Buckingham, Open University Press.

POLLITT, C. (1990) 'Doing business in the temple? Managers and quality assurance in public services', *Public Administration*, **64**, 4, pp. 435–52.

SCHRATZ, M. (1992) 'Researching while teaching: An action research approach in higher education', *Higher Education*, **17** (1).

SILVER H. (1992) *Student Feedback: Issues and Experience. Council for National Academic Awards Project Report 39*, London, CNAA.

Suggested Reading

GIBBS, G., HABESHAW, S. and HABESHAW, T. (1988) *53 Interesting Ways to Appraise Your Teaching*, Bristol, Technical and Educational Services.
Like much of the material that Gibbs co-authors, this is a good anthology of ideas, but

you must provide the analysis and place the suggestions within a values framework. The book contains a variety of evaluation schedules, which you can adapt for your own purposes.

Journal of Assessment and Evaluation in Higher Education.

This journal colloquially known as *AEHE*, includes items from every discipline and various countries. This means that there should be some papers of interest to you, whatever your discipline. It welcomes thoughtful, qualitative studies and many of the papers are not written in too impenetrable a style. It is worth exploring if you are interested in looking at evaluation issues in any depth.

SILVER H. (1992) *Student Feedback: Issues and Experience. Council for National Academic Awards Project Report 39*, London: CNAA.

This might make a useful halfway house between the purely instrumental Gibbs *et al.* (1988) and the sometimes highly theoretical *AEHE*. It is reasonably short, but deals with the main issues in seeking student feedback for a variety of purposes and their practical implications.

Chapter 11

Action Research

Introduction

If you were asked to say what distinguished a satisfactory teacher from an excellent one, you would probably guess at qualities like enthusiasm, communicative skills, depth and breadth of knowledge. Keeping up to date and enthusiastic about the content of one's teaching is probably unproblematic for most tutors. How to keep enthusiastic about the processes of teaching and learning may be more difficult, since most tutors lack the long period of training, reflection and research given to their subject study.

This is particularly problematic where imposed changes, such as increased numbers in seminar groups, make traditional methods of teaching difficult to sustain. The experienced tutor is able to reflect upon a large repertoire of methods and instances and can learn how through reflection to continue learning. The novice who necessarily lacks this resource for reflection, needs nevertheless to know how to reflect systematically in order to sustain development beyond the initial stages. Another way of putting it is to say that experienced tutors need to know how to reflect as a means to improve their practice, and novices need to know how to reflect as a goal (McIntyre, 1993).

The aim of this chapter is to help experienced tutors to articulate their pre-suppositions about teaching and learning. To set up a small-scale action research project, and to introduce the novice to ways in which practice can be systematically researched and improved.

Action Research and Teaching

Action research is one model of reflection on practice. The model is a very power-ful way of orienting yourself, systematically, to the challenges of professional practice where situations are either problematic or where you feel they could be improved. The model was first outlined by Kurt Lewin (cited in Kemmis, 1988) and has since undergone many refinements. In this chapter we will explain the early version of the model as suggested by Lewin, consider its advantages and disadvantages, suggest how such research can be set up and supported and finally how such research can be disseminated to colleagues and the research community.

What is Action Research?

Lewin derived his model of action research from his observation of the pattern of Allied bombing during the Second World War, which graphically, if tragically, illustrated the basic processes involved in learning and acting in systematic and directed ways in order to get things done. The problem for the pilots was how to hit strategic targets. Hence there would be a preliminary trip by a reconnaissance plane. Photographs would be taken and examined back at headquarters, a plan would be made, pilots would be instructed, they would deliver their bombs, another reconnaisance trip would be made, photographs brought back, new plans made and the whole process repeated until there was the required outcome.

This unfortunate example of the process of systematic learning in a practical context has the advantage of making two things clear. First, that action can be based on evidence (rather than habit, intuition, or custom and practice), and second that action should be directed to a clearly specified problem or focus. The steps can thus be summarized as:

- idea or focus for research;
- general plan;
- reconnaissance or fact finding;
- planning an intervention;
- implementing the plan;
- evaluating the results of the intervention;
- amending the plan, if necessary;
- implementing a revised plan;
  and the cycle is repeated.

Each step involves reflection, description, analysis and evaluation.

The method is inductive in the early stages. That is, it requires a certain amount of experience of the object of study and the ability to notice aspects of the situation which seem to reoccur, which are a problem, a puzzle or of interest for some other reason. When the focus has been located, the initial fact finding (the reconnaissance stage) should lead not only to a description of the present state of affairs, but also to a hypothesis or hunch about what kind of intervention might bring about the desired end of action. In the analogy of the bombing raid presented above the desired end is all too obvious and the means by which it is to be attained is also obvious. In educational action research we may not be clear about what the desired end might be, nor the best means of achieving the end, until we have started on the investigative journey. We might revise our initial focus during the research. It is not uncommon during action research to realize that you have started with the wrong problem.

The method is empirical, since it utilizes observation, and 'scientific' in the sense that any claims to knowledge arising from the investigation should be verifiable. On the other hand the method is also 'unscientific' in the sense that it does not use experimental methods (Stenhouse cited in Murphy and Torrance, 1987), for the perfectly good reason that in the educational setting it is impossible to control all the variables. However this does not necessarily mean that action research is less rigorous in its procedures than other forms of educational research.

Elliott (1991) presents an elaborated form of the model (Figure 11.1) that allows for the inclusion of a number of action steps at each stage, which apply more readily to educational settings. His model also emphasizes the need to monitor

Figure 11.1: *Curriculum action research — The context*

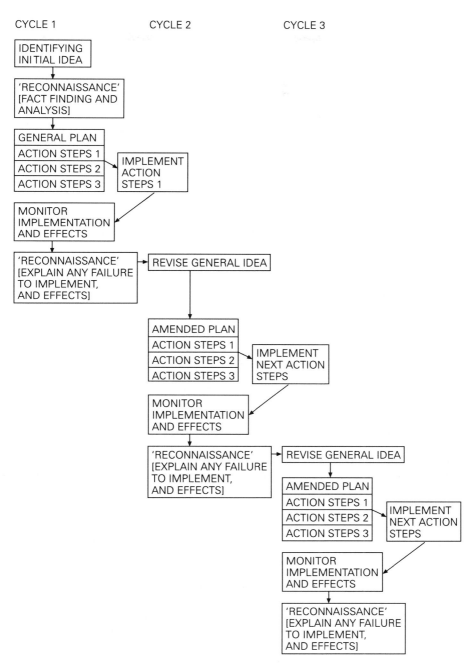

Source: Elliott 1991

implementation steps. In our experience this is a crucial point, especially where you are working with a team of people.

Elliott has argued that teaching is a theoretical activity and that the source of such theoretical activity should be the tutor's own practice (as opposed to theories derived from educational thinkers). Improved practice involves tutors developing their own theories through reflection on their own presuppositions about the situation and beliefs about teaching, as well as empirical data. The central idea is that we develop interpretations of practical situations and use these to build our personal theory of teaching. When we are faced with a problem in the classroom, these theories give meaning to our actions. This is one reason why it is sometimes hard to evaluate tutors' actions in the classroom until we find out what their intentions are and how they construe the situation.

In some areas of the curriculum, such as in literature teaching, there are competing ways of construing teaching and there is no such thing as consensus (Foreman-Peck, 1986). This means that you can only understand a person's teaching in the light of their theory of teaching. A complicating factor for the novice who is trying to learn through the experience of others is that experienced teachers are often unable to articulate their theories and intentions. This is because they are operating with tacit knowledge (Polyani, 1973). This is not to say that they could never come to make their theories explicit. In the normal course of events they are not called upon to do so. Personal theories (whether held implicitly or explicitly) and actions are intimately related. A consequence of this is that poor theorizing leads to poor practice.

Elliott's model has been called a 'practical deliberative' model in contrast to Lewin's 'scientific technical' model. The first is directed to understanding a complex situation, the second to implementing an action in what is construed as a relatively simple situation where the meaning of the situation is not in doubt. The problem is a technical one.

In complex situations understanding is crucial for informed and principled action but does not specify the action. However, both models retain the elements of induction, forming hypotheses, planning and discussing with others, implementing, monitoring, systematic data collection and evaluation.

A consequence of Elliott's insight into the importance of personal theories is that more attention is paid to the frameworks tutors use in describing and analysing the data or information collected in the reconnaissance phase. If you become engaged in this kind of practical deliberative action research, you will need to concern yourself with the way in which all the actors (the students, other tutors, yourself and so on) understand their situation and the assumptions they are making. The data you collected will probably be qualitative, such as accounts of the communication that occurred, or close descriptions of what seemed to happen.

In addition, in order to judge whether the result of an intervention has led to an improvement you must make clear what would count as an improvement. Useful questions to ask yourself include 'Where do my analytical concepts or descriptive vocabulary come from?', 'Are they adequately capturing what is happening?', 'What does my preferred description tell me about my implicit theories of teaching adults and this subject matter?', 'What would an improved state of affairs be like?', and 'Are these frameworks morally and therefore educationally defensible?'. The role of others is crucial in forming appropriate personal theories, as is access to a good education library.

Interpretations of data, and the way in which you are thinking about them should ideally, be checked out with others, so that different viewpoints are brought to bear on the same situation. Reflective practitioner can then benefit from the checks and balances on their construing and perhaps advance their thinking. In the scientific technical mode of action research, which Lewin's model can be said to represent, frameworks for analysis and the interpretation of data are seen as independent of a person's preferred mode of interpretation. Although it is a democratic process and agreement in judgments is sought, the element of making and developing personal theories is absent. During wartime there was no room for disagreement about ends.

A third model has been advanced by Kemmis (Carr and Kemmis 1986) called the 'critical emancipatory' model. This model aims to help tutors not only to discover and become critical of their own implicit theories or interpretative understandings of situations but also to organize action in order to overcome obstacles in the path of rational or just goals. The outcome of this model is a critique of unjust or irrational practices. The associated fieldwork methods place a new emphasis on discursive, analytical and conceptual skills. Although critique is meant to be grounded in the interpretative categories of practitioners, the aim is not the development of personal interpretative theory, but the development of group understanding through critique. Furthermore, proponents of this position hold that the concern for evidence and systematic analysis and evaluation of the two other models of action research tends to mislead the practitioner into thinking that educational problems are first and foremost technical. Rather curriculum problems are value-laden, moral and political in character. In this model the domain of concern is widened to include social and political arrangements. Critical action research is about the control of education and is concerned with political action.

This extends the idea of tutors' professionalism from the narrow classroom focus to the questioning of policies and the consequences of those policies for the institution, the community and society. In this model, the problem or focus for research would not necessarily be confined to the classroom. It might be an aspect of policy, such as admissions policy, equal opportunities, appraisal, anti-racist policy. This form of action research involves collective deliberation and is more likely to be the concern of the experienced tutor.

It is, however, important for the novice to be aware of how policies and debates have an impact on their own experiences and to examine the ideological underpinnings of institutional arrangements. It is important to be aware of the way in which certain practices disadvantage some and privilege others (see Chapter 9). Reading, discussion and enquiry into institutional policy and practice can serve to inform understanding of what is happening in the classroom.

Finding a Focus for Action Research

Argyris and Schön (1974) made a useful distinction between theories that we espouse and theories that we actually use — theories in action. Both take the form of personal imperatives that we use when we are acting professionally. Espoused theories are those we make explicit to ourselves and others. Theories in action are those that we actually live by. Schön and Argyris claim that all our action, whether consciously held or not, can be construed according to the following formula,

'in situation S, if you want to achieve consequence C, under assumptions A1
. . . . . . An, do A'.

It is important to be aware of our espoused theories since there is often a
disjunction between what we think we are doing and what we are actually doing
in practice. It may be that one source (but not the only source) of felt dissatisfac-
tion has to do with this disjunction. Making explicit your own theories of teaching
and learning is not easy. For the novice, theories of and in action will be derived
from past experiences of being taught and from the ideas picked up from mentors
or colleagues. The experienced teacher is much more likely to have to 'dig' and
reflect on data about their teaching in order to recover theories in use.

The scope of action research may be broad or narrow, the issue may be
general or specific. Areas that you might consider researching include aspects of
students' learning (your ability to match the work to their abilities and interests,
their learning strategies, their perceptions, their prior experience, their involvement
in learning, developmental issues and so on), teaching issues (changes in classroom
organization, patterns of interaction, issues in equal opportunities, time management
and so on) or institutional issues.

You might use Enquiry Task 11.1 to examine your implicit theory in use. It
might provide you with a starting point for collecting and reflecting on data.

Enquiry Task 11.1

Think of a visual image that symbolizes the way you think of your role as
  an educator.
Draw it (some examples of images given by tutors have been 'sponge',
  'architect', 'shepherd', 'tray', 'tree').
Discuss your image with an experienced colleague.

What are the assumptions about education implied by your image?

What does the image imply about your view of yourself?

Does your image imply that you behave in certain ways?

Are there any aspects of your image that you would like to change or challenge?

Another way to identify an area for research is to start with a feeling that
something isn't right or that something is puzzling. For example, it might be that
you sense an unproductive tension in the group or you are not sure whether the
level of difficulty of the work is matched to the levels of understanding in the
class. Students may be expressing concern about the assessments and you may
suspect that they do not adequately reflect course objectives. You may be concerned that your students are not developing enough critical acumen, or you
may be concerned that group work projects seem to flounder for some students.
Problems or puzzles do not have to imply failure. It maybe that your inquiry is
motivated simply by the desire to understand and improve a situation that is
already 'good enough'.

Action research should be focused towards problems or puzzles that it is possible for you to investigate. Where solutions are not within your control, the situation will not be suitable for action research. In other words the project must be feasible and within your sphere of action.

Enquiry Task 11.2

Kemmis (quoted in McKernan 1991) suggests the following three questions as a way of focusing on the research area or question.

What is happening now?
Why is it problematic?
What can I do about it?

Take a problem or a situation that is concerning you at the moment.

List the kinds of evidence you will need to collect in order to find the answer to the first question above.

Write down your reflections about the second and third questions.

What do your reflections tell you about the way in which you are construing the situation?

Discuss the problem or situation with a colleague.
Add to your list and your reflections in the light of this discussion.

Feasibility: Making Time

Tutors in higher and further education often find that there is not enough time to fulfil all their obligations. It is therefore important that you integrate any action research project into your teaching time as much as possible and build action steps and data collection into the normal teaching process as much as possible. In the early stages it is probably better to choose research questions that seem to you to be solvable and within your control. (Later you might tackle more intractable questions. It is our experience that action research sometimes enables one to reconceptualize a problem in a way that transforms its nature.) You may find it useful to decide how much time you can realistically set aside for collecting, transcribing and analysing data and fit your fieldwork to that. We have found that it is helpful to use a calendar with provisional dates for collecting data at each stage of the research, constantly revised in the light of contingencies. This provides one way of guiding the research in a purposeful way and monitoring your own progress.

We have found that it is useful to set up a collaborative partnership, since it helps to sustain the research, it helps tutors to feel less isolated, and it provides another person's perspective on the data. However, there is nothing to stop you proceeding alone and you can invite students to give another perspective on the data. There are, however, important limitations to doing this, not least the problem of motivation over a period of time.

Data Collection Points: Reconnaissance, Monitoring, Evaluating

One needs to collect data in a systematic way at three points: at the reconnaissance stage, at the monitoring stage, and at the evaluation stage. In the reconnaissance stage you will need to collect data that are likely to illuminate your focus or problem so you can gain a better understanding of it. Methods might include documentary analysis, observation, interviews, recordings of classes or lectures. These data are then scrutinized, first in order to get a better description of the area of study, but also for what they might suggest by way of possible intervention.

Once a line of intervention has been formulated, you will need to decide on the action steps and then implement them. You will need to decide how you will monitor the success of your action. You may find that particular steps need to be repeated or modified in the light of experience. You are likely to find a research diary or log for monitoring the implementation and noting what happens is indispensable.

If the intervention went according to plan you will need to collect data about its actual consequences and/or processes. Methods for looking at the consequences and processes could include interviews, observations, recordings, rating schedules or questionnaires.

Enquiry Task 11.3

List ways of collecting evidence about an intervention.

Think about what each is good and not so good for.

For example:

Technique	Good for	Not so good for
Fly on the wall observation	Looking at actual behaviour	Getting at people's feelings
Structured observation		
Interviewing		
Questionnaires		
Diagnostic marking of students' work		
Videotaping		
etc.		

As we have said, you may find that it is useful to keep a log of your activity for future reference, noting for example to whom you spoke, when and for what purpose throughout the research. Systematic records of time, place, persons, activity and intention are part of your total data base.

Some action researchers also recommend keeping a diary. This might record personal feelings, hunches, things said 'off the record', things overheard, attitudes, motives, circumstances etc. These details can help capture the reality of the research and help others to gain a sense of what it was like to be there in that situation. For instance, in one of the authors' research she included a descriptive passage to convey a sense of what it was like in a particular classroom that was in fact one half of the dining hall with a constant clattering of plates, pots and pans and the chatter of cooks getting lunch ready while the class was being taught.

It may be useful to construct a well indexed, well ordered, and easily retrievable case record. This will provide you with an 'archive' of materials, selected from the total data record, of those parts that are most relevant to your research issue. It can include photographs, documents, transcripts of interviews, field notes, in short any piece of data that provides evidence.

In addition to a log and a system of indexing, you may find it useful to keep a reflective diary that tells the story of your thinking. This narrative can be reread periodically and examined critically for what it shows you about your own thinking and for ways in which you might reconstrue the situation you are researching. Periodically you might wish to make analytic memos, notes that summarize thinking so far, explore different ways of conceptualizing the situation as it has changed, elaborate new hunches, or that specify additional data you might need to collect or new problems arising.

Enquiry Task 11.4

Think about the ethics of action research. Draw up a set of ethical rules that will guide your action.

For example:
Participants will be informed about the nature of the research and the uses to which it will be put.
No data about any participant will be divulged to a third party without their knowledge and informed consent.
No participant will be harmed by the research, etc.

Discuss your list with a colleague who has some experience of research.
Add to it in the light of this discussion.

Data Collection Methods

Your aim in collecting and organizing data is to describe the focus of research, the action, the effects and the circumstances as accurately as possible. The data collected might consist of video and audiotapes, written materials, eyewitness accounts, interviews with participants. A fellow collaborator might be able to make observational notes, read data and contribute different viewpoints. More ambitious action research projects might involve teams of tutors sharing the planning, implementation, analysis and reporting (for example see Ashcroft and Griffiths, 1989).

Diaries

We have already recommended that you keep a research diary and/or log of the course of the research. It may also be useful to ask other participants in the research to keep diaries. You will need to decide from the start who the readers of the diaries are. You may decide to disclose only those parts that participants (e.g. students) feel comfortable about. Alternatively, you may decide to organize a discussion where diary evidence is utilized in the discussion but not read out or handed in. Whatever you decide, it is important that all those participating in the research are clear about the extent of confidentiality that they can expect and the ways that the data may be used.

The advantage of diaries is that you get different viewpoints of the same events. You can also ask participants to focus in their writing on certain aspects of a situation. On the other hand, other participants are probably not as motivated to keep them up.

Structured Observation Schedules

Structured observation schedules are lists that are designed to focus observation. They can be used to note the presence, absence, or frequency of an aspect of a behaviour in the 'field' (usually the classroom). They can help you to build up a picture of events over time. Some you may be able to do yourself during the event. Others may be carried out by an outside observer.

The first step in designing a schedule is to specify categories (such as teacher questions). The second step is to specify the rules for employing the system (for example noting behaviour at three-second intervals). The third step is to specify how the data is to be analysed. For example, the Flanders system (Flanders, 1970) had ten categories of teacher–pupil talk. During the first minute, twenty marks can be made on a tally sheet recording who was speaking and what type of speech they were using. One of us was interested in promoting discussion that was not tutor centred. She created a simple observation schedule to map the pattern of interaction in a classroom and to note the number of student–tutor interactions, as opposed to student–student interactions, when she used various teaching methods. In this way a certain picture of the nature of the interaction can be built up.

Checklists tell us whether a certain behaviour is present. They do not capture information about the interaction that is outside the category system, nor do they tell us anything about the quality of the behaviour. Nevertheless if you were concerned that your students did not engage in critical reflection during group work, an observational checklist could be a useful way of confirming or disconfirming your hunch.

Document Analysis

Some documents can help illuminate your research problem, for example course documentation, course papers, samples of students' work and syllabuses. These can be read, not only for literal information, but also for what is omitted and for tone. Omissions and apparent contradictions in documents can lead you to formulate lines of inquiry. Even if these are not central to your research focus they can help you get a better picture of the context in which you are operating.

Recordings

Audio recording is a good way of capturing verbal exchanges. Problems arise if the quality of the sound is poor. Radio microphones and good quality equipment help. One of the authors found that two tape recorders, strategically placed, provided more information in large classes. Video cameras can be useful in capturing non-verbal exchanges and other aspects of behaviour which might have some relevance. If fixed in one place they are less distracting, but may not pick up crucial information if the participants are moving about. Moving the camera is a possibility but may make participants nervous and alter the nature of the interaction. Using equipment regularly in a routine way helps participants to become accustomed to its presence. Explaining its presence can also take away some of the distracting effects.

You might ask a colleague to do the videotaping. This can be particularly helpful since there will be a recording of the same event seen by two people. You may wish to make a further audio recording of any discussion of the video that may take place, in order to record different viewpoints.

Recordings do not always have to be transcribed. Where time is short other methods have to be used. It may only be possible to listen to the tapes, index them by topic or episode and transcribe those sections that seem most pertinent. It has been estimated that every five minutes of recording takes one hour of transcription. This is immensely time consuming but it can be valuable. A recorder that has index numbers will save you time, since topics or episodes can be quickly relocated on the tape. It is also useful to leave wide margins on each side of one's transcript since you are likely to want to write notes, note categories, themes or key phrases. You may also find it useful to give each 'utterance' a number. Where you have a number of tapes it may be useful to use topic index cards and to collect together all references to that topic. This helps at the writing up stage.

Interviews

It is important to interview those participants who can give another viewpoint or account. This could mean interviewing a sample of students or colleagues.

Interviews are usually thought of as being structured, semi-structured and unstructured. In the first the questions are predetermined by the interviewer. The semi-structured interview involves some predetermined questions, but also gives the interviewee the freedom to digress and raise their own questions. The interviewer can be opportunistic and ask supplementary or probing questions which were not anticipated at the outset. Allowing digressions, even if they seem irrelevant, allows the interviewer the opportunity to be divergent and creative in thinking. In the unstructured interview the idea is to enable the interviewee to raise their own questions. The interviewer's role is to help the interviewee to expand and clarify, and if need be challenge, their thinking. The stimulus for this kind of exchange may come from considering a record of some kind, such as a set of photographs, or you might take the interviewee back through their personal history, or ask them to reflect on fairly recent events.

The approaches differ from one another in the extent to which the interviewer controls the agenda. In our experience it is useful to use a combination of different sorts of question in any of the approaches to interviewing described above. Predetermined questions, which are closed in nature, can be useful for evaluating the weight one might put on what someone says. So for example the question 'How long have you been teaching on this course?' might help you to assess the likelihood that someone has a distorted view because they are newcomers. As the research proceeds this kind of question can be checked out.

Similarly, open-ended requests can be very useful for generating new ways of reconceptualizing a problem. Examples of this sort could be 'If you were in charge of resources what would you do to bring about an improvement?'. This sort of hypothetical questioning can arise out of predominantly structured, unstructured or semi-structured interviews. It is a fruitful way of accessing how people construe situations and it can be a way of helping them to further their thinking.

Interview questions suffer from many of the problems of those included in questionnaires (see below). These often boil down to a lack of shared meaning or a lack of understanding of the concerns of the person being interviewed. In addition, in the face-to-face situation people are particularly reluctant to make statements that might reflect badly on themselves or seem critical of the interviewer.

Questionnaires

A questionnaire is a list of questions that one would like other people to respond to in writing. The questions can be open (allowing an unpredictable variety of responses) or closed (allowing a yes/no answer, or a choice of answers from a preset list).

A major problem with questionnaires is that your questions may not reflect the issues that others may think are important. This can be overcome to some extent by piloting it. The other major drawback of the closed question variety, is that they force participants to express their views in a black and white way. Many questions raise ambivalent responses. Open-ended questions can also miss important aspects of participants' experience. One way of increasing the likelihood that a questionnaire will be relevant to the respondents' experience is to decide on the categories of the questionnaire in the light of those issues that emerge from unstructured interviews with a sample of the targeted group.

An advantage of closed questionnaires is that they can provide quantifiable data. They tend to be easier and more time efficient to analyse. However, the questions themselves have to be very carefully phrased to ensure that they are not leading, threatening or ambiguous. People will often express their views more honestly and openly if they can be assured of anonymity.

Questionnaires might be more appropriate where the target group is geographically dispersed, for example if you were interested in employers' views of your students (although you might consider telephone interviews). However, the rate of return on questionnaires is usually disappointing unless they are administered face-to-face and collected immediately. Questionnaires are the most efficient form of research tool where you are trying to collect very specific information from a large number of people. They are a valuable tool in whole course evaluation but in research with a small number of people interviews might be more useful.

Inventories

Inventories are a form of questionnaire with statements with which you ask others to agree or disagree. The respondent is usually asked to tick one of the following categories: Strongly Agree, Agree, Uncertain, Disagree, or Strongly Disagree. This is a quick way of checking whether others agree with your interpretations. Categories for the inventory need not come from your own point of view. You can ask other people to generate statements about a shared experience. The data will tell you how many people see things similarly. Inventories may be used to complement data collected in unstructured or semi-structured interviews.

Field Notes

These are descriptions of observations made in the research setting 'on the hoof'. They are written either during the event or as close to the event as possible. The point of keeping them is to record as much detail as possible, before you forget.

Enquiry Task 11.5

You may find it useful at various stages in the research to draw out your understanding of the theoretical underpinnings of the descriptions you use to describe the situation.

Having decided on a focus for action research collect as much data as possible.
From time-to-time discuss the questions below with a colleague and try to answer them:

- What would a better situation look like?
- Why would it be better?
- Are there alternative explanations for the problem?
- Are there actions that might improve the situation?
- Do any key words or phrases reoccur in your written records?
- Do your data need examining in more detail?
- Are new ideas emerging from the data?
- Does the initial focus or question for the research need to be reformulated?

If you are working with someone else:

- Are there areas of disagreement?
- What causes the disagreements (misunderstandings, competing theories, value conflicts or vested interests)?

Record your responses in analytic memos.
Use them in the writing up stage.

Again, find a sympathetic colleague with whom to discuss your ideas.

Triangulation

Triangulation is used by researchers in several different senses. Elliott (1978) argues that triangulation is a method for bringing different kinds of evidence together for the purposes of comparing and contrasting different points of view. For example classroom events can be seen from the point of view of the tutor, the students, and an observer. The tutor is the best person to give an account of intentions and aims. The students are in the best position to give an account of the way in which the tutor's actions influenced them. The observer is in the best position to give an account of the observable features of the interaction. In triangulation each person's point of view can be reviewed in the light of data from the other two sources. In comparing different accounts, the points at which there is agreement, disagreement and difference should be noted. Disagreements can be checked by reference to the data and by further discussion between the parties involved.

Another version of triangulation is given by Denzin (1970). This is called 'methodological triangulation'. He argues that different data-collection methodologies (for example, observation combined with survey) should be brought to bear on the research problem because each method has limitations and strengths. By using different methods you maximize the confidence you can place in the findings. Apparent discrepancies can be the focus for further reflection and investigation.

Enquiry Task 11.6

List three kinds of method you might use to triangulate data arising from the intervention you have decided upon.

Try to work out how you might minimize the disadvantages of each.

Method   *Ways of minimizing the disadvantages*
1
2
3

Writing up the Research

You may want to write up your action research for a variety of reasons. The process of writing it forces you to become more orderly and to re-examine your evidence and interpretation. This can lead to new insights. Much action research has policy implications. A well written report can provide weight to your arguments. Perhaps the most common reason is that you found the process interesting and think others will be interested in what you found out. Much action research has application to more than one situation. (Journals sympathetic to publishing action research are listed in the annotated reading list at the end of the chapter.)

Action research is often difficult to write up and present in a way that remains close to the experience of doing it and keeps the reader interested and on track. Elliott (1991) suggests that a report of an action research project should adopt a historical framework, telling the story of the research. This might include the general focus; how it changed and how your understanding of the situation changed over time; the action steps you took in the light of your understanding of the situation; the extent to which proposed actions were implemented; how you dealt with these problems; the intended and unintended effects of your actions and explanations for why they occurred; the methods used to collect data; and problems encountered and resolutions. Ethical problems encountered in negotiating access to and release of information and any attempted resolutions, any problems in negotiating action steps with others, or in negotiating the time, resources, and cooperation during the course of the research might also be mentioned. You might also want to include an account of any research literature drawn upon.

This model of the correct way to 'write up' assumes a particular type of academic audience (for instance, an MEd tutor). It might not always be the best approach for your purposes. For instance, if you want to affect policy, your message may be lost in the detail. The audience for your report might have limited time and be most interested in the scale of your investigation and what you found out.

Dissemination is taking an alternative form through action research networks in some areas at school level (McKernan, 1991). In Britain there is the Collaborative Action Research Network (CARN) coordinated through the Cambridge Institute. More informally, case study reports of action research projects can be used as a basis for discussion in departmental meetings.

Criticisms of Action Research

Some important criticisms of action research have been made by Hodgkinson (1957). The outcome of action research may only be valid for the cohort with whom it was carried out. If the other cohorts of students are different in some way (different social and cultural composition for example) the findings may not be generalizable. In other words, the validity of action research tends to be localized and temporary in nature.

It may be a mistake to think that action research can provide prescriptions for action. Part of the value of action research case studies is their contribution to the literature on action in complex educational settings. Readers will find similarities and differences in their own situations and the case studies can open up new lines of inquiry for their own investigations. Part of it is also in the learning process and the changes which occur in the skills, attitudes and values of the person undertaking the research.

Summary

Action research is a systematic way of finding solutions to problems, gaining deeper understanding of situations that puzzle us. For the novice tutor, action research is a goal of professional development. For the experienced teacher it is a method of continuing professional development.

Action research method involves interpreting data. It is therefore important that you have an understanding of your own presuppositions about education. You need to ask yourself:

- Are you working with prejudices or assumptions that are unsupported?
- Are your values translated into principles and practices that are fair and equitable?

Action research requires some familiarity with methods of organizing, monitoring and collecting data. Ideally you should work with a colleague or a mentor, not only to sustain your motivation but to share perceptions and interpretations of the data.

Action research reports can be used to inform institutional debate and departmental thinking.

Entry for the Reflective Diary

Write about:

- areas of your work that puzzle or intrigue;
- areas that you would like to improve;
- critical incidents that have challenged the way you normally think;
- legislative change or change in institutional arrangements that have given you problems;
- areas of sensitivity in your institution related to change or innovation.

References

ARGYRIS, C. and SCHÖN, D.A. (1974) *Theory in Practice: Increasing Professional Effectiveness*, London, Jossey-Bass.

ASHCROFT, K. and GRIFFITHS, M. (1989) 'Reflective teachers and reflective tutors: School experience in an initial teacher education course', *Journal of Education for Teachers*, **15**, 1, pp. 35–52.

CARR, W. and KEMMIS, S. (1986) *Becoming Critical: Education, Knowledge and Action Research*, London, Falmer Press.

DENZIN, N. (1970) *The Research Act*, Chicago, Aldinc.

ELLIOTT, J. (1978) 'What is action research in schools?', *Journal of Curriculum Studies*, **10**, 4, pp. 355–7.

ELLIOTT, J. (1991) *Action Research for Educational Change*, Milton Keynes, Open University Press.

FLANDERS, N.A. (1970) *Analysing Teaching Behaviour*, New York, Addison-Wesley.

FOREMAN-PECK, L. (1986) 'Teaching Response to Literature in the Secondary School Classroom through Verbal Interaction', unpublished PhD thesis, University of Newcastle Upon Tyne.

HODGKINSON, H.L. (1957) 'Action research — a Critique', *The Action Research Reader* (1988) Australia, Deakin University.

KEMMIS, S. (1988) 'Action research', in KEEVES, J.P. (Ed) *Educational Research, Methodology and Measurement: An International Handbook*, Oxford, Pergamon.

MCINTYRE, D. (1993) 'Theory, theorizing and reflection in initial teacher education', in CALDERHEAD, J. and GATES, P. (Eds) *Conceptualizng Reflection in Teacher Education*, London, Falmer Press.

MCKERNAN, J. (1991) *Curriculum Action Research: A Handbook of Methods and Resources for the Reflective Practitioner*, London, Kogan Page Ltd.

MURPHY, R. and TORRANCE, H. (Eds) (1987) *Evaluating Education: Issues and Methods*, London, Harper and Row.

POLYANI, M. (1973) *Personal Knowledge*, London, Routledge and Kegan Paul.

STENHOUSE, L. (1987) 'The conduct, analysis and reporting of case study in educational research and evaluation', in MURPHY, R. and TORRANCE, H. (Eds) *Evaluating Education: Issues and Methods*, London, Harper and Row.

Suggested Reading

Educational Action Research. (Wallingford, Oxon, Triangle Journals Ltd.) and *The British Educational Research Journal*, Oxfordshire, Carfax.

These journals are sympathetic to publishing action research at tertiary level. *Education Action Research* supports the Collaborative Action Research Network.

ELLIOTT, J. (1991) *Action Research for Educational Change*, Milton Keynes, Open University Press.

An excellent introduction to action research in educational settings. Chapter 6 has a practical guide to action research.

MCKERNAN, J. (1991) *Curriculum Action Research: A Handbook of Methods and Resources for the Reflective Practitioner*, London, Kogan Page Ltd.

This book contains many useful suggestions for collecting data. A good introduction.

Chapter 12

Conclusion

Drawing the Threads of the Book Together

In this book we have attempted to introduce you to various aspects of teaching that are more or less within your control which you can therefore influence to a greater or lesser extent. In Chapter 1, we outlined the values and principles on which the book is based. These included qualities of open-mindedness, responsibility and wholeheartedness and the need for analysis within a real life political, social and economic climate, based on evidence. Central to this analysis are notions of the need for alternative perspectives and for the analysis to be contained within a moral framework and the idea of managing oneself, people and resources. We see these issues as threads that run though the whole book and provide its principal justification.

Given this framework it was impossible for us to write a book that lists 'things to do' or 'tips for tutors', first of all because of the basic requirement of reflective practice to move away from a consideration of 'what works' towards one that has issues of worthwhileness at the heart of the educational process. Second, the more we enquire into the reality of the educational process within real educational contexts, the less we have come to believe that education works as a science, with laws and rules that 'work'. Values have slowly become the fixed points for the evaluation of our practice. We have found that other measures are only as sound as the values that underpin them. Our values include a consideration of the needs and interests of individuals and groups. These are highly variable and therefore preclude simple solutions.

Linking Teaching to the Reflective Practitioner Model

The view of reflective practice underpinning this handbook relates not just to you as a tutor but also to your relationships with colleagues and to managers. We hope that the content of the book, the enquiry tasks and reflective exercises have started you thinking about issues in your teaching and your institutional context (in which you are an actor as well as an object) in new ways.

We have introduced the idea of responsibility as it is defined by reflective practice. Responsibility does not just refer to your interactions with your students, but also refers to your 'duty' to look at the nature of the institution in which you and they work and learn. This duty goes beyond a responsibility to examine, understand and in some way interpret this environment for your students, although it encompasses this. In addition, it implies that you seek to influence and change that environment because it fundamentally affects the education your students experience and the extent to which you can facilitate their learning. We recognize that this can be very difficult in some circumstances, and that any victories may be small. Nevertheless, unless tutors somehow retain the optimism to try, they may become cynical. Cynicism is totally and completely incompatible with reflective practice.

Fortunately the process of enquiry is almost always an empowering one. Enquiry generally reveals that institutions are not monolithic. We have found that even highly authoritarian institutions have islands of democracy and some people with power who are susceptible to informed argument. Understanding how systems and people within the institution work is central to your exercise of responsibility.

We also hope that, through your reading and enquiry, you have come to see the link between reflective practice, responsibility and open-mindedness in new ways. Open-mindedness is essentially linked with responsibility. The more inauspicious the setting, the more that this linkage matters. The chinks in the institutional settings and the understanding of those with power can only be achieved with open-mindedness. Without it, you may be tempted to believe that nothing will or can change. Enquiry that has a fixed view of the outcome will not help you to change yourself, your practice or the context in which you work.

Much of the book has been about the way that you relate directly to your students. Here again there will be tensions between what are desirable and what are possible causes of action. The enquiry base of the reflective practitioner model may help you to find transformational solutions to some of the dilemmas inherent in education, for instance, about who should control the curriculum and how principles relating to justice, equality and fairness should operate in a context of limited resources. Reflective practice can provide a model for conceptualizing the needs of the various 'players' in education, their interests and values, as against your own, and the consequences for each of these players of the various courses of action open to you and to them.

We have stressed that reflective practice is an essentially moral activity. Without this, all values become equal and it becomes acceptable to ditch principles of justice in favour of those of value for money, to damage the innocent individual for the good of the group, and so on. We have tried to create a series of tasks and reflections within this book which may help you to define what your fundamental values are, how they relate to education, and the extent which you are putting these values into operation. This process, if entered into wholeheartedly, will be painful. You may find that some of your actions have unintended consequences, that some of your values are changed, or that your ideals and your practice are not always compatible.

You may also find that your wholehearted pursuit of reflective practice is not necessarily good for your career. We do not apologize for this. In trying to find out and then do what is right, you may have to ignore expediency. Ultimately, you have to decide what is more important. You could use the information within this book and that which you collect through the enquiry tasks for your own ends or for those of the students.

Enquiry Task 12.1

List the four main things that you have learned about your teaching from working through this book.

List the ways how what you have learned has affected your practice.

Identify an aspect of your teaching which should now be a focus of your enquiry.

Design your own enquiry task to find out more about this aspect.

Linking Student Learning to the Reflective Practitioner Model

We have also suggested that part of your job as a tutor may be to help your students to develop as reflective practitioners of their subject. We have implied that this will require you to focus on certain enabling skills and qualities. The qualities that they may need to acquire parallel those that have concerned you as a reflective tutor, in particular, open-mindedness, responsibility, and wholeheartedness.

Open-mindedness in the case of students refers to qualities appropriate within a vocational context, but also that required by the purely academic study of a subject. It may include a consideration of the social significance of the subject, the values that underpin some of its central concepts and also the views and interests of other students and teachers. It also implies a student orientation to study which stresses the intrinsic worth of the subject and an intrinsic interest in the perspectives on that subject of fellow students, of tutors and of people from other times and places whose ideas may be accessible only through the literature.

Responsibility on the part of the student implies that they are willing to become independent learners but at the same time to help others to learn where that is appropriate. Responsibility implies an acceptance by your students that certain actions will have long-term good or bad consequences for themselves and for others. Therefore, the responsible learner is one who does not rely on others for their motivation, but who is willing to act as a motivator for others. This implies that matters of character and integrity should be a part of the intended outcomes of further and higher education, and that these have an important place alongside more formal measures in determining the success or otherwise of a student's educational experience.

Wholeheartedness implies that the students take a deep approach to their study; that they look beyond the gaining of approval or marks; that they seek to enquire into the subject and beyond subject boundaries, because this is something that they want to do for its own sake.

The tutor's role in the students' movement to reflective practice has been described within this book as one of structuring student experience and providing the climate for such development. This includes the provision of opportunities and the interpersonal climate for the student to practise open-mindedness, responsibility and wholeheartedness, but also to develop a whole range of enabling skills. These skills include skills principally within the affective domain including self-assessment, personal development and interpersonal skills and those mainly within the cognitive domain such as advanced and basic study skills and research skills.

Enquiry Task 12.2

List the four main things that you have learned about your students' learning from working through this book.

List the ways how what you have learned has affected your practice.

Identify an aspect of student learning that should now be a focus of your enquiry.

Design your own enquiry task to find out more about this aspect.

Reflective Practice and the Content of the Book

In each chapter of the book we have linked the focus to the notion of reflective practice as a process of enquiry into the perspectives of those with an interest in education and into the consequences of action. This enquiry we have located firmly within a values framework.

Because education is first and foremost about students learning, we started by looking at models of student learning. It became clear that the process of learning is a dynamic one, where students are influenced by the teaching they experience, the way material is presented, and the context for learning but must also develop responsibility for their own learning. The tutor does have influence, and in particular can, through sensitive or insensitive action, promote or impede the students' ability to develop a range of learning styles and approaches, and in particular the qualities needed to take a deep approach to learning. Learning can be conceptualized as the students' progress towards reflective action. Students can develop their skills and understanding, and so develop a greater choice of perspectives to view subject matter and techniques for analysing it. Thus, your student may not abandon earlier skills and frameworks, but rather develop a greater repertoire and opportunity to make decisions about fitness for purpose when solving particular problems or exploring particular issues.

It is evident that a conception of learning as more than the transmission of information implies that the teaching becomes a complex process. The skills students need include more than the ability to remember facts. Many of these skills are in the personal and interpersonal domain. The complex issues involved in personal development and the development of interpersonal skills were explored in Chapter 3. They are of particular interest to tutors who wish to develop their students as reflective learners.

The issues of assessment in learning are more complex than they appear at first sight. Assessment may be conceptualized in various ways, as a process of 'testing' of student learning or competence; as the 'quality control' mechanism for assessing student outcomes; or as a tool within the learning process itself. Each of these notions about assessment will affect its form. If assessment tasks are seen as opportunities to extend learning itself, the tutor's or course designer's implicit theories of learning and teaching will also influence the forms of assessment. In Chapter 4 we explored the ways that assessment schemes may facilitate or impede the students' intellectual, personal and interpersonal development and their central interest to reflective teachers.

Change in the way that higher and further education have been funded has led to a search for 'efficiency savings' in colleges and universities in Britain during the late 1980s and 1990s. These efficiencies have nearly always included increases in class size. These increases pose particular challenges for tutors who are interested in teaching and learning as complex processes aimed at meeting the needs and interests of students. In Chapter 5 we explored these issues and the dilemmas posed, and suggested that the tutor may find transformational solutions to these dilemmas through a reconceptualization of their role within the learning process, and some practical techniques for achieving these solutions.

The needs of a variety of groups of students traditionally underrepresented in further and higher education can only be met through an increased openness of the system. In Chapter 6 we discussed the variety of forms this openness may take, for instance, through a permeability of subject boundaries; the openness of access and exit points; or through programmes that validate locations other than colleges and universities as legitimate locations for teaching and learning. Open learning poses many problems and demands a variety of skills. They are detailed along with some suggestions as to processes which may help to resolve the problems open learning poses.

Teaching can proceed in many ways apart from through the spoken word. In Chapter 7 we explored the range of aids to teaching and learning available to the tutor and the opportunities each offer. The need for criteria relating to quality and fitness for purpose was discussed as well as the ways that such aids can help you and your students' development towards reflective practice.

Tutors who are concerned about their students in some way as 'whole people' will inevitably come up against some who are in difficulties with their personal lives or with their study. The tutor has a responsibility to their student, but also to themselves in these circumstances. In Chapter 8 we explored some of the issues raised by these responsibilities, and suggested practical solutions and techniques which may enable the tutor to work with greater sensitivity.

Since values are central to reflective practice, we believe that it cannot occur where the interests of some major groups in society are ignored. Issues of equal opportunity are, therefore, integral to reflective teaching. The dilemmas raised by issues of equality were discussed in Chapter 9 as well as opportunities for good practice in the teaching and learning process that the consideration of equal opportunities offer.

Reflective teaching is based on the collection of evidence, its review and the examination of practice and values in the light of that evidence. Therefore, to this extent, it is an evaluation-led model. In Chapter 10 we explored the relationship between good practice in teaching and learning and evaluation and suggested a number of ways that you can explore your teaching and the students' learning using evaluation instruments. 'Quick and dirty' evaluation can be as appropriate in certain circumstances as more sophisticated kinds of data collection. The important point is that you should have the evaluation tools available to make the appropriate choices.

Evaluation also relates closely to the focus of Chapter 11, action research and teaching. Within this chapter we explored action research as one method for the development of practice, the opportunities it offers as well as its limitations. We suggested a modification to the classic action research model to make it reflect the 'messiness' of real time research and to make it more responsive to the variety of 'insider research' that is appropriate to reflective teaching and learning.

Reflective Practice in a Cold Climate

Tutors within further and higher education are having to contend with a macro-political climate in which it is not always easy to practise reflective action. The British Conservative government of the 1980s and 1990s introduced a new emphasis on the interests of employers and the rights of students as customers (a misleading analogy), rather than on education as a 'good thing' in its own right, at the same time as a resource squeeze. This might have created a climate of pessimism and despair about the future of reflective teaching. What we have found instead is a willingness on the part of many tutors to take the developments as a starting point for enquiry and the creation of transformational solutions to the dilemmas they pose.

Examples of this kind of reflective action abound. For instance, tutors have discovered opportunities to investigate the needs of a variety of students who had not been served well by the educational system. In the search for appropriate ways of meeting these needs they have found out much about the nature of teaching and learning. Other tutors, faced with larger and larger teaching groups, have examined their traditional assumptions about tutor-centred learning and the role of the tutor in such learning. Again they have reconceptualized teaching, for instance from a matter of instruction and skill development to one of empowering students to become independent practitioners of their subject.

Reflective teaching does not require a perfect climate. Indeed, it may be the most rational response to tutors' needs to retain their integrity within difficult situations. It is one method of searching for the kind of creative solutions that may take practice forward, but that might not have been discovered without constraints that required new methods of working. In the course of your movement towards reflective practice, you are likely to find that you are empowered to deal with complexity and difficult circumstances. The processes of critical enquiry can help you to find appropriate ways of solving problems you face, while at the same time enabling you to examine these solutions within a framework of articulated values.

We have described the management of teaching and learning as part of a life-long process, which encompasses the aspects of the life of the educational institution, the community and the wider educational context. The aim is that you and your students, once equipped with the skills, knowledge and qualities for reflective practice, are able to assess various courses of action, to examine alternative perspectives on change, not in order to accept automatically these perspectives or actions or to reject them, but rather to weigh up each and consider how they relate to ideas of 'worthwhileness' and the context of the action or change.

Reflective practice is an ideal to be worked towards. It will not be possible for you or your students to reach the point where you say: 'That's all right then, I'm a reflective practitioner now'. Instead, we hope you and your students will seek to build a greater and greater understanding of your values and practice; that you will retain earlier skills and insights, but also develop more sophisticated ones, so that in a particular circumstance, you have a greater choice of strategy and choice open to you. We believe that the understanding of the problematic nature of much 'knowledge' and the process of self-critical problem-solving based on real evidence is the basis for lifelong learning and development.

Summary

Our aim in writing this book has been to link the central concepts within the reflective practitioner model to your teaching and the students' learning.

The factors that influence reflective teaching include personal qualities, such as:

- open-mindedness;
- responsibility; and
- wholeheartedness;

skills, such as:

- research skills;
- personal and interpersonal skills;
- communication skills;
- study skills;
- skills of analysis; and
- skills of self-assessment;

and processes, including:

- evaluation;
- critical enquiry;
- the collection of evidence;
- problem-solving; and
- collaboration.

Reflective practice influences all aspects of teaching and learning including, student development, personal development and interpersonal skills, assessment, teaching methods, modes of curriculum delivery, student support, equal opportunities, evaluation and research.

Reflective practice is an approach to the development of effective and moral practice within a contextual framework which includes:

- values;
- the needs and interests of all parties to the educational process;
- institutional ethos and systems; and
- the political, social and economic climate.

Entry for the Reflective Diary

Define your personal theory of teaching.

Define your personal theory of learning.

Write about:

- how these theories are linked;
- how these theories have changed in the light of your developing understanding, experience and enquiry;
- how these theories relate to your fundamental values; and
- how these theories affect your practice.

Suggested Reading

ASHCROFT, K. with FOREMAN-PECK, L. (will be published in 1995) *The Tutor's Guide to Quality and Standards in Colleges & Universities*, London, Falmer Press.
This book has the same format as *Managing Teaching and Learning in Further and Higher Education*. It takes as its premise the idea that you need to know about the formal and informal systems within your institution in order to develop your own teaching and the students' learning. It explores the ways that the quality of teaching and learning can be improved by your understanding of and interaction with aspects such as quality control, academic standards, student support, appraisal, management and team working, course design, resource management, bidding for funds and marketing.

Index